REACHING YOUR FULL POTENTIAL

Richard Furman, M.D.

HARVEST HOUSE PUBLISHERS
Eugene, Oregon 97402

Cover by Paz Design Group, Salem, Oregon

*The names of certain persons and places have been changed
in order to protect the privacy of the individuals involved.*

REACHING YOUR FULL POTENTIAL
Copyright © 1984 by Harvest House Publishers
Eugene, Oregon 97402
(Original edition published 1982 under the title *To Be a Surgeon*
by Frederick Fell Publishers, Inc.)

Library of Congress Cataloging Card Number 84-81210
ISBN 0-7369-0713-0

Printed in the United States of America

01 02 03 04 05 06 07 / BC-CF / 10 9 8 7 6 5 4 3 2 1

To my wife Harriet,
who supported me through it all
with her unfailing love and understanding.
"She is worth far more than rubies"
(Proverbs 31:10).

Contents

The Secret to Success

MOST PEOPLE LIVE IN A SEA OF MEDIOCRITY. They neither fail nor succeed. Seldom do they think through and set goals for achievement.

Mothers rise every morning, cook breakfast for the family, then begin rushed routines toward exhausted bedtimes. Some begin the day as mothers and wives, then abruptly change into individuals employed outside the home, with all the stresses and problems of professional people.

A husband may work with the same company for years—drawing his paycheck monthly and advancing automatically when the time comes for a promotion, never realizing that life is passing rapidly—then one day realize that the dreams he used to have are simply not going to happen. A few more years pass and he finally begins to accept his status and slowly sinks into mediocrity.

I am talking about ordinary people. Ordinary people have dreams, and they dream to become great. They know the type of person they want to become. They know the kind of home they would like to have. They know what kind of clothes they would like to wear. The problem is that they are not motivated to set goals for themselves which will turn these dreams into reality. They lack the desire to begin paddling toward shore and to climb out of the mediocrity and to stand firm on the shore of opportunity. They have no framework for goals and no guidance for accomplishing goals once they set them.

This book is written to encourage you to begin right now to change your life for good. It is written to show you how to reach your full potential in whatever you do. It deals with motivation and goals that you can apply to your life right now where you are, no matter what you are or want to become. If you are a homemaker, it will show you how to reach your full potential as a homemaker. It is better to be a full-potential secretary than a mediocre one. The life of a businessman working toward a specific goal is more fulfilling than one who is simply doing his job—doing only what he is supposed to do and nothing more.

A life that is reaching toward its full potential is exciting. It imparts new meaning to taking care of your children. It gives being a wife or husband new perspectives. It makes time a newly appreciated commodity. Once you set a goal to try to have a more meaningful relationship with your mate, you begin to evaluate time spent watching television versus time invested taking a walk with your spouse. How differently we treat our children once we set goals concerning them and then begin to center our attitudes and actions toward making these goals happen! How different a secretary's life becomes once she decides to reach her full potential as a secretary! Not only does her life change at work, but individuals also begin to notice a marked difference in all areas of her life. Once you start to set goals in one area of life, you'll find that it carries over into all aspects of everything you do.

You need to set goals. You may not have realized that need, but it is there. This book will explain to you a proven structure for setting goals that can apply to any and every situation. This structure is one I developed in order to ensure acceptance to medical school, then applied in order to get through medical school and surgical training. But in no way are these principles limited in their application because they were used for medical training. They relate to *you* and to what you are doing right now; they deal with realizing your dreams for your life.

—**Richard Furman**

PART I

MEDICAL SCHOOL

1

The Long Road Begins

I became a Christian when I was twelve years old. That tells how long I had been on the road but doesn't tell how far I had traveled. I was, you might say, an average American Christian. I had been brought up in a churchgoing family, had read my Bible (mostly at night just before going to sleep), and had considered myself a better Christian than many of my friends. I had been on the Christian road for quite a few years when I began my first day of medical school, but I did not realize that I had not traveled down the road very far. I had been lulled into believing that the way I was handling my spiritual life was the correct way.

I was making essentially no effort to mature spiritually. I was doing very little serious study of God's Word. Ninety-five percent of the time I was living the kind of life I wanted to live. The other five percent of the time I was fooling myself into believing I was living the Christian way.

> There is a way that seemeth right unto a man; but the end thereof are the ways of death (Proverbs 16:25 KJV).

I was really living for self, learning how to set goals that glorified self—and it was working. I had made it through four difficult years of college and premedical studies and had earned the right to begin the most grueling and competitive environment I would ever face in my life—medical school.

Ever since Mrs. Avery's husband died of a heart attack, she has surrounded herself with medical students. We are not physicians, but she feels safer, I guess. There are three large rooms upstairs. The rent is cheap, the accommodations are clean, and best of all, we are left alone and it is quiet. I choose the corner room with its big bed, big desk, and two windows, where studying looks natural. My desk would be worth 700 dollars at an antique shop, yet it is only a piece of unmatched furniture left over from a partially successful insurance business owned by Mrs. Avery's husband.

My eyes focus on some words underlined in the upper right-hand corner of the felt desk pad: *Set your goals high.* I suppose every college student who has ever been accepted to medical school worked on the goal of being accepted.

I remember back to my senior year in high school, when I made the decision to go to medical school. That was a major decision in my life, and a major goal. Once that goal was decided on, I never thought of changing it. No matter how bad the odds became, I never played with the idea of changing that goal. I believe that is the basis of being where I am today: adhering to a major decision, a major goal.

I reach for my pen, and under *Set your goals high*, I add, "MAJOR GOAL: Set it and never change it."

I remember my high-school teacher sincerely advising me against a premedical curriculum in college because I was barely passing chemistry and we both knew that chemistry would be a major concentration of premedical studies at college. To me, this brought about the realization that in order to reach my goal of being accepted to medical school, I had to excel in chemistry once I was in college. The day prior to starting college I sat at my desk and set another goal: to excel in chemistry. This would be necessary in order to reach my major goal of being accepted to medical school. This goal of excelling in chemistry was directly related to the major goal, but was *intermediate* in the span of time of college. I realized at that time that if I did not attain this *intermediate* goal, the *major* goal would never be reached.

I lean forward and write again on the felt pad. Just under "MAJOR GOAL: Set it and never change it" I add, "INTERMEDIATE GOAL: Necessary to reach major goal."

Goal-Setting Structure

I begin to see a definite structure to the goals set for reaching medical school. First came the major goal of being accepted to medical school. Then came the intermediate goal of excelling in that first chemistry course in order to reach the major goal. The intermediate goal did not seem nearly so prestigious or glamorous as the major goal, but it was more important than the major goal because it was closer to the present time. It was something I would have to do very soon.

Not until my second night in college—after having attended the first chemistry class—did I happen upon the cornerstone of the goal structure I would follow in the remaining college courses. It was during the second night that I realized that making an excellent grade in chemistry depended on what I did that night. I had the feeling of impending doom or impending excellence. The outcome of my goals depended on the action I took *immediately*. And that action meant that I had to sit down and study *now* and not go with friends or take a break or practice for the intramural football team. My major goal, my intermediate goal, and in essence my *goal structure* depended on what I did not tomorrow, not in the morning, not later tonight, but *immediately*.

I lean forward and add to the goal structure that has proven successful in getting me into medical school:

MAJOR GOAL: Set it and never change it.

INTERMEDIATE GOAL: Necessary to reach major goal.

IMMEDIATE GOAL: Right now, get it done.

These goals got me to medical school, and I decided to use them again to get through medical training. I pick up a small, black, pocket-sized notebook and write a new set of goals for a new chapter in my life. On the first page I write, "MAJOR GOAL: Become a surgeon." On the second page, "INTERMEDIATE GOAL: Successfully complete anatomy and histology." These are my first two courses and will let me and everyone else know whether I am capable of completing medical school. On the third page I write, "IMMEDIATE GOAL: Set study time for each day and never depart from it."

I decide to carry this notebook with me in my lab coat pocket and write down any new immediate goals that I may realize are necessary for attaining my intermediate goal of getting through anatomy and histology successfully. I will call the notebook my *Goals Rule Book*.

I begin the first day of medical school with all the apprehensions and uncertainty that a person could endure, with my entire future at stake. My schedule shows four months of anatomy in the mornings and histology in the afternoons. In keeping with the immediate goal, I write in my *Goals Rule Book*: "I resolve to spend every minute of my life for the next thirty days either studying, eating, or sleeping— nothing else. I will make no telephone calls, write no letters, attend no movies, think of nothing but anatomy and histology for this period of time." The first test in anatomy will be in one month.

Between anatomy and histology, anatomy is the more difficult course, claiming ten times more victims and requiring three times the amount of study.

Life with the Cadavers

The first morning of classes arrives, and I meekly enter a huge lab that contains the cadavers—bodies that have been preserved solely for dissection by medical students. Entering the room, I feel confident, yet within me is a small twinge of insecurity. I wonder whether I can learn all there is to know about the anatomy of the human body.

The freshman class numbers one hundred. I try to size up as many of my fellow students as I can as we crowd into the anatomy lab. A few are laughing and joking, but for the most part everyone else appears uneasy as well. We are motioned to the front of the room, where Dr. Glenn, the head of the department, is arranging papers on a clipboard and getting ready to speak. I doubt that I will ever forget this moment. The odor of the cadavers is indescribable; plastic sheets cover the bodies; plastic aprons, one for each student, lie over the bodies; and two jars of petroleum jelly are set on the portion of the cadaver I guess to be the abdomen. There is an excitement in the room that has no comparison.

Dr. Glenn speaks: "This morning you will be split into groups of four and draw lots for the bodies." He paces up and down in his long white coat, which looks as if he had slept in it for a week. Even sitting three rows back, I can detect that it has the same odor as the cadavers—an almost putrid smell. In fact, everything in the room smells like the cadavers—the floor, the old wooden tables which the bodies lie on, the high stools around the tables, and the bookstands which hold the atlases with pictures of the different parts of the body to be dissected. But after ten minutes the odor becomes less noticeable; all attention is focused on Dr. Glenn. "The small skinny ones are the best to get. Some have arms missing, some have been operated on, some are fat; but you are stuck with the number you draw. If anyone doesn't like his cadaver, I will bring up 'the Chinaman.' He weighs 305 pounds and is five feet two inches tall. We have preserved him for eight years now and won't hesitate to use him if someone complains about the condition of his cadaver." This statement puts us all at the mercy of fate. Whatever number we draw we have to keep.

The dissecting group I elect to be with consists of three of my friends. We attended the same college and were classmates in most of our premed courses, with the exception of Bill Warren, who had been three years ahead of the rest of us. Persistence had made it possible for him to be here. We were all rooming together, and each of us had agreed to do nothing but study for the first month. We would give any earthly belongings in return for a good cadaver, but that will be determined by lot. We elect Bill to draw for the cadaver. We get table number six. Anxiously we walk over and pull back the sheet.

"Not a bit over eighty-five pounds," Bill boasts. Sure enough, there is the cadaver we will be living with for the next four months, a black female, about eighty years old, with almost no fat on her body to speak of. We stand motionless and stare at her without speaking. Her skin is dry and feels unnatural. We are instructed to rub two jars of petroleum jelly on her from her toes to the holes in her ears to keep the skin from cracking. Her hair and fingernails look perfectly natural, but her eyes are dull, the whites cloudy. Her tongue lies unnaturally—slightly stiff and very dry. She has pierced ears and skinny fingers with wrinkled skin. We couldn't have picked a better cadaver if given the choice of the entire room. We slap Bill on the back and congratulate him as if he had just won a million-dollar sweepstakes. It brings a good feeling knowing there will be less time spent on dissecting, with more time left for review at the end of the day.

"She looks like her name ought to be Minnie," Pokie says. Pokie is the nickname we have given Larry Pike because everything he does is slow and deliberate. He walks slowly, eats slowly, talks slowly; everything he does is slow except his thinking. He is a rapid learner and quick to grasp new ideas. He has the best scholastic records of anyone in our group and will have no difficulty getting through medical school. Even though we kid him about his slow ways, we all have some envy of his quick learning ability. Minnie is the cadaver's new name, and Minnie is what we begin to call her.

Goal-Thinking

The days pass quickly as we enter the routine of freshmen medical students. I realize something new to write in the back of my goals book that I am carrying around. It occurs to me that becoming a surgeon is what I think of when I first awaken and it's the last thing on my mind when I go to sleep. I think that such focus may be one essential factor in making a dream come true. I write: "A major goal is something you first awaken to and the last thing you think of when you go to sleep."

During those first few days, everyone in our group becomes tense when it comes time to put a knife to Minnie's skin and cut through the tissues. As we get used to doing this we become more relaxed, and as our confidence builds, our attentiveness slackens.

This is the time I feel the need to push. The newness of medical school has worn off. Some of the students are beginning to talk about programs they saw on television the night before or movies they went to, and another student spent two hours after dinner shooting pool at the fraternity house. There is definitely a relaxed attitude creeping into the class, and I must guard against becoming a part of it. I need to keep a clear view of my goals in preparing for the first test to the very best of my ability.

I also remind myself of Bill Warren. The odds of being accepted to medical school are about 20 to 1. Only about five percent of those who apply are accepted. Bill beat the percentages by persistence. He was rejected three years in a row before being accepted. What he lacked in grades he made up in persistence. That has to be one of the secrets of attaining goals. Bill's goal was not reached initially, but he never changed his mind. He was going to enter medical school if it took 20 years. He didn't say he would make it to medical school if there wasn't a death in the family. He didn't say he would make it to medical school if he didn't wreck his car. He didn't say he would make it to medical school if he didn't run out of money. If he had not had persistence he would not have been accepted, because each of those things did happen to him. Yet he persisted, and he reached his goal.

Persistence, Persistence, Persistence

I again turn in the small notebook to the page labeled "Thoughts" and write "PERSISTENCE: Vital to reaching the goal."

Closing the notebook, I realize that I am somewhat more relaxed about studying and the everyday chores of school. I've even noticed I have a different attitude toward the cadaver. She is no longer a smelly old body, but has taken on some character. We now greet her with "Good morning, Minnie," and always leave with "Good night,

Minnie." We realize that she is only a body without a spirit or soul, but after a while it seems almost as if she does sense what we are doing. Soon it is normal to converse with Minnie without feeling foolish about the one-sided conversation.

"Minnie, you don't have a radial nerve?"

"I believe you are hiding your stellate ganglion, and if you don't show it to me, I'll pinch your carotid artery."

I talk, Pokie talks. In due time we find that her mouth will stay in the position in which we place it. If one of us feels particularly happy, we turn up the corners of her mouth and work all day on a smiling little old lady. If someone feels grouchy, down go the corners and we work in a "grouch" atmosphere.

2

The Day of Reckoning

I DID PRETTY WELL THAT FIRST MONTH of medical school. I had devised a structure for setting goals and had begun to learn the anatomy of goals along with the principles of human anatomy. I was well on my way to developing a vision about goals which would help me through many years of medical training. I was also becoming caught up in my own world, which was rotating around myself. I was doing things I considered religious, but I did not understand what it meant to have the indwelling power of the Holy Spirit within me to face every situation I encountered every day. The life of self and the life of the Spirit are so different—as different as night and day—but I did not understand.

> Those who let themselves be controlled by their lower natures live only to please themselves, but those who follow after the Holy Spirit find themselves doing those things that please God. Following after the Holy Spirit leads to life and peace, but following after the old nature leads to death (Romans 8:5,6 TLB).

I was not mature enough as a Christian to understand what being constantly in the Lord's will at all times was all about. I needed to grow a lot to comprehend the full meaning of letting God control my life under the lordship of Christ.

The first four weeks of medical school passed more rapidly than any other time in my life. We cover Minnie's shoulder, neck, and arm, dissecting each muscle, vessel, and nerve. No sooner do I finish studying the hand than the time arrives for our first test. I feel stunned that the showdown is actually upon me. This is the test that we hear so much about from the sophomore students. They keep shaking their heads and laughing every time one of us mentions the upcoming test, telling us that studying is useless. I have noticed a slight amount of diarrhea the past three days, a sure sign that my nervous system is overworking.

In only one month I have acquired full appreciation of the often-quoted statement, "Getting into medical school is one thing, but staying there is something else." The pace is fast; we cover as much material in one week of medical school as we would be expected to learn in a whole quarter in college. There is no time to go over the subject four or five times in preparing for a test; the material has to be learned the first time around, for there is too much to know to try to rely on recall from a cram study period the day before the exam. This first test is to cover the neck, shoulder, and arm region in minute detail. Every day I have gone over the gross specimens assigned for the time allotted, and each night I have reviewed the atlas and text-book covering the area I dissected that day. Our class has even paid the janitor to come back and unlock the lab on Saturdays so we could have more time to dissect the cadavers.

Goal Structure—First Test

Now the cards are on the table. Approximately 15 percent of the class will flunk this first anatomy test. This test is *the* deciding factor—the one material object that puts all the talk, all the specu-lation, all the self-esteem on the line. At last someone is going to give me a number that I can interpret any way my conscious mind will let me. If I get a low grade, my mind will tell me I will do better next time. If my grade is the class average, my mind can tell me I am going to make it in medical school. If I make a high grade, I must strive just as hard on the next test to keep myself there.

Nine o'clock. I glance at my watch while sitting at my desk the evening prior to the test. I am not really learning anything, only staring at notes I have reviewed numerous times before. It seems almost wrong to go to bed early the night before a test, but I decide that sleep will be more beneficial than staring, so I go to bed and get ten hours of restful sleep.

I walk into class at 8:50 A.M. and take a seat near the back. The cumulative result of my immediate action goals is at hand.

Numerous "Right now, get it done" events have occurred. After supper, when should I start studying? *Right now, get it done.* Finish dissecting a particular nerve, or wait until morning when I am fresh? *Right now, get it done.* Look up a word in the medical dictionary, or let it go? *Right now, get it done.* Find the location of the artery in the atlas tonight, or wait and look for it tomorrow on Minnie? *Right now, get it done!*

The immediate goals are complete. Now let's see if the goal structure works, if it holds water, if it has laid the proper groundwork for the intermediate goal of completing anatomy and histology.

Most of the class is already present, but no one is talking. I can sense the tension in the air: There is some doubt in everyone's mind; there's not a single student here who doesn't have at least a small unsureness about this exam. But I know I am as well prepared as I will ever be. If I can't pass this test, I don't need to be here. What a horrible thought—"don't need to be here." Would my mind let me set an unreachable goal? Surely I can think of some goals I would not be able to attain no matter how hard I tried. Could it be possible? Could I have set an unreachable goal before I took that first chemistry course in college? I have to think I am going to pass this exam, finish medical school, and become a surgeon—I have to believe that my mind would never let me set an impossible goal. There has to be some unknown mechanism that prevents the mind from allowing one to write down an impossible goal.

I mentally write a note for my goals book. "Is it possible for a person to set an impossible goal? I think not, but I am about to find out what goals, desire, and persistence are all about. I will know a lot more about all of these about four hours from now when the test is completed."

The first two hours of the test comprises the writing part of the exam, covering the origin, insertion, and innervation of all the muscles in the region we have dissected. There are several discussion questions concerning the plexus of nerves in the neck and shoulder as well as what type of injury would result if a particular nerve were injured. There are other questions. Some I know completely and remember even more than is asked; some I only vaguely remember reading about.

After 45 minutes, minutes that seem like hours, I sense movement in the room. I look up to see someone turning in his paper and leaving. I can't believe he has completed the test when I am not halfway through. I finish the test in one-and-a-half hours, but am not about to hand it in until the two-hour limit is announced. I still have time to go over the questions once more and make sure I have not misread a question or given a wrong answer when I know the correct one. The announcement is then made that our time is up; everything is answered the way I intend it.

The next two hours brings a test not only of intellect but also of nerves. There are 25 bodies, each with yellow tags attached to particular parts that have been dissected. Some are obvious, some vaguely obscure. Everyone picks a station to begin the test. The instructor stands at the head of the room with a large clock that will sound off with a loud buzz every two minutes. Each time it sounds, we are to move to the next station, whether or not we have identified the tagged portion of the cadaver.

Look at the specimen.

Think!

Eyes closed. Try to remember!

Buzzer.

Move to the next specimen.

Easy one—write it down and think back to the last one.

Think! Name of the branch of that nerve. I can't think.

Buzzer.

Move to the next specimen.

Think! Think! Think! Got to come up with this one! I know I can come up with this one if I can slow down and think.

Quit listening for the buzzer.

Think! Ansa hypoglossal! That's it. Write it down.

Think back to the one I missed.

I don't know it! I don't remember—no, I don't know.

Buzzer.

I near the cadaver I began with, signifying the end of the road, and realize that there are six blanks on my paper. I had planned to answer these as I had time to think, but that time never came. I decide to fill them in as best I remember from the little notes I have written in the margins of the answer sheet. Then the final buzzer sounds. The test is over.

I turn in my paper and find myself with absolutely nothing to do. I have studied so much in the past month that I couldn't possibly read anything more about medicine.

Romance Time…Finally

Today is Saturday, and we won't start another section on our cadavers until Monday. This is the first free time I have had since beginning anatomy, and it is too nice a day not to drive 120 miles to surprise that girl I told not to expect to see me until Thanksgiving.

In the meantime I notice a strange phenomenon: It is 24 hours into the weekend, and I am just beginning to relax. My mind has been running in high gear for a month, and it won't let me ease back into the free and easy style I was used to in college. Does this mean I will soon be geared to run at a higher speed for the rest of my life, or will I still be able to slip back into a frame of mind that will occasionally allow me to waste a little time here and there?

I quit thinking about that and begin to enjoy what little free time I do have. Harriet is so excited to see me this weekend. We have dated for a one-and-a-half years; I think it's time to get married. She is starting her junior year at college, and I know we can't wait until she graduates before we get married. I haven't asked her to marry me, but I know she is thinking along the same line as I am. After our second date in college I decided she was the girl I would marry, and I have just assumed that it will eventually happen. She is just right for me. I guess the first step is to figure out how to get her education taken care of. The real problem is the fact that there is no college near the medical school. We will have to talk this situation over and come up with a workable solution before discussing it with her parents. Which is more important: our happiness or her college education?

I present the idea to Harriet. It is fun to actually start thinking along the line of marriage. We arrive at no solution to our problem, however. Sunday afternoon approaches, and it is time to quit thinking about Harriet and begin thinking about what grade I made on the anatomy test.

Monday morning comes quickly. I can feel butterflies creeping into my stomach as I walk up the steps to the anatomy class. The test papers are to be returned this afternoon. Where is my faith in my analogy of goals? As the day progresses, the butterflies worsen. I keep trying to convince myself I did okay, but do not feel like eating lunch. The grade curve is announced: 48-98. The papers are returned at 5 P.M. Mine has big red numbers: a nine and a four. All I can do is stare at them. My eyes fix on the grade at the top of page one—94. I'm within the upper one-fourth of the class. The feeling is the same as when I learned I was accepted at medical school. I know now that I am going to make it. This strengthens the idea that whatever I strive for I can reach. Still, I am not 100 percent certain if this is true. I have so much ahead of me to tackle. New immediate goal: next section of anatomy and histology, continue same study habits. *Right now, get it done.* I write this neatly on the "Immediate Goal" page of my book.

Goals Rule Book

Because my immediate goals cover small increments of my progress, I realize they will always be changing. I'll be glad when anatomy and histology are over and I can change my intermediate goal for the first time. I review the *Goals Rule Book* again:

MAJOR GOAL: Become a surgeon.

INTERMEDIATE GOAL: Successfully complete anatomy and histology.

IMMEDIATE GOAL: Next section of anatomy and histology, continue same study habits. *Right now, get it done.*

As time progresses, my rotation on anatomy becomes more enjoyable and less demanding. I develop a routine consisting of going to class all day, studying until 12:30 at night, going to bed, getting up, and going back to class. No movies, no television, no breaks—just sticking to the routine. However, a big change in my original plans has developed. Each weekend I pack my books into the car and take off to see Harriet. I guess I can now call her my fiancée, even though I haven't really asked her to marry me. This particular weekend is special, at least to my way of thinking. We dissected the heart during the week, and I slip a heart out of the building as I leave, rationalizing the act by telling myself I want to study the valves and arteries in the heart over the weekend. But I know the real reason is to show Harriet what a real human heart looks like inside and out. I can hardly wait to get to her house with my "surprise package" floating inside a jar of formalin.

After two-and-a-half hours of traveling, I arrive. After the usual ritual of giving her a hug and kiss, I remove the jar from the sack to demonstrate my newly learned knowledge of the heart.

Harriet shifts away from me and takes three steps backward.

"It's only Minnie's heart. Look, this is where the blood comes in," I authoritatively point out. "It goes from here to the lungs and back into the heart."

Harriet shows slight interest, but it is evident that I will not be able to take it out of the jar for a closer look. I find it difficult to believe she doesn't have the interest I think she ought to. If she is to be a doctor's wife, she ought to *want* to hold a real heart; at least that's the way I look at it. However, I accept reality and place the jar back on the front seat of the car.

As we finish dinner, Harriet and I go over the game plan we have decided to present to her folks. We have decided that there is no real reason for her to finish college. What is important in our lives is our happiness, our being together. The best way to accomplish this is for Harriet to quit college and take a secretarial course, and in less than two months be typing away in someone's office. She can make enough for us to live on, and after four years of medical school I'll be starting internship and making some additional money.

We get our story straight and ask her parents to sit down. I begin, "We would like to go over something with you to see what you think. We have decided that there is no real reason for Harriet to finish college. What is important in our lives is our happiness and our being together. The best way to accomplish this is for Harriet to quit college and take a secretarial course." I pause because I can tell her father wants to say something.

"I have always wanted Harriet to finish college. I think she should."

For some reason, the rest of my story doesn't want to come out of my mouth. He hasn't said we can't get married; he won't say that. But he has told us exactly what he is thinking. We end the discussion fairly coldly, with no one knowing how not to say anything wrong. Harriet and I will have to reconsider our plans. So I return to class and we postpone any decision for the time being.

By the time I finish anatomy and histology, most of the excitement of being in medical school has worn off and I'm beginning to feel more like I'm in an overdemanding postgraduate school. I find some of the courses only vaguely related to what I think necessary to become a doctor, much less a surgeon. I force myself to study by remembering that the entire gamut must be taken, and passed, in order to receive a degree. On this I have to rationalize. Many of the courses do not pertain in the slightest to surgery. I am not particularly interested in some of them and will never use the knowledge once the final exam is over. Why not relax and just get by rather than knock myself out for good grades? I come to realize that I must reassess my major goal, intermediate goal, and immediate goal before I can decide what action to take: major goal—surgery; intermediate goal—whatever course I am taking; immediate goal—knowledge of a course I'm not interested in.

Setting Goals Positively

What do I do with courses that are not of interest to me? Can I utilize my *Goals Rule Book* to help answer this question? Perhaps I will have to come up with a new rule that will help me deal with this dilemma. I am sure this will become a greater problem as school progresses.

I analyze this problem carefully by considering the known goals. MAJOR: to become a surgeon. To accomplish this, I must be accepted to a superb residency training program. To accomplish *that*, I must be accepted to a superb internship. Now to the truth of the matter. Internship acceptance depends on two things: recommendations and grades.

Good grades are easier to obtain if I have a genuine interest in the course. Therefore, I need to somehow develop an interest in a course I am completely disinterested in. But how?

AGGRESSIVE POSITIVE THINKING. This will be the only way. Any negative thoughts about a course will ruin it for me. I must erase the negatives as they appear and replace them with positives. I have to seek the good points in the professor, the book, the hours spent in class, and so on. This is the secret to controlling my mind in order to get good grades in uninteresting courses. Attack them with positiveness of mind and beat them with repeated attacks. Just like the proverbial bad apple in a barrel, the negative thought must come out and be replaced with a positive thought. I jot on the "Thoughts" page of my book: "POSITIVENESS OF MIND: beat the negatives. Replace negatives with positives."

I move on to the studies of pathology, physiology, pharmacology, and a few minor courses to fill any time slots left vacant. The first year goes well, and I start on the second year. I find that I have much less enthusiasm now than I had on the first day of medical school. I have to rely on the goal system of study more and more. Fortunately it is working; I cannot live on enthusiasm alone.

Harriet and I continue to discuss our marriage situation. This first year has passed so quickly. She is now only one year away from graduation. We decide that she should finish. We are somewhat reluctant but know that there is some virtue in her completing what is begun. We decide to write each other every day. As I drive back to medical school, this weekend comes to a close. However, one thought is certain in my mind: We *will* get married. As far as setting a date, I am also certain when the marriage will take place. That is simple: look up the date of Harriet's graduation, and we will get married the following weekend. I reach Mrs. Avery's upstairs apartment, take a seat at the desk, and start preparing for my new classes in the morning.

I begin studies in parasitology, biochemistry, hematology, introduction to clinical medicine, and several courses that will help bridge the gap between the basic sciences and actually treating the patient. The first part of this year turns out to be a gradual transition from all bookwork to a minute amount of time being spent actually seeing patients. It seems too gradual to me. It is six months into the year, and I am anxious to stop looking at books and start looking at patients. I haven't even seen a patient, much less talked to or touched one. All I do is read until the information is coming out of my ears, then go to class, take notes, and study the thick medical books on my desk. I am introduced to people as being a medical student, which immediately triggers them to talk of some ailment that either they themselves have or that some friend or relative has. I do not know any more about the ailments and diseases of the body than a biology major in college, yet these people expect me to have the knowledge of a practicing physician. This increased my drive to start learning something about patients, about sick people, about the treatment of at least the more common diseases. I was tired of reading about how the body works, how it is put together, and what medications can be used. I feel ready to start applying my knowledge; all the learning compartments of my brain are overflowing…saturated…supersaturated. I try to make myself realize it's all part of the system.

Desire: The Essential Element

Lamar Owens is not as concerned about those issues as I am. He has much more to think about—whether he will pass or fail. I attended college with Lamar, who had excellent grades back then, but for some reason he began having real difficulty academically as soon as he started medical school. The last year and a half has been a tough, almost terrifying, experience for him. This is verified by the fact that he vomits every morning as soon as he is awake enough to realize he is in medical school and has to go to classes. What makes someone go through such torment? He is not enjoying even 60 seconds a day of his life. Why does he continue this way? I confront him with the question. "Desire," he says. The only thing that keeps him getting up every morning and going to class is *desire*. I think about that.

DESIRE.

This is not the type of desire expressed by a college student who says, "I would give anything to be a doctor," and all the while he is having a good time and getting Cs. He may desire to become a doctor, but he does not desire it the way Lamar does.

As I think about this more, I begin to realize that this special desire is what it takes to accomplish day-to-day, immediate actions. We all have a goal, but the difference lies in whether someone does something about it. Lamar's compelling desire is the difference between what he dreams of becoming and what he actually becomes.

This new finding impresses me enough to jot it down in my goals book. "COMPELLING DESIRE: the necessary force between wanting and having."

The year ends, and both Lamar and I pass, but each with a different psychological reaction to our grades. He paid the price of compelling desire and will be rewarded for it. I am sure he will find a spot in medicine that he likes.

Medical school is basically divided into two segments: the first two years consist mostly of studying books and doing classwork, and the last two years are devoted to the clinical aspect of becoming a doctor, which means time spent working with patients. I look back on the subclinical years as 100 percent work. I learned much but am now eager to get into the hospital, to work the wards, to get into the operating room, to learn from residents. Now the time has come to take a big step in becoming a doctor: I move into the hospital. My major goal remains the same: become a surgeon. My intermediate goal centers on completing medical school. Now is the time to change my immediate actions from reading books to that of adding patients to the books.

3

Marriage and Medicine

AS THE SECOND YEAR OF MEDICAL SCHOOL ENDED, I began life as a married man. I knew so little then about how a marriage ought to work. I was preparing to run my marriage the same way I was running my life—centered on self.

As long as things went the way I thought they should go, everything was fine. Whenever something happened that didn't suit me, life was pretty rough around the house. I felt marriage ought to be a 50/50 proposition. I would give my 50 percent as long as Harriet gave her 50 percent. But if I thought I were right and she were wrong, then my 50 percent was negated immediately. I had not yet read Paul's letter to the Ephesian Christians, where we find this difficult command to husbands:

> Husbands, love your wives, just as Christ loved the church
> and gave himself up for her to make her holy, cleansing her by
> the washing with water through the word (Ephesians 5:25,26).

I had not yet realized that God's instructions in this passage do not say, "Husbands love your wives as long as you are treated a certain way, as long as she is wrong and you are right, as long as she upholds her 50 percent of the marriage." It would be many years before I realized that marriage is not a 50/50 proposition; it is a 100/100 proposition for both the husband and the wife. I am required to give 100 percent of Christ in me to the marriage, whether or not my wife gives 100 percent or even 10 percent.

On June 6 the dream becomes reality. Harriet and I become man and wife. The long-awaited honeymoon ends all too quickly, and the time has come to begin the exciting clinical years of school. We find a small garage apartment. Our bedroom is hardly big enough to call it a room. Our double bed is pushed against one wall, and you have to turn sideways to walk between the other side of the bed and the wall.

"Why did you choose this small room to be our bedroom?" Harriet asks as we move our furniture in. "The other room would have let us walk on both sides of the bed and would make it much easier to make up the bed."

"The tin roof," I reply. "There is a tin-roofed shed just outside the window in the small room. You can't beat the sound of rain beating on a tin roof for a good night's sleep. I even stuck a piece of tin in my window when I was in college so I could hear the rain. You'll see; you will like it."

"Okay, if it means that much to you, I guess I can make the bed with it against the wall."

We finally get our little bit of furniture moved in and settle down for our first night in our new home. We talk of the coming year.

"You know that once classes begin we won't be able to spend much time together. I'll be on call at the hospital every third night and will need to study the other two."

Harriet smiles and replies, "Just being here is going to be so much better than last year. At least we'll have your study breaks and weekends to call our own."

One Goal Fulfilled

It certainly is a nicer life with Harriet as my wife, and she is such a sweet girl to come home to. I feel good about the days ahead.

This year of medical school will consist of rotations devoted to certain specialties. One of these, internal medicine, seems to be the epitome of medical science: detailed workups of patients, with all the special studies that are at the fingertips of the internist. New medicines are being used daily. The field seems wide open for anyone who is willing to give three extra years of internship to study the more unusual types of diseases.

Obstetrics and gynecology comprise another field I will rotate through this year. Some surgery is performed, but is limited to that of the female organs. I would rather be able to operate on all the organs in the abdomen if I am to operate at all. I will also rotate through pediatrics, but I doubt that my disposition will allow me to be a pediatrician.

Obstetrics and gynecology are my first clinical rotation. While I feel limited by these, I take comfort in knowing that at least I am on my way to becoming a "real" doctor. I am assigned to the city-county hospital for the first part of the rotation. There are numerous charity cases, and most of these deliveries are done by the interns. It doesn't take long to find that a student is the low man on the totem pole—even lower than the nurses, since most of the nurses have been working on O.B. for years, and delivering babies is second nature to them. Much of the practical work of delivering babies will be learned from them.

Labor Pains

Our group completes the usual first-day orientation and is about to go eat dinner when we are told to report to the delivery room immediately for our assignments and introduction. Just as we enter, a woman lets out a yell so loud that we stop in our tracks, looking at one another as if someone ought to be doing something. We are told she is only having labor pain, which will soon end. The intern introduces himself and instructs me and three fellow students to get into scrub suits in preparation for assisting with deliveries. We are designated to be "on call" tonight. The rest are free to leave, but everyone is so anxious to see a delivery that the entire group of 16 changes into scrub suits and stays. Soon a patient is wheeled into the delivery room as we curiously gather around. I am actually going to see a real live patient deliver a real live baby! This is real, genuine medicine—nothing artificial, nothing to read about, just "doing." The intern scrubs his hands hastily, then quickly puts on a sterile gown while the nurses place the woman on the delivery table. One nurse puts restraints on the patient's wrists, another places her feet and legs in stirrups. The contractions are coming at short intervals, and with each one the patient writhes around on the table and moans continuously.

"Go ahead and give her the Demerol," says the intern as he makes his way to the foot of the delivery table. The nurse injects the pain medication. She has already prepped the vaginal region with surgical soap and has placed drapes around the site of the delivery. To one side of the intern is a stand about the size of a kitchen table which is covered with a sterile sheet. On it is an array of instruments—sutures, needles, basins, a suction bulb, test tubes, sponges, umbilical cord clamps, and forceps. The Demerol has been given, but it seems not to have had any effect, judging by all the noise the patient is making. The intern picks up a needle and syringe, fills it with Xylocaine, and proceeds to inject the numbing medication into the top portion of the birth canal. The contractions are coming just a few seconds apart, and suddenly I see black hair on the baby's head making its appearance. For five minutes the patient continues to contract, but it doesn't seem as though the delivery is making any progress. The intern becomes nervous and mutters, "She having her first delivery, and the head is rotated; we're going to have to turn the baby."

I don't know if this is serious or not, but I become more concerned as I watch perspiration begin to appear on the intern's forehead as he moves around a little quicker than he has been. All attention focuses on him, and somehow the noise and fuss coming from the mother recedes in my mind, even though only a few minutes ago all I could think of was how much pain she was experiencing, and could not see how any doctor could concentrate on delivering a baby with all that going on. Now the intern takes center stage. I concentrate on his performance only.

Delivery Complications

The intern persists at turning the baby in the womb, and finally it is evident that he is going to be successful. The baby's head comes well into view, and the intern grabs a pair of scissors, and with two snips of the blades, performs an episiotomy, making the outlet of the birth canal larger by incising its outer rim. Within a few seconds the baby is out, and the intern holds it in one arm as he picks up the bulb syringe with his free hand and suctions the mucous material out of the baby's nose and mouth. Next he places a clamp across the umbilical cord and cuts the cord in two. The baby begins to cry and the intern passes him to one of the nurses, situating himself again at the foot of the table to deliver the afterbirth, the placenta. He does this by applying gentle traction on the portion of the cord remaining attached to the placenta. The placenta comes with ease and all appears well until the intern inspects the episiotomy site. A few choice curse words explode from his mouth as he exclaims: "Call Dr. Harman. Tell him to come right now. I have a laceration into the rectum and need help." The episiotomy has torn into the rectum and left a direct communication between it and the vagina, and now must be sewn in such a way as to close the tear.

By this time the mother is quiet and resting, the nurses are busy with their duties, and the whole scene is one of anticlimax, except for the intern, who is still looking at the episiotomy and shaking his head in disbelief. "Never had this happen before," he says. "I just can't understand it." He keeps repeating those two sentences and says nothing more. All of us are afraid to ask for an explanation of what went wrong or of his plans to redeem the situation; we stand quietly watching.

I feel sorry for him. I know it was the mother who went through the pain and agony of delivering the baby, and it was the mother who had a tear in her rectum which would have to be closed. It seems only sensible that I ought to have empathy for this poor mother, but somehow the only person I felt badly for was the intern. I somehow sense that he is having the worse experience and enduring greater mental stress than she. He is obviously affected by this complication, saying very little until the attending staff physician enters the room. The physician is a short, obese man in his mid-forties with almost no hair. The town doctors call him Curly, but this intern addresses him as "Doctor." The patient is soon taken to the operating room, where the tear is closed under general anesthesia.

Our student world of medicine changes completely once the patient leaves for the operating room. Our world does not yet include the total care for the patient. We will not yet learn how to close a rectal tear or how to treat a patient post-op. On this particular patient our world is a shallow one: We do not have the worry or responsibility for the woman. Instead, we turn to other patients. We are fed the milk problems of obstetrics and gynecology; the meat will come later.

My First Patient

Each of the four in our subgroup is assigned a patient to follow through labor and delivery. I am assigned a mother of four healthy children who is having weak and irregular contractions about every 20 minutes. I am told by the nurse that this means she is not near delivery, and I am to sit beside the bed with my hand on her abdomen and record each contraction her uterus makes. She is an obese, jolly, and talkative patient, telling me about her other deliveries—that the first two were born at home, and the next two in the hospital. She states that the first child had been difficult to deliver, but the more babies she had, the easier it became. As I sit with one hand on her abdomen, and the other propping up my chin, I keep thinking about the woman who had just been taken into surgery. I know all deliveries can't be that bad, and wonder if she will ever desire to have another baby after what she had been through.

Hours pass, and the contractions increase to every seven or eight minutes apart, but are still not very forceful. I have used three sheets of paper, writing down the actual time of the contraction, the duration, and the strength, using an arbitrary plus one through plus four. Another hour passes, and the contractions get stronger and closer together. By three in the morning the nurse tells me the patient is having true labor and that I should wake the intern to inform him of the progress of the patient if I don't want to deliver the baby in bed. This I certainly do not want—neither in bed nor on the delivery table. I was overly eager to deliver a baby the minute I came on the service, but after seeing how difficult delivery can be, it has become the last thing I want to do. I awaken the intern and tell him how close the contractions are; he gives me instructions to go ahead and get her on the table; he will be right in. This I do, or, I should say, the nurse does while I stand to one side trying to put on a gown and gloves. This is an ordeal in itself, for everything must be completely sterile from the time I scrub my hands all the way to the end of the delivery. There is a special way to put on sterile gowns in order not to contaminate them, and a unique way to get the gloves on without touching the outsides of them. Presently I can scrub, gown, and get my gloves on in a correct, orderly fashion, but that's about as far as I know what to do. Only a few hours ago I had watched everything the intern had done to get ready to deliver a baby, and he had prepared with ease, but each small movement I made seemed like a major thought process. Where do I put my hands? I feel awkward standing on both feet—it seems as if I am standing at attention. I don't know what to say to the patient. I smile and nod to her, but because I have a mask on she saw only the nod, not the smile. I now wish the intern were here. Only a few hours ago I watched him go through the "ten easy steps of delivering a baby," but now I realize there are at least a thousand steps involved in getting ready for a delivery. The nurse begins to tell me what to do until the intern arrives—how to drape the patient, where and in what order to place the instruments, how the umbilical clamp works, and so on.

By this time the patient is having good contractions coming very close together. She is having some pain, but is keeping quiet about it and is not moving all over the table, as did the previous patient. The nurse who is standing beside her asks what she plans to name the baby.

This is more like it, I think to myself, still not feeling very sure of myself delivering babies and wishing the intern would show up. Had he fallen back to sleep? I begin to feel apprehension like I'd never had before. Do I dare show it by asking the nurse where the intern might be? I ask myself this question three times before the intern sticks his head in the door and stares commandingly. "They just called me to the emergency room. Someone is bleeding, and they want me quick. You stand there and catch the baby. That's all. Don't try anything special; she's had four already, so this one ought to fall out."

"What about an episiotomy?" I inquire, trying to sound like I know at least a little about what could happen.

With that comment he looks directly at the nurse and says, "I've got to go. Don't let him do anything other than catch the baby and put the umbilical clamp on. I ought to be back by then." He turns and disappears, leaving me the loneliest individual in the world.

With Opportunity Comes Responsibility

I sense I am about to take that giant step toward becoming the doctor I have been thinking so much about. I step right up to the foot of the delivery table and try to act knowledgeable about what I am doing. I can't seem to visualize how to look busy by just standing, waiting for a baby to fall out. I am sure the intern is right and this will be a routine delivery, but then again, I am not sure this woman won't be just like the previous patient and end up in the operating room. I begin to realize why babies are delivered by obstetricians. Nine times out of ten, anyone can deliver a baby with only a little knowledge of what to do, but it is the tenth time that makes all the difference in the world.

I see the little head pushing down. I awkwardly reach out and place an apprehensive hand on the head and let the baby glide into my nervous fingers. I know I am supposed to clamp the umbilical cord, but where did the intern place the clamp? The umbilical cord is two feet long; I don't know where to put the clamp. Does it even matter where? I remember now. I place it adjacent to the umbilicus, then suction the mucus out of the nose and mouth of the baby, and hand the child to the nurse. The placenta comes with ease. The nurse breaks the silence barrier between us by saying, "I'm giving the Pitressin now, doctor." I am startled at being called a doctor. I decide I must have done okay because she used this term. After all, I do know that Pitressin is a drug used to make the uterus squeeze down after delivery, and not many people who are not doctors know that.

"Sure, go ahead," I say confidently. I realize I haven't done much, but I have experienced something new, and it is a great feeling. The intern calls to see how things are, and is relieved to hear that it was indeed an uneventful delivery. I take a moment to talk to the mother, telling her it was my first delivery. She smiles, and I somehow sense she realizes that this is a bigger event for me than it is for her—it is my first, and her fifth.

I remove my gloves and gown, buy a Coke and a pack of cheese crackers from the vending machines, and head toward the bed. It is now 6:00 A.M., and it takes about three seconds for me to fall asleep—with my clothes on.

Discipline: The Foundation of Goals

The new day starts early, with time for only one hour of sleep. Tonight is an off night, which should allow me some time to catch up on my rest. Our group meets in the residents' lounge and decides who has to draw blood from the patients. The only fair way is to rotate four at a time, and since we already have a schedule for who will be on call each night, we decide to let the students draw blood the next morning. All that means to me is that I am supposed to draw blood. I have never stuck a needle into anything; yet I am now required to insert a needle into every patient on the floor for blood. I have to remind myself of the rule I discovered back when I was taking courses that weren't of interest to me: I must discipline myself to do things I don't like in order to achieve my major goal, which, in turn, will reward me for my work. I knew this rule worked in those courses, and I knew it would work now. I did not want to cause pain to the person by learning how to insert a needle into his or her veins, yet I knew I had to take immediate action—right now!

I muster up some courage and walk into the room of the first patient. I explain my mission as best I can to the patient as I place a tourniquet around her arm. My conversation sounds as if I were reading my sentences. I insert the needle through her skin on top of a vein in plain view just below the tourniquet. The needle slid to one side of the vein, so I had to withdraw it and try again. I finally got the needle through her skin and into the vein, with the patient leaning closer and closer to my face. I glance up at her with a slight smile and say, "Your veins are really hard to hit." She replies that they were not that hard to hit yesterday, and that no one else had ever had this much trouble getting blood from her. I can't bring myself to tell her that the student who drew blood just the morning before had a year's experience, while I am having my first try.

I withdraw enough blood to fill one test tube. I have to fill two tubes, but can't withdraw any more blood. Evidently the needle has slipped out of the vein. I withdraw the needle and hold pressure over the site, but blood continues to come out of the needle hole.

The patient starts wiggling her fingers. "That tourniquet is hurting my arm and making my hand tingle."

How stupid can I be? Obviously the vein will keep building up pressure and bleed as long as the tourniquet is on. I take it off, and the bleeding stops. My big worry now is to get the other test tube of blood, but I don't want to see this patient again in my life, much less insert a needle into her again. I am sure the feeling is mutual. I walk out into the hall and meet a fellow student who is waiting for me. He was unable to get any blood at all from his patient, and wants me to try my luck. It suddenly dawns on me that my problem is solved. After all, I have drawn one tube of blood from my patient; he ought to be able to draw one. We agree to swap patients and try again.

I walk into the room of the other patient. "Are you any better than the last doctor that was in here?"

"Well, I've had a little more experience," I reply. I am honest. I have drawn blood, he hasn't.

We both are successful due to some unknown fate, but I decide right away that I am not going to settle for a blood-drawing rotation every fourth morning. I am going to be here *every* morning until I can draw blood from any patient I try. I glance at the *Goals Rule Book* from time to time just as a reminder. Immediate action—there is no problem with that. There are few minutes in the day when I am not actively working on my goal on O.B. With a subject this interesting, I don't have to work so hard in making myself stick to the rules.

As the rotation progresses, I begin to hit the majority of veins I attempt—one hurdle passed. I am also delivering babies with some regularity and no longer feel out of place standing at the foot of a delivery table. The excitement and newness of the first clinical rotation wears down as the clerkship draws to an end. I have enjoyed O.B., but I don't think I want to do this for the rest of my life. I refuel my eagerness to learn something new and prepare to move on to the next rotation—pediatrics.

Do It Now!

Before starting the next rotation, I review my goals book and bring it up to date, something I have started doing from time to time.

MAJOR: surgeon; INTERMEDIATE: medical school; IMME-DIATE ACTION: study pediatrics—RIGHT NOW. Don't wade into it for a week or two; get aggressive now and learn all that is possible on the first day. I am learning more and more that immediate action is the key to successfully reaching a major goal. What I do right now determines what the outcome will be. The price is paid *now*.

As I think of goals, I think of Harriet and our achieved goal of marriage. Harriet is an ideal wife. She is teaching a second-grade class at a school near our apartment. We are living on her salary alone, and our meals reflect this fact.

"Sweetie, do you realize I have now eaten tuna fixed 38 different ways?" I remark as I dish up a big spoonful of tuna casserole onto my plate.

"I made tuna only because you complained about the Spam last night," is her brisk reply.

We have been married just long enough for me to develop a sense about Harriet. My sense tells me I have said enough. In fact, I have probably said too much. I will be glad when next year comes and she gets a raise. She does do a good job with tuna; for this I am thankful.

4
The Maturing of a Medical Student

AFTER NEARLY THREE YEARS IN MEDICAL SCHOOL, I have made great strides toward maturing as a medical student. From the beginning I had realized that to accomplish my goal of becoming a surgeon, I had to give of my time and myself. Since then, I had read the right books and listened to respected instructors lecturing on how to be a better physician. I was serious. I was dedicated. I pulled out all the stops.

It is a shame I was not wise enough to see that maturing as a Christian requires similar devotion to studying and obeying the Scriptures. Had I understood the need to set goals for my spiritual life as well as my medical career, I could have begun breaking down the domination of self and relying upon the direction of the Holy Spirit.

No one told me, however, about the battle that rages in one's life between self-rule and rule by the Holy Spirit. No one told me how to allow the Holy Spirit to begin working in my life on a daily and hourly basis. The only spiritual goals I set centered on making sure I went to church at the proper time and that I read the Scriptures just enough to give me a superficial sense of well-being. My progress in spiritual living paled when compared with my progress in medicine.

I was not eager to study the Bible. I had no desire to read spiritual books. I wanted to know that which was righteous, but I didn't have a genuine hunger for it. I was hungry and thirsty to grow as a medical student, but I did not possess that same appetite when it came to spiritual growth.

After only two days of orientation, I can see that the pediatrics rotation is completely different from the O.B. rotation. The diseases, diagnoses, medication, and treatment are all on a much different scale from that of an adult. After the first few days of ward duty, I become somewhat discouraged with working with infants. Unlike adult patients, they cannot tell me or show me where they hurt, and I can't seem to find where they hurt by direct examination because they usually cry from the time I begin the exam until I quit. I had a difficult enough time memorizing the dosages of adult medicine in O.B., and now this mental process has to be redone but on a much more accurate basis, since a small difference in the dose makes a big difference to a small child or infant.

The rotation begins at the university hospital, and I am placed on a team of doctors consisting of a staff man, a senior resident, a junior resident, an intern, and four students. I am assigned to Tom Moore, the junior resident, and am to take orders from him. We make rounds and attend conferences in the mornings, and hold clinics in the afternoon. The students are required to remain at the hospital every third night to be on call and check on patients if anything happens to them. After seeing a patient, the student is to decide whether he can handle the situation or needs to call an intern. Likewise, the intern is responsible to the first-year resident, and so on up the ladder until, on a complicated case, the whole team might be on hand to see the patient.

Learning Experiences

I soon realize the whole basis for medical teaching has to be this chain of command, and there is no cut-and-dried method of knowing where the chain stops. One first-year resident may be able to handle a situation superbly while his fellow first-year resident may have no idea what is going on, necessitating aid from the second-year man. The one important lesson I learn from this rotation setup is that if there is any doubt at all about the proper treatment of the patient, call the next higher man. This does three things: It gives more assurance that the patient will be treated correctly; it transfers the responsibility from someone with less experience to someone with more experience; and it presents the opportunity to learn from someone with more experience. After working with this chain of command a few times, I begin to understand an important fact of life. There are basically two ways to learn anything: one is by direct experience, and the other is by being smart enough to benefit from the experience of others. On the one hand, there is the "I have to go through it myself" experience, and on the other hand there is the "I don't have to go through it myself" experience. Medical training is set up for me to learn directly from the individual above me in the chain of command. I shouldn't have to make the same mistakes or go through the same experiences just to learn what someone above me knows. If I am smart, I will observe him and ask as many questions as I can to keep from having to reenact everything he has done wrong. And if I am really smart, I will look ahead to the entire chain above me and learn from their experiences, even though I am not far enough along to directly benefit from them at this time. This will help me to be better equipped and possibly help lessen the suffering of patients.

A Madhouse Rotation

Dr. Keith Milton is the chairman of the pediatrics department and is a perpetual whirlwind of activity. The entire staff likes and respects him, but there are very few students or residents who don't get reprimanded by him at least twice. He is everywhere at once—on rounds one minute, in a conference the next, and grabbing a student by the arm to go see an interesting patient the next.

By the fifth night on call, I feel comfortable on the service. The awkwardness of being a new student on a new rotation has vanished; I know the patients and some of the treatments. All is quiet until I am awakened by an intruder in our sleeping quarters. The lights go on. Someone is stomping around the room, yelling, "Let's go! I don't have all night to pussyfoot around. I've got to fly to Chicago in the morning, and I want to see how those patients are doing." I rise up in bed and look at my watch. It is 2:30 A.M. All of a sudden I realize that Dr. Milton is the "intruder." He had been out of town for three days and he had just arrived from the airport.

This fellow must be crazy, I think. *He hasn't even been home, and now he wants to make rounds in the middle of the night.* I drag myself out of bed feeling sure it won't take long to make rounds, since we have very few sick patients on the ward.

I am proven wrong. We finish rounds at five o'clock, and the intern has five or six items to be ordered for each patient. These are things that even Tom, the resident, had not thought of, much less told us to do.

Dr. Milton then took off to the nurses' station, poured each of us a cup of coffee, and started talking. At least it was a nice gesture to pour our coffee, and I thought he was going to become more informal, and possibly even talk about his recent trip. I was ready for a few minutes of discussing something other than patients.

Instead, he said, "I don't ever want to leave town and come back with the pediatric service looking the way it does now. Tom, I'll see you when I get back. Now, let's get to work." And with that verbal order, he was off down the hall and gone for another week. We all sat calmly drinking our coffee, saying very little. It was difficult to believe the preceding events had actually happened. All the responsibility lay on Tom's shoulders, even though many of the things that had not gotten done were the fault of the intern and me. There was nothing I wanted to do more than return to bed, but I knew I wouldn't even *see* the bed until after another full day. We were too far behind on our work to think of a nap now.

Associate with Winners

The weeks pass. Often during this portion of my pediatric rotation, I caught myself becoming annoyed with Dr. Milton's dictatorial, authoritative role in running the service. Only as I near the completion of working with him do I realize the fantastic amount of knowledge I have learned from this man and his unique form of teaching. He *makes* his students learn. He doesn't leave it to the prerogative of the student to read his assignment, depending on whether he has time or wants to. He will ask questions on the subjects he expects us to know. I regret that I realize only now how great a teacher he is. I could have learned more from him had I made that observation earlier.

I now realize that Dr. Milton's goal makes him the way he is. His goal is to have the best possible pediatric department. His goal is not to be the best-liked professor on the staff, because the two goals are not in harmony. He can't be very well-liked if he wakes us in the middle of the night and keeps us up for several hours. But that may be the reason he has one of the best pediatric departments in the country. The goal makes the man's character what it is. I pledge to surround myself with teachers like Dr. Milton in the future, if at all possible.

I try to think more about what it is that makes Dr. Milton so successful in his field of medicine. What makes him the chief? What sets him above everyone else in the department? If I can figure that out, then I can decide how to conduct my activities accordingly. I first rehash in my mind what I have already put together and see if there is anything to add to the picture of attaining goals—my goals. One thing I noticed is that Dr. Milton has made a habit of doing things that the other staff men don't like to do. He has made a habit of working at any time of the day or night because there may not be any other time for his work. He has repeated this work habit so long that it has become a part of his character. I conclude that I should be able to determine my own work character by deciding to do things that the other students don't particularly like to do, and then continue to do them until they become habit. Dr. Milton's life is one big habit. He doesn't have to stop and think about how he is going to handle rounds; it is automatic. It is a habit to him.

I turn a few pages in my *Goals Rule Book* and write, "CHARACTER: Summation of one's habits. HABIT: Repetition of immediate actions."

Also, Dr. Milton is persistent in his character. There is no question in my mind exactly where he stands when it comes to caring for his patients: It has to be completely right. I add a new word and definition to the list on the "Thoughts" page in the back of the *Goals Rule Book:* "PERSISTENCE: A necessary ingredient to success."

Immediate actions, persistence, habit, character. These form a logical plan to build goals on. I will try to remember these as I continue through the rotation, which consists of Pinewood Hospital and the nursery. Tomorrow I start at Pinewood, which is a state institution for mentally retarded children.

The Pinewood Rotation

I have already read extensively about retarded children and have quickly grown to dislike looking at the terrible pictures I see in the textbook. After beginning rounds the first morning, it takes only minutes to realize that the actual patients are ten times worse than what is written about them. After ten minutes I am ready to go back and ask for an extended rotation with Dr. Milton. These grotesque figures of human anatomy send the eyes searching, but at the same time make one try to block out from one's mind what he is actually seeing. There is nothing proud, nothing ambitious about these children. They will not have goals or master habits. These children are not like the ones seen on television in campaigns for the mentally retarded; these are the ones that only a fraction of civilization ever sees. There is one four-year-old child who has a head as large as a basketball. During his waking hours he only sits and stares. Another child is tied with a sheet in a chair while he makes uncoordinated movements with his arms and head, saliva drooling off his chin onto his chest.

After being at Pinewood only ten hours, I am more depressed than at any other time since starting school. All these helpless children, and so little to do to help them. I am glad there are doctors who are interested enough and dedicated enough to spend their lives studying and treating these children, for I know I don't possess what it takes to practice this type of medicine.

I elect to avoid this ward of the hospital in the future; I cannot control my mind enough to cope with such problems. I know I should be able to, but as yet I have not found a way. I flip through what I have written in my goal book, but cannot come up with a convincing argument that it is necessary to dwell on these patients in order to become a surgeon.

There are patients in another section of the hospital who can function adequately in the institution's environment. These are children with low IQs—many of whom are very pleasant and affectionate. These are the ones I have seen in public and on television in the "Special Olympics." I can envision these children being helped enough to make their own way in society; in fact, I see many in this ward exerting more effort to accomplish something that 90 percent of the people in the outside world do. I'm sure many of us could learn more about accomplishing goals from these patients than from the successful people in the world around us.

I begin spending more and more time with these patients, looking for some insight to better understand what makes them go. Why do they try so hard? What is their secret? I am aware that they are the less endowed ones; yet I think they may have something that the rest of us don't have and could use. I spend some of my thought time at night trying to solve the riddle of what drives them so hard. Obviously they cannot think of a multitude of goals at any one time. They can't learn to ride a bicycle, shoot a basketball, play dodgeball, and dress themselves completely all in the same day. Yet there are some riding bicycles, others shooting basketballs, and others very proud that they have buttoned their own sweaters correctly. If there is something to learn from them, it lies in the fact that they go at things one step at a time. They don't attempt to learn to dress, to ride a bicycle, and then shoot a basketball all at once. *One step at a time* seems the answer to their major accomplishments.

I write in my book for future reference: "ONE STEP AT A TIME—The path to accomplishment of goals." I have just proven that I can learn even from these children.

I soon become accustomed to being around the retarded. I say accustomed because I felt like an outsider invading the privacy of these children's lives when I first arrived, and it has taken over a week for me to get over that feeling. By contrast, the children adjusted to me and accepted me immediately. Here I was, a learned medical student, but unilateral—that is the irony of it all; I was the one learning from them!

"Fool John"

There are several adults who have been here since childhood, and many of these are the most interesting to observe. There is one patient who is about 30 years old. Even though his IQ is low and he can't read, write, or take care of himself, he has the unusual ability to know what time it is within two minutes of the correct time without looking at a clock; he doesn't even have a watch. "Fool John" is the only name I have ever heard people use for him. Every time I see him I always ask him the time, and he is always correct. I wonder how he does this so precisely. One day I ask him, and he smiles, makes a motion like he is winding a watch on his forehead, and replies, "I have a clock inside my head and I keep it wound all the time." I watch as he walks down the hall making the same winding motion on his ear, his chin, and his nose. It is fascinating to see how someone like John can pull this ingenious feat time and again. There is much about the mind that we don't know, especially John's mind.

This happens to be my night on call, and it turns out to be a work-less evening. I read for a while and drop off to sleep, only to be awakened by the ringing of the phone. The nurse on the line says there is a boy, six years old, with a temperature of 101 degrees, and she wants me to check him. I dress, walk to the next building, and go through the usual examination of his ears, throat, neck, and lungs, but find nothing to explain the fever. I don't want to give him antibiotics without locating the source of infection, so I know I need to find some reason for the fever.

The nurse senses my bewilderment. "Doctor, do you think he could have a fecal impaction? That causes a high fever in these children lots of times."

I perceive this as a nice way of her telling me to do a rectal examination and check for an impaction. Sure enough, he is impacted. Looking at his chart, I find that he has not had a bowel movement for five days. I order enemas and laxatives, and, after performing the messy chore of cleaning out his rectum, return to my room. Usually I don't have any trouble going back to sleep after getting up in the middle of the night, but occasionally when I return to bed my mind stays awake no matter how much I want to sleep. I begin to think about my next test, which I didn't even want to think about, and let the thought fade into darkness. Then another thought arose in my mind: Fool John. The more I think about John and his strange ability to tell time, the more I wonder if his ability is functional in the middle of the night. I have observed that I can look at my watch in the morning, and if I keep up with the time throughout the day, I can guess fairly close to the correct time. I think perhaps this is what John does. I have thought that all along, but there is only one sure way to find out.

I get up again, dress, and walk to building number three, where John rooms. I slip quietly through the main lobby, past the nurse's desk, and down the hall to his room. I ease the door open and walk to his bed. "John...John," I whisper, as I shake his shoulder. "What time is it?"

John doesn't move an inch; he simply opens his eyes at the same time his customary smile appears on his lips. "Twenty-five after three," he whispers back, and then shuts his eyes. He is still smiling when I leave his bedside. As I walk toward my on-call room, I know John must feel some sense of superiority at being able to make me get out of bed in the middle of the night to ask him what time it is. I wonder how many other students have tried to "fool" John. I get back in bed at 3:30 and actually glance at my watch to check the time. For some reason I feel foolish as I realize I'm looking at my watch only five minutes after Fool John told me the correct time.

I finish the rotation at Pinewood Hospital almost in disbelief that there are so many normal, well-formed children in the world. After being here only three weeks, I am almost afraid to try to have a family. I have never known before that there are so many possibilities of a malformed or retarded infant being born. Very few people realize how blessed they are to have normal children. Perhaps it is best for most not to know of the possibilities. From one viewpoint I wish I were ignorant of the facts, but this portion of my medical education has been enlightening, although depressing.

Motherhood—A Worthy Goal

During my rotation at Pinewood, I tried to tell Harriet about what I had seen. However, she seemed content to remain ignorant of the facts.

"I don't want to hear about it," Harriet cuts me off as I start to recount my rotation with the mentally retarded. She is preparing for tomorrow's class, and I am taking a little break from my reading.

"I don't think just talking about it will have any effect on whether we have a mentally retarded baby or not," I reply, trying to get her to put her books down and talk to me for a minute.

"I don't want to talk about it!" She never even gives me a glance.

"When do you want to start planning a family?" This question catches her off guard and causes her to put her books down immediately. She looks up and smiles.

"I don't know. I would like to be able to stay home with the baby whenever we do have one. So I guess that puts it just after you start internship. You will make a small salary, I can quit teaching, and we can start having our children. I will stay home and cook you something more than creamed tuna on toast." Harriet comes over and sits down on my lap. She likes to talk about the children we will have; I think she is going to make a good mother.

With my rotation over at Pinewood, I return to the medical center to complete the pediatric rotation. However, I have mixed emotions. Though I have left the physical location of Pinewood and tried to leave behind the memory of that first ward, I find that it is indelibly stamped on my mind.

The last portion of pediatrics rotation will be spent in the nursery, which requires being present at all deliveries, checking the infants immediately after they are born, and carrying them to the nursery. We are taught to examine the newborn and give them a rating in proportion to how good their reflexes are, their color, and their general response.

It feels good to be back under Dr. Milton's wing, even though the workload will be ten times greater than at Pinewood. Pinewood was one of those experiences you have to learn firsthand. No one can quite tell you what it is like. It is an "I have to go through it myself" experience. Dr. Milton is a great one to learn from, especially for the

"I don't have to go through it myself" situations. He doesn't mind telling you the things that have not worked for him. And he is quick to tell you they won't work for you either.

A Baby Born Dead

We walk into the lecture room a few doors down from the nursery to attend his first lecture on the care of the nursery infant. Dr. Milton clears his throat and begins: "On certain occasions a newborn does not breathe properly, so the pediatrician has to place a tube through his mouth and into the windpipe and breathe for him. This consists of putting a laryngoscope, which is like a small tongue blade with a light on the end, into the infant's mouth to visualize the back of the throat and on down the windpipe. Next, a hollow rubber tube about half the size of a pencil is placed through the mouth and down the larynx." Dr. Milton picks up the laryngoscope and an endotracheal tube and holds them for all to see. He walks over to a small oxygen tank and continues his lecture. "Oxygen can then be delivered directly to the lungs by connecting the oxygen to this bag that fits onto the rubber tubing. You can breathe for the infant. This is like mouth-to-mouth respiration except that there is a direct tube to the lungs and a bag is used for the ventilating process. This can be a lifesaving procedure, but you have to remember that the most critical point of the entire situation is the time factor. You are working with a very small baby, with very small instruments, and are in a life-or-death situation. The outcome depends on whether the tube can be placed correctly and quickly."

Dr. Milton pauses for effect, and then as he turns toward us he drops everything he is holding. All of us jump and shift in our chairs as we watch the instruments bounce as they hit the floor. Now that he has everyone's attention, he continues. "Someday you will be the only one around to put the tube down an infant's windpipe. Will you be able to do it, or will you try unsuccessfully and see the infant die? Think about that." His eyes shift from one student to another until he has "contacted" every student present. "I want every one of you to be able to intubate a newborn infant by the time you leave my service. The first infant born dead, day or night, I want the entire group to be called in and each of you to take your turn passing the tube until you can do it on the first try, five times in a row."

My immediate reaction is how inhumane this seems. I attempt to switch my mind from that of a layman to that of a physician. As a "layman medical student," I think of the poor, innocent infant who has come into the world without life or breath. I have to concentrate awhile before I express my displeasure at intubating a dead infant. I make myself look ahead to the next time an infant is born who may need intubation. I know Dr. Milton is correct and accept his reasoning, knowing it is something I must learn to perform even though it will be difficult to do. I think back on one of my rules—I must go ahead and do what I don't want to do in order to reach my goal. If I do only what I *want* to do, I will never learn to intubate a baby. After all, I surely would not want to be passing a tube at a critical time without ever having practiced at a noncritical time. When that situation really does occur and no one else is around with any experience in intubation, the infant may survive only because I know how to do the job correctly and quickly by previous practice on a dead baby. Call it rationalization, call it whatever, but I convince myself to do it because it is the right thing to do.

Paying the Piper

Our first stillborn comes in the middle of the night, and we are called in from home. Sleepily I drive to the hospital and climb the stairs to the nursery. Within the next few minutes our entire group of eight students is present, and the resident goes through the procedure of intubation step by step, ensuring that each of us knows what to do. Then he leaves us with a dead infant, a laryngoscope, and several endotracheal tubes of varying sizes. One by one we start to practice with the tube. Then my turn comes. It looked easy enough for the resident, but I can't find the epiglottis, the beginning of the windpipe. Within the next 30 minutes the worth of this night exercise becomes very evident. I can see myself trying to do this on an infant in distress without having done it in practice many times before. We practice until proficiency is obtained, and by the time we are through, each of us can intubate in less than six seconds from the time we pick up the instrument to the time we connect the breathing bag to the tube.

I drive home in the chilly morning air with a feeling of accomplishment and know at last that I have learned something that gives me the ability to save a life in a situation in which perhaps no one else can help. This is the first time I have ever experienced this feeling, and in these early-morning hours I have a small taste of what becoming a doctor is all about. Some of the immediate goals of action are beginning to pay off, and for the first time I get a fleeting taste of what my intermediate goal tastes like—being a real doctor. Not only that, but I am also realizing that the "I have to go through it myself" experiences are the most difficult experiences, and that no one could teach them to me. They are absolutely necessary, even though I don't relish going through them. If I am ever to be successful, I must, I *must*, do the necessary things I don't want to do. That is a point. These are things that no one else likes to do and most won't do. Few do them, and it is these few who will reach their goal successfully.

I finish pediatrics learning much about the practice of pediatrics plus learning much about goals. With these thoughts implanted, I begin the rotation I waited two-and-a-half years to start—general surgery. I look to surgery as having all the excitement I will ever want to deal with in everyday work. There also seems to be some intangible significance of actually doing something with your hands rather than just prescribing medicine for the patient. At last I get to find out—firsthand.

5

Surgery Rotation—My First Love

Seek first the kingdom of God, and his righteousness; and all
these things shall be added unto you (Matthew 6:33 KJV).

*MY LIFE'S GOALS WERE BECOMING INCREASINGLY centered on medicine
and my future surgical training. I was beginning to think about
surgery through the day. A person can have "other gods" and not
even know it. Surgery was becoming my god, and it would soon command top priority in everything I did. I was seeking surgery first,
above all else.*

*Things seemed to be going so well. I was setting goals and
accomplishing them one by one. It was only a matter of time before
these accomplishments would all add up to what the world calls
"success."*

*To be a growing Christian and also in medical school, somehow,
did not seem to mesh. The narrow road Jesus spoke of seemed far
removed from the broad road of my world of medical training.*

*To me, that narrow road was a little road off to the side that I
would travel for a short distance every Sunday when I went to church
and every evening for a few minutes when I read the Bible. The broad
road of the world was the main stream that I was living in. It was
medical school; it was studying; it was learning medicine; it was
what meant most at the time.*

*I did not know the wide road was controlled by self and the
narrow road by the Holy Spirit, and that only one road can be traveled at any one time. Either self is in command, or the Holy Spirit.*

*The wide road of surgery was enticing me away from the narrow
road of Christ's lordship. If I had realized that I could travel that
narrow road all the way through my surgical training, how different
my life would have been! At the time, though, all I could think about
was developing myself as a surgeon—seeking first the kingdom of
surgery, as I prepared for the start of the surgery rotation.*

My first day of surgery begins by reporting to the ward and meeting with the residents. The chief resident is the "big gun" who calls all the shots because he has the most experience on the team. Our chief resident is Ben Harris. He is pleasant and easygoing, but best of all he likes to teach. Formal lectures are given by the attending staff each day, but much of the practical teaching is done by the residents. Ben greets us and introduces the rest of the team, consisting of a third-year resident, a second-year resident, a first-year resident, and two interns.

While making rounds the first morning, it appears that there is a definite pattern concerning which resident performs which operation. The first patient on rounds is a man who was admitted to the hospital because of poor circulation to his leg. An above-the-knee amputation, called an "A-K" amputation by the intern presenting the patient to us, has been performed. This is an "intern case," meaning that it is easy enough so that someone just starting in surgical training can handle the procedure. Other intern cases we see on the rounds include an appendectomy, a hemorrhoidectomy, and a split-thickness skin graft, in which a thin piece of skin has been taken off a burn patient's thigh and placed on the site of the burn, his chest.

The first-year residents make formal presentations of their patients to us, and these operations seem to be a little more difficult than the intern cases. There are several hernias, a patient who had a V-shaped wedge removed from his lower lip in order to excise a small cancer, and several types of cases which seemingly could be done by either the intern or the first-year resident, depending on whether or not the first-year man would give the case to the intern.

Obesity and Infection

The second-year resident presents a huge woman with gallbladder disease. The resident removes the dressing and notices that the wound is red and swollen. He takes out some of the stitches, which results in foul-smelling pus pouring out between the skin edges and down the side of her abdomen. He grabs a handful of gauze pads from the dressing tray and tries to catch as much of it as he can without getting it all over the patient's abdomen. "I knew she was too fat not to get infected." He appears angry as he slaps a dressing over the now-open wound. His anger melts into an understanding smile as he looks at the horrified patient. "That will be a couple of weeks healing, but it will be okay. It just means we'll have to clean it several times a day, and show you how to take care of it. In a few days I think you will be able to clean it at home and get out of the hospital on time."

The patient lies there nodding her head and staring at the dressing. I am about as horrified as she is. I have never seen an infected wound drained before and am sure the patient has not witnessed such a sight herself, much less experienced it. It looks awful. I think it should merit much more than a brief comment from the resident in assuring the patient, and me, that the infected wound is going to heal rather than fall apart and allow all her intestines to protrude through the wound. I will accept his statement for the time being, but plan to watch the wound daily to see exactly how quickly it heals or whether the intestines end up falling out. This experience affirmed what I've observed to be true with much of life: What is common to one person is assumed to be common to all. The first time this resident had a patient with a wound infection, he probably spent an extra hour reassuring the patient, convincing her it would be all right. But after seeing several infections and seeing them all heal, he forgets that his knowledge is one-sided, that the patient has not had the privilege of seeing ten infected wounds heal.

The same resident next presents a woman from whom he has removed a lobe of the thyroid gland and used a subcuticular stitch to close the incision. He points out that the stitches were placed just under the skin and would be absorbed by the body; no stitches are visible on the skin. This closure has been done so nicely and meticulously that even now the incision can hardly be seen. I can tell he is proud of the closure because he jokingly asks one of the students if he can detect where the patient was operated on.

Man Without a Jaw

The most difficult and spectacular cases are performed by the chief resident. He has had more experience than anyone on the team and has to take the responsibility not only for his patients, but for all the cases done on the entire service. He walks into the room of a patient who looks like he has lost half his face. Ben places his hand on the patient's shoulder and addresses us: "This man had a 'commando' procedure. We call it that because after the operation it looks like a commando dropped a grenade on his face and then expected us to close the wound. He had cancer on the floor of his mouth, which we resected along his mandible, and a radical neck dissection on the same side. That means resecting his jawbone and all the lymph nodes and fat tissue in the neck from the collarbone up to the jaw." Ben looks at the student standing beside me. "I want you to be able to tell me the chances this man has of being cured. In fact, you can discuss cancer of the floor of the mouth on rounds tomorrow afternoon." Turning to the patient, he says, "I think your chances are good myself, but let's see what our new student has to say." And with that we are off to the next room.

Ben introduces the patient as we gather around his bed. "Mr. Smallwood had a blockage of his superficial femoral artery, one of the main arteries in the thigh, and was developing what we call intermittent claudication. He could walk only about a block and then would have to stop to rest because there was not enough blood getting to his leg. This made the calf muscles cramp. Intermittently, he would stop to rest and allow enough circulation to return to enable him to walk another block before the pain hit again. I did a femoral arteriogram on him. For those who flunked radiology, this means I injected dye, which will show up on X ray, into the main artery in the thigh and could then outline the block inside the artery very nicely. We will go over those films in X-ray conference this afternoon. Anyway, I put in a bypass graft, which is a cloth tube sewn above and below the block in the artery which diverts the blood through the tube and around the blockage. You can now feel his posterior tibial pulse—his ankle pulse—which means there is an adequate blood flow, resulting in a pain-free leg."

This time he points to me: "I want you to look up the symptoms and progression of peripheral vascular diseases and be able to explain them in detail by tomorrow."

When to Operate

Ben steps to the next bed and looks at Bart Moore, probably the most intelligent student in our group. "This patient had surgery for a duodenal ulcer. Do you know anything about ulcers?"

"Yes, I have read about them," he replies confidently.

"What percent of patients can be treated medically?"

"I'm not sure. Most of them."

"Eighty-five percent. What percent are *cured* with medicines?"

"Most of them."

"Wrong. Only 5 percent become asymptomatic with no recurrence of symptoms. What are the indications for surgery?"

"Bleeding, perforation, obstruction," Bart answers without hesitation. He had memorized these indications straight out of the textbook just for this moment as if he knew Ben was going to ask that very question. In all of medical school, I have never had that set of circumstances happen to me; if I know the answer, I am not asked the question.

Ben finishes Bart's answer, "…and unsuccessful medical management. There are four indications, but I guess three out of four isn't bad." Ben realizes he is questioning one of the smarter ones in the class and uses him to teach the rest of us. "Okay, now you have decided to operate. What procedure are you going to perform?"

"A vagotomy—cutting the nerves to the stomach and pyloroplasty."

"What does a vagotomy do?"

"Decreases the acid secretion of the stomach."

"What is pyloroplasty?"

"I am not sure just how you do it, but it enlarges the outlet of the stomach. That also decreases the amount of acid in the stomach."

"What other operation could you perform?"

"A vagotomy and antrectomy."

"How does that differ from a vagotomy and pyloroplasty?"

"The bottom portion of the stomach is removed."

"Dr. Moore," Ben addresses the not-yet doctor, "I hope you realize you have only scratched the surface of knowledge about peptic ulcer disease. Before you leave the service, I hope we can teach you the thorough physiology behind your answers." Ben heads for the next room.

Traumatic Steps to Success

I hate to be put on the spot as Bart was, but I have come to realize that this is the best way to retain knowledge—to actually be the one called on in class to discuss a subject. A poor second best, I have concluded, is to be the spectator at such a session. Worse yet is to try to learn it from a book. At the beginning of medical school, I thought learning from a book was the only source of knowledge, but I am coming to learn that facts on the pages are only the first layer of cement and steel in the foundation of a skyscraper. This conviction relates back to the two basic sources of experience I learned at Pinewood Institution. The "I don't have to go through it myself" type of experience is beneficial, but merely being an observer isn't the best way to learn. The "I have to go through it myself" experience Bart had just gone through is the most traumatic kind of learning, but is also the most rewarding when it comes to remembering a subject for the future.

As I follow our group to the next patient, I begin to realize that there is something distinctly different about the surgical residents and the residents on the other services. For example, their morning rounds begin at 6:30 A.M. instead of the usual 8:00. There is always something to do either in the operating room or with the patients on the floor—dressings to be changed, wounds to be cleaned, burn patients to be continuously taken care of, post-operative checks on seriously ill patients. This is truly a working service that never stops.

Also, the lesson learned from the children at Pinewood begins to fit here at the medical center. The children learned to button their sweaters and coats. The intern learns to do an appendectomy. The children next learned to ride a bicycle. The first-year resident learns to do a hernia. The children learned to dribble a basketball. The second-year resident learns to perform stomach surgery. And finally, the children could get up, dress themselves, get on a bicycle, ride to the playground, and play a game of basketball. Likewise, the intern becomes resident, then chief resident, putting all his skills together to do it all. The same chief resident was once an intern who had to complete one immediate action goal at a time to achieve a successful year of internship and go on to complete his intermediate goal of junior residency in order to fulfill his major goal of chief residency and becoming a complete surgeon.

Goals—Now

Speaking of immediate action goals, I need to get over to the library to study peripheral vascular diseases as soon as I can find time. Immediate goal for the moment: Read all I can on peripheral vascular disease *today*.

When we finally finish evening rounds at 6:30, I waste no time heading straight for the library to study my assignment for tomorrow. I am elated, and think I could study surgery all night for sheer enjoyment. There is so much to learn, and I need to begin building my storehouse of knowledge. By midnight I realize how little I know about vascular diseases and how much more reading I will have to do by tomorrow afternoon to be able to discuss it. I roll into bed at

1:00 A.M., but I think back over the first day on surgery rotation and can't go to sleep. I have the same kind of excitement I used to get on Christmas Eve or the night before going on a trip. Four years of college, almost three years of medical school, and at last I am studying what I have thought so much about: surgery.

Harriet senses my excitement as I keep her awake talking about how busy we're going to be on surgery. She doesn't say much; she just lies in bed staring at the ceiling, listening. After ten minutes of my chattering, she leans over and gives me a kiss on my cheek, telling me I had better go to sleep or I won't feel like getting up in the morning. However, I lay awake long after I hear her breathing deeply in slumber. It's going to be fun becoming a surgeon.

Standing at the Table

My excitement carries over to the following morning as I awake easily. I beat the residents to the hospital for 6:30 rounds. Today is an operating day for "our" team, and I am scheduled to scrub with Ben on a patient with cancer of the colon. I am listed as third assistant, which means there will be Ben, a first-year resident, an intern, and then myself to scrub on the case. "First surgeon" carries the same connotation as being labeled "president of the corporation." The surgeon given this title is in complete command at the operating table; whatever he says is final. He takes full responsibility for the patient, and everyone else is subordinate. I am listed as third assistant and must work my way up the ladder of surgical study and expertise until I am listed as first surgeon. Even when Ben has the chairman of the department scrubbing on a case with him, he is still listed as first surgeon and assumes complete responsibility for the patient. If anything goes wrong with the case, it is the first surgeon who explains the situation to the patient's family. It is the first surgeon who takes the credit for whatever happens, no matter whether the results are successful or not. It is not a label given without forethought and deserving credit, and is not received without the self-assurance required to perform the particular procedure. One of the more senior residents had recently dropped out of the surgery program solely because he was not willing to take the responsibility that coincides with being first surgeon.

After rounds, I change into a scrub suit and follow the intern into the operating room. Ben makes a midline incision in the lower abdomen and soon is packing the intestines out of the way by covering them with a moist towel. He places two metal retractors on top of the towel and turns to me. "Now's your big chance to get in on some surgery. Hold these." Two-and-a-half hours later I am still holding them. I admit this isn't a very large part of the overall procedure, but at least I have a front-row seat to what is going on, plus the fact that I feel just as successful right now doing what I am doing as Ben does performing the operation. I feel this way because I can see myself as a surgeon, just as Ben is. I don't actually possess all the required skills, but there is no doubt in my mind that someday I will. Therefore I can enjoy a similar feeling of success being third assistant as I will have when I become chief resident. I realize I have already been successful for as long as I have been working toward my major goal, but this is the first time I have really felt any feeling of being successful. I am actually standing at an operating table working on a real-live patient. I have reached a milestone—I have experienced the tangible reality that I can actually become a chief resident.

Importance of the Minute

My mind wanders from what I am doing and I relax my hold on the retractors for only about two seconds, but the intestines begin to slip around the retractor blades and fall down into the operative field. I am not sure what to do. All he said was to hold the retractor, which I am doing. Ben stops, places the intestines behind the retractors, and speaks to me without lifting his eyes from the operative field. "You've got to keep looking. If you can't see, I can't see. And if I can't see, I can't do the operation. And if I can't do the operation, there's no use in your being here, so keep those guts out of the way." I nod and continue my grip on the retractors. He does an excellent job getting the cancer out and the large bowel is reconnected.

He starts the closure by placing a large suture through the tough fascia layer of the abdomen. "This is what holds the wound together," Ben states. "This fascia layer and nothing else." He looks up at me. "You thought the skin held the incision together, didn't you?"

"I thought it helped."

"Nope. Sewing the skin together just makes the skin edges grow properly. This deep fascia layer is the one that does the job. This is the important layer—the layer the patient can't see. The patient judges the whole operation by the way the skin is put together, but that is actually the least important part of the procedure." By now Ben is almost ready to start closing the skin.

"Do you know how to sew skin?" Ben delays starting his sewing and looks directly at me.

"Yes. I have never closed skin in an operation, but I know how it is done." I see a chance to get to do some operating, even if it is only to close the skin—the most important part of the procedure, according to the patient.

Ben hands me the needleholder and tissue pickups. I feel awkward. I feel that everything in the room has stopped, and everyone is watching me. I start sewing, but my hands don't seem to want to do what my mind tells them to do. They work as stiffly as chopsticks. My shoulders are the only joints that want to try to coordinate my hand movements. My elbows, wrists, and fingers are frozen. It is as if my two hands were connected to two separate people rather than both being fed by one central nervous system. It looked so easy when Ben was holding the instruments. Finally I manage to get the incision closed and hope the patient realizes how insignificant the skin closure is in this operation.

As soon as the case is over, Ben takes me to the residents' lounge and explains what he did in surgery. He discusses cancer of the colon, goes over the prognosis, the symptoms the patient usually presents to the doctor, and how much bowel to resect. This 15 minutes of individual lecturing makes the entire morning worthwhile. Much of medical learning is done in this way. Yesterday Ben could have spent the same 15 minutes telling me about cancer of the colon, and by today I would not recall 10 percent of the knowledge he taught me. However, standing at the operating table for three hours watching the cancer being removed and seeing a patient being cured before my eyes enables my brain to make an impressive recording of what Ben tells me during those 15 minutes, and I will be able to recall 90 percent of it tomorrow. Not only that, but I will be able to use that 90 percent as a base for further information to be built upon. Even though it appeared to be much wasted time while I stood at the operating table holding retractors, this time was used very efficiently in preparing my mind for knowledge of cancer of the colon, which will be useful to me the rest of my surgical life.

Considering Success

My mind races back to something I thought at the operating table: "I can see myself already as a surgeon, just as much as Ben is... I can have a similar feeling of success." As long as I am working toward becoming a surgeon, I will have this feeling of success. In my own mind, I will be successful as long as I am working *toward* the goal of becoming a surgeon. I add this to the *Goals Rule Book:* "SUCCESS: I am successful as long as I am working toward my major goal. I don't have to wait until I actually complete surgical training to be successful. I am a success *now!*" (In fact, I became a success that day in high school when I decided to become a doctor and began working toward that goal.)

I decide to spend lunch break going over the notes I made on vascular disease last night in preparation for afternoon rounds. Before I can finish, I hear about a patient coming in from Jenkins, a small town about half an hour away. It is a Mr. Paul Bennett, who was seen in the surgery outpatient clinic three weeks ago. Ben tells us that at that time Mr. Bennett had a large abdominal aortic aneurysm along with some back pain. He reviewed the anatomy for us, explaining, "The aorta is the large artery that receives blood from the heart, traverses the chest and abdomen, and finally divides into the large arteries that go to the legs. Mr. Bennett's aorta is ballooning out of his abdomen, much like an inner tube will balloon out through a crack in a tire. This is called an aneurysm. An inner tube can rupture going 90 miles an hour on the highway or sitting still in the driveway. Similarly, it cannot be predicted when the aneurysm is going to rupture, so these aneurysms are usually taken out and replaced with a cloth tube as soon as they are discovered. If they manifest themselves by causing some pain in the back, as in Mr. Bennett's case, there is usually little time before it ruptures. I had seen Mr. Bennett in the clinic and had explained the seriousness of his aneurysm, but he had elected to wait a while on the operation." Ben begins to shake his head. "He has waited too long, because the aneurysm is now rupturing and he is on the way for a very bloody operation; his chances of survival are ten times worse now that he is leaking."

The Price of Procrastination

Within a few minutes Mr. Bennett is on the operating table with type-specific blood being pumped into him. He is breathing heavily and groaning with each breath. Both flanks are blue due to the blood leaking from the aneurysm. His feet have a waxy white appearance because no blood is reaching them. The look on his face is one of sheer terror. His eyes keep searching, but never finding. He looks anxiously at Ben, at me, at the I.V. pole, then his face relaxes as the sodium pentothal is injected and the merciful anesthetic begins to take its hold.

The chairman of surgery, Dr. Self, is present to assist on the operation. Ben quickly opens the abdomen from "tip to stern," and as soon as he enters the peritoneal cavity that holds all the intestines and abdominal organs, a huge blood clot can be seen around the aneurysm. "Get proximal control first," snaps Dr. Self.

Ben eases his hand up the aorta very slowly and deliberately to just above the beginning of the aneurysm. "I think it's above the kidney arteries," he says with a single negative movement of his head.

"Well, clamp it and let's go!" Dr. Self replies, underlining the necessity of speed in controlling the situation. From the reading I did last night, I know it is a bad prognostic sign if the aneurysm extends above where the arteries to the kidneys come off the aorta, as Ben is implying in this case. I also know that the survival rate of taking out a *ruptured* aneurysm and replacing it with a cloth graft is very low indeed. As Ben attempts to get control of the pulsating aorta, the bleeding begins. It looks like the dam broke. So much blood is coming out of the aorta that it literally fills up the peritoneal cavity. Ben finally gets the clamp placed across the vessel and the bleeding slows, but doesn't stop.

"Are you sure you have the whole thing clamped?" yells Dr. Self.

"I think so, but I don't have any idea where the arteries to the kidneys are located—don't want to clamp them," Ben replies.

"Go ahead and clamp the iliac arteries to the legs, and get it out of there," Dr. Self orders as he continues to suction blood out of the abdomen. There is still a considerable "ooze" even with the aorta clamped above and below the aneurysm, but Ben ignores this uncontrollable bleeding and steadily works at getting the aneurysm out.

The anesthesiologist at the head of the table pumps blood into the patient. "I don't get any blood pressure at all, and I am pumping in the twelfth unit now."

It seems a hopeless case, but Ben keeps sewing as fast as he can. The graft is in place; the clamps are removed—four hours have passed. The kidneys have not made any urine, there is still no blood pressure, he has been given 18 units of blood, and is still bleeding from everywhere. Everything Ben touches bleeds. What else is there to do? The graft looks all right. There are no gross bleeding areas in the graft or where the graft is sewn to the aorta, but the blood continues to come from everywhere, and all efforts at getting it stopped seem futile.

Dr. Self steps back from the table, takes off his gown and gloves and says, "Close him up. I'll go inform the family that things are going poorly."

Ben puts the last stitches in the abdomen. Blood fills the peritoneal cavity and seeps through the wound. Mr. Bennett is dying and Ben knows it, but he continues to work as hard as he can and gets him off the operating table and into the recovery room. I can't understand why all the details and rush. What difference does it make if he dies on the operating table or in the recovery room? He is going to die. I realize that Ben has taken the whole responsibility for the patient. I am only a shadow of insignificance concerning Mr. Bennett, but I ask Ben some questions concerning my unsureness of the situation. He attempts to explain the recent action. "Have you ever played in a game where your team is way behind and you know you have no chance of winning? Well, whatever it is that makes you play those last two minutes as hard as you can is the same drive that makes me not want to have my patient expire on the operating table. Whether that 'something' is pride, hurt, care, concern, or hope for a miracle that the patient quits bleeding, I don't know."

Ben and I both know that everything possible has been done, but we also know that his best was not enough to save the patient. Twenty minutes later, Mr. Bennett dies in the recovery room.

Moving Onward

The next few days are spent mainly thinking about my becoming a surgeon. I get more excited the more I think of it. If I am to be a surgeon, now is the time to set the proper goals necessary to fulfill such a position. I will try to formulate these in my mind as I begin dog surgery. This portion of the rotation is spent actually performing operations on dogs. I will be able to act on my own ideas at a real operating table in a true surgical setting. My immediate goal changes once again. I must take action to be the best dog surgeon I can possibly be. My attitude must be kept positive toward all the negative situations that might occur.

6

The First Operation—Dog Surgery

> Whatever you do, whether in word or deed, do it all in the
> name of the Lord Jesus, giving thanks to God the Father
> through him (Colossians 3:17).

*IT WAS NOT THAT I WAS LEAVING GOD OUT of my plans; it was not that
I was purposely choosing to ignore Him. It was just that I was cen-
tering my life around becoming the best dog surgeon I could.*

*There is nothing wrong with setting goals to excel in dog surgery.
The problem comes when one sets goals without first seeking direction from the Lord, when one's ultimate plan is to exalt self rather
than God. I was setting goals and doing them in my name rather
than the name of the Lord Jesus Christ. Whether a goal was worthwhile or not, I could accomplish it with the goal structure I was
using. I was getting deeper into running my life in the way that
seemed right to me at the time.*

*Something may seem right, but that doesn't make it right by
God's standards. If I had stopped 100 people on the street and asked
them if what I was doing—training to become a surgeon—was right,
most of them would have agreed with me that it was. Could doing
what seemed to be right lead to something wrong? With hindsight,
it is easy for me to see that I could have continued the rest of my life
doing things considered right in the sight of 100 people, yet missed
the mark of God's will. I could have become a surgeon, helped a
poor family every year at Christmas, and gotten active in the community raising money for worthy causes. If I had done all these right
things and yet missed God in my life, it would all have been in vain.*

*The only right ways in my life have been the ones in which I have
sought the Lord's direction. So many times I have tried to do good
because I wanted the world to look at me favorably. And as I began
the first day of dog surgery, I wanted to do everything possible to
make a positive impression on my instructors.*

❖ ❖ ❖

For dog surgery, we are divided into groups of four, with one student acting as the first surgeon, one the assistant, one the anesthesiologist, and one the scrub nurse to pass instruments. Before each operation, a real surgeon from the staff performs the procedure while we take notes on the technique of the operation and then perform it ourselves. There are four different operations planned, and each of us will be the first surgeon on one operation. As first surgeon I will actually get to do the cutting; as assistant I will act as the surgeon's helper—cut his knots, clamp bleeding arteries, retract tissue out of the way so he can see better, and do anything else he instructs me to do. There is much preparation. There are pages and pages to read about the associated diseases and the surgeries we will be doing, and in addition we have to read all we can about how to put a dog to sleep and keep him alive during the procedure.

Goals Progress

Dr. Wright is in charge of our dog surgery, and greets us with a stern face as we enter the dog lab for our first demonstration. The room is cold and bleak, with no chairs—only the troughlike tables that hold the dogs. Dr. Wright is in his early fifties, has graying hair cut short, and is dressed in a green scrub suit covered by a long white lab coat. He neither smiles nor says any unnecessary words. As we gather around him, eager to hear every word, Dr. Wright discusses the operating tables. The setting is similar to our first day in anatomy, but now there is so much more excitement since we will be dissecting live animals rather than cadavers.

"In the middle of the trough you will see this long thin pan that catches blood or irrigating solutions used during the operation. The pan drains into that bucket at the end of the table. The height of the blood in your bucket tells how well you control bleeding during the operation. It can be a 'full-bucket' case, a 'half-bucket' operation, or a 'just-covered-the-bottom' procedure. It's all a matter of pride—if you have any. I can teach a monkey to do these operations, and I'll try to teach you. Anyone off the street can learn to operate, but only a surgeon knows when and why. I expect you to read all the assignments and have a thorough knowledge of the disease process related to the operation you are performing and be able to apply that to back up any decision you make."

We seat ourselves on the floor in front of him as he hands out a list of references for each procedure. "You're expected to read and know the information covered in these references, and any additional reading is up to you."

Just looking at the list I can't see how it is going to be physically possible to take enough time from our regular surgery rotation to read this material, much less read it well enough to be questioned about it.

"The first two procedures will be a splenectomy (removing the spleen) and a gastroenterostomy. All a gastroenterostomy entails is a communication made between the stomach and a piece of small intestine by cutting a hole in the side of the stomach, another hole in the side of the intestine, and sewing the two holes together so that food entering the stomach will fall through the hole into the intestine.

Death Under Anesthesia

"There will be an oral exam following these first two procedures, after which you will perform a cholecystectomy (removing the gallbladder) and a small bowel resection. You will take out a portion of the small intestine and sew the two remaining ends together. That covers the operations, but does not cover everything you will be held responsible for. Anesthesia is vital to general surgery and not something to be taken for granted," he continues as he paces back and forth in front of our group. He seems to be in his own little world, talking and walking, looking at the floor, an occasional glance toward us. I am certain he must attain some satisfaction from flunking a student in dog surgery. My initial thought was that this would be the most enjoyable part of surgery rotation, but after listening to him, I think it may be the most difficult portion. "Anesthesia is vital to surgery, so we have made a rule. If any dog dies while under anesthesia, the one putting him to sleep has to write a paper on 'anesthesia deaths' with an adequate review of the literature."

Everyone responds to this news in the same way: The deeper the dog is asleep, the greater the chance of an anesthetic death, so each of us decides that when our turn comes to be anesthetist, the dog will be asleep just deeply enough to keep him on the table. After all, a live dog is better than a dead one, especially when a dead one means hours and hours of reviewing the literature and writing a paper.

The Necessity of Preparation

Dr. Wright calls us to the scrub sink and starts his spiel on how to wash our hands prior to surgery: "The scrub initially consists of washing the hands and forearms just the way you do at home before dinner. Take a scrub brush out of the sterile container and start scrubbing each finger, hand, and forearm for ten minutes. You will miss areas; to prove it, I'm going to have you do the 'black scrub.' I want you to paint this black dye on your hands and arms. I will blindfold you, let you scrub for ten minutes, and then remove the blindfold so you can see what you missed. If you scrub properly, the dye will come off—all of it." He points to a large plastic jar with the words "Black Scrub" painted on the side.

After applying the dye to our hands and arms, we scrub every inch of skin from elbows to fingertips for ten minutes. I feel sure I have covered the entire area more than adequately, and will surely be one of the few who ends up with no dye remaining on the skin. I remove my blindfold. There is black dye under my fingernails, the web of skin between each finger, and a whole strip up the back of each arm.

Dr. Wright picks up a scrub brush and starts demonstrating the proper technique for scrubbing. "Scrub your fingertips and each web of skin between your fingers 20 times. Visualizing each finger as a four-sided box, scrub each side 20 times. Then scrub 20 times the back of each hand, your palms, and—again imagining a box—each side of your forearms. Then repeat the entire procedure, this time scrubbing each area only ten times." Dr. Wright briskly goes through scrub for us and begins to rinse off the soap. "When rinsing, hold your hands up and your elbows down, so that the water always runs from the tips of your fingers, a cleaned area, toward your elbows, which is considered a contaminated area. In this way, dirty water from around your elbows will not run back down onto the areas just scrubbed."

The first day in dog surgery ends with all of us back at the scrub sink trying to get the black dye washed from under our fingernails.

I stop by the operating room of the hospital on the way home and ask one of the nurses for some silk suture to practice tying knots. "This ought to do," she says as she gives me a handful of 2-0 silk suture. "We'll give you more when you are ready for one-hand knots," she laughs.

I know there are two ways to tie knots: a two-handed tie, which is similar to tying shoelaces with both hands, and a one-handed knot, which is much quicker but more difficult to learn. I will stick to learning the two-handed method for now.

Developing the Habit

After supper I set my chair directly in front of the refrigerator while Harriet does the dishes. I clumsily begin practicing tying knots on the door handle. One hour later I announce: "Okay, time me." Harriet plays my game and tells me when to begin. One minute later I've tied 44 knots. I mentally set a goal of 100 before I finish my surgery rotation.

Three nights later I decide to try one-handed knots. They can be tied much more rapidly than the two-handed knots once you learn them, but I only do eight in the first minute. My fingers just don't "think" that way. I glance at the refrigerator door handle on the way to bed; hundreds of black silk sutures dangle loosely. Those silk sutures represent more than the fact that my fingers are ready for surgery; they have become a symbol in my mind. They are a tangible representation of my major goal: to become a surgeon. The thread itself would be worth perhaps 50 cents to most people. But to me it is worth hours and hours of study and numerous immediate actions performed. I suppose symbols have always been important to me. These silk surgical threads tell me I am a surgeon, the ball-point pen advertising a drug company tells me I am a medical student, and buying a small wooden box filled with dissecting instruments for frog anatomy told me I was a premedical student. All these symbols would be worth very little to anyone other than an aspiring surgeon, medical student, or a premedical college student. But for me they are a strong reinforcement for the goal set in my mind. And for some reason, which perhaps a psychiatrist can tell me, I want to leave those silk sutures on the refrigerator door handle. They are my trophies and encouragement. They reinforce the fact that I will become a surgeon. In my mind, they represent that I am now a surgeon, and that is the way I see myself tonight. Because I know I will achieve my goal, I can see myself as already having achieved it. I look back at the definition of success written only a few days ago in the *Goals Rule Book:* I am successful as long as I am working toward my major goal.

I go to bed feeling very successful and ready for our first day of "live" dog surgery. As I lie in bed, I think back over the black scrub routine a few days ago. The word *honesty* comes to mind. How honest am I with myself? Do I apply a "black scrub policy" to the way I look at things that really matter? I know that in some instances

I put on a blindfold and say something or do something that can probably get me by just the way it is. But what about taking the blindfold off and really seeing what it is that I am saying or doing?

A few nights later at home, Harriet and I both finish our book work early. For the past several days I have been reflecting on the smoothness with which dog surgery went after we all decided to work together toward one goal. I think this same principle should work in marriage as well, so I decide to put it to the test.

I put my feet up on the stool and move to one side of the over-stuffed chair—my favorite study spot. Then, motioning for Harriet to sit beside me, I say, "Come on over." She squeezes in sideways and snuggles up to me as I place my right arm around her shoulders and give her a squeeze.

"I've been thinking about our money situation." I speak to her, but I put my head on the back of the chair and look straight ahead.

"We're not doing too badly, are we?" she looks up at me questioningly.

"No, but we don't have a plan. We save a little, spend a little, and give some to the church. Let's set a goal. Let's give 10 percent to the church and put 10 percent in savings. We can do it."

"You have to cut out Cokes at lunch. We can't do it and buy Cokes."

"How about making me a lunch every day, a couple of sandwiches or so?" I respond, happy that Harriet has accepted the idea of setting this goal. I am realizing something that is becoming more and more apparent as our marriage progresses: It is important for both of us to develop the same goals and work toward them together. That makes for a greater sense of oneness.

So, as we begin working on our saving and giving program, I begin the last portion of the surgery rotation, which is at the Veteran's Administration hospital. It has been converted from an old resort hotel into a hospital, the grounds kept as they were in the 1930s, with huge trees scattered around the front lawn and five acres of lush green grass. The hospital itself is a four-story white-painted brick building. The old golf course is still preserved in excellent condition behind the hospital. There is definitely a sense of relaxation and informality here, in contrast to the university hospital I just left. It even seems more appropriate to be carrying a lunch here than at the university hospital.

The Opened Door of Opportunity

I am the first student to arrive on this initial day of the V.A. rotation. There is one resident in the surgery office flipping through the latest issue of *Annals of Surgery* while leaning back in his chair, feet propped up on the table.

"Come on in. My name is Charlie Stern. Call me Charlie. Make yourself at home—coffee's in the bathroom. The rest of the crew will be here shortly." Charlie is a tall, lanky man about 30 years old. He wears his black hair longer than most men, and keeps most of it brushed out of his face. He puts the surgery journal down. "I'm a third-year resident. Bruce Conner is first-year, and John Baker is chief. We don't have any interns out here. John runs a loose service, lets us do pretty much as we like. You play golf?"

Less than 60 seconds have passed, and I already know Charlie. I have heard a lot about him from other students. He is known as the student's friend; he doesn't mind taking up time teaching and talking with students. He is supposed to be very practical in patient care, and lets the students do as much "cutting" as possible. This usually amounts to taking off moles and lipomas—fatty tumors.

The other students arrive, and Charlie orients us to the floors and office. John Baker, the chief resident, comes in only long enough to announce that he is going out of town. He glances at Charlie and says, "Take them on rounds and see if you can't get Pollard's temperature down today. He might have an abscess."

How different this is from the university hospital! There we had a routine for everything, and a time and place for everything. Here the residents work whenever they want to, so long as the work gets done.

John turns toward our student group and continues with his instructions: "We don't have any surgery scheduled this morning, so split up the patients and write an up-to-date 'on-service note' on the chart giving the summary of the patient's history and course while in the hospital. This will be beneficial for a quick reference review when you have to present your patient on rounds or in a conference." John leaves following his short appearance for the day.

"You come with me," Charlie says, pointing to me. "I understand you're interested in going into surgery."

I am not sure how he knows that fact, but evidently he has taken enough initiative to research the students coming into his service. No one has ever mentioned my going into surgery directly to me, and I feel awkward discussing my future following such a superficial acquaintance. I hesitate and then reply, "I hope to, if the time ever comes for me to finish med school."

"I'm taking charge of assigning new patients to the students. You just take all my patients and work them up when they come in and then you work with me. When I come in early, you be here; when I have to stay late, you stay late. I occasionally sleep late when I don't have an early case. I'll let you know the day before and you can do the same. Oh yes, I play golf every Thursday afternoon. Students are scheduled for a conference with Dr. Dover at that time, but go ahead and skip that and I'll teach you a few new swings with the clubs. Old Dover is a terrible teacher, and everybody ends up falling asleep before it's over anyway. You won't miss a thing."

I fit into the pattern Charlie sets up, and find that I have a little more work to do than normally expected on the V.A. rotation, but it is well worth it. By the third week I have scrubbed on a total of 14 hernias and am sure I can do one. I decide to discuss the situation with Charlie to see if there is any possibility of that.

First Hernia Operation

I catch Charlie in his office. "You know Mr. Barker, the hernia that came in today? It certainly does feel like a small one."

Charlie puts down the journal he is reading and smiles. "Buba [the name he calls all the students], I guess you're gonna tell me it's so small that even Bruce won't want to do it."

I sit down, but say nothing.

"All right, if it is okay with Bruce, I'll let you steal it from him."

Those are the very words I wanted to hear. "It's fine with Bruce. I've already asked him," I reply.

"You fox, you. I'll tell you what. I'll let you start the case and go as far as you can. When you start bogging down, Bruce takes over. Fair enough?" Charlie becomes serious in his manner.

"You give me an hour and a half to finish, and I'll guarantee you I'll get it done correctly." I really feel good. This is an unusual opportunity for me because there is no intern on the service, and Bruce has done more hernias than he wants and doesn't mind turning the case over to Charlie and me.

Fifty-two minutes and I do it all. I even surprise myself with how fast the operation goes. It marks the high point of my career to this date. I go to the doctors' dressing room to change out of my scrub suit. I have just performed an actual operation! Elation is no word to describe my feelings. I could not be more satisfied than any surgeon who has just completed his first open-heart surgery case. I have been given a small nibble of what it is all about, and I hunger for more.

Desire from Within

I realize that my desire has just been given a boost. What makes desire build in a person? What causes the hunger to reach the proportions that make me want to do a hernia operation? And now it is even greater. It is a *compelling desire* that centers all thoughts upon one goal—that of becoming a surgeon. That is the direct offspring of that small *initial desire* to become a surgeon—the desire I had after finishing high school! I know that this compelling desire is related to that original desire. And now that I have actually performed an operation, the original desire has been rekindled tenfold. I am glad I acted on the initial desire in high school. Looking back, the initial desire seems so small and insignificant. It is like a fetus still in the uterus compared with the compelling desire I now have. There is no doubt in my mind that I would have gotten straight A's in college if my "fetal" desire had matured into a compelling desire before I started college. I must keep this in mind the next time I have a small inkling to do something. I must look ahead and see what the outcome might be if that desire matured into a compelling desire. I bet it would multiply my potential tenfold in whatever I undertook.

Right now I had better come down off my cloud and think about how much of a surgeon I really am. Charlie lets me write the admitting orders on the chart; he lets me write the post-op orders after surgery; he has even let me perform an operation. But I really do not have day control over the patient. If my orders are incorrect, he changes them; if I had started to make one wrong move at the operating table, he would have taken over. He, not I, is in charge of the patient's well-being. None of my decisions are worth writing in the chart without Charlie's approval. True, I can learn from these experiences, but I must never let the little corner of my mind labeled "make-believe doctor" grow to include any of my useful mind. I must reserve the useful portion for reality. It is real; I am still just a medical student with 99 pages out of 100 yet to learn.

I do not get to do any more major surgery during my stay at the V.A., but I do pick up some of the basic knowledge I need to become an M.D., and I finish the rotation with a self-satisfaction that I have never before experienced. I have taken the first real steps toward becoming a surgeon, and I regret that the overall rotation is nearing an end. My desire to become a surgeon has kindled to the point that it is now a compelling hunger, a compelling desire.

As the surgery rotation ends, I leave with a generally satisfying memory of what I have just gone through. I have matured quickly, having to face the realities of life and death. Not all patients get well; not all patients just have a baby and go home. Some have an incurable cancer, and no matter how much surgery is performed, no matter how much medicine is given, no matter how "good" a patient is, that particular patient is going to die. This is difficult for me to accept, but I have been exposed to it.

It has been a good rotation, one I hate to leave. But there is much more general medicine yet to be learned, and so I start the last rotation of my junior year in medical school: internal medicine. It is a specialty that deals with diagnosing a disease and treating it with medicine. There are many overlaps between medical and surgical patients, and these two divisions of medicine must work together to give the patient the best possible care. Patients with diabetes, heart failures, chronic kidney disease, lung problems, hematological diseases, and many chronic multiple systems diseases frequently develop coexisting surgical problems that necessitate operations regardless of the associated medical difficulties. In such cases, it is important for the surgeon to realize the severity of the medical problem and to seek advice from his medical associates. It is equally important for the internist with patients who have a surgically related disease to consult the surgeon early. However, as with many overlapping situations in life, certain surgeons and internists have little regard for each other's ability to care for the patient. Thus the old adages, "An internist knows everything, but does nothing" (according to the surgeon); and, "A surgeon knows nothing, but does everything" (according to internists).

7
Internal Medicine

Study to show thyself approved unto God, a workman that
needeth not to be ashamed, rightly dividing the word of truth.
(2 Timothy 2:15 KJV).

*I CONSIDERED INTERNAL MEDICINE SLIGHTLY FOREIGN to surgery. It did
not include the hustle and bustle of surgery. It was not the sport of
surgery. It required a lot of reading, a lot of studying out of books—
large books. It did not include the excitement I yearned for, but I
realized I must study and learn internal medicine in order to be a
complete surgeon. One must know internal medicine in order to be
a better surgeon. Even though a surgeon may not be very interested
in internal medicine, he must study it in order to see how the two specialties work hand in hand, how interrelated the two are, how one
builds upon the other.*

*At the time, I did not perceive the correlation between studying
medicine and surgery with studying the Bible. Now I see a similarity.
There are exciting passages in the New Testament that I enjoy
reading over and over. I think of the New Testament as the surgery
portion of the Bible. To me, it relates to the present much more than
the Old Testament. It moves at a faster pace, without listing the
names of tribe after tribe. But to understand the Bible thoroughly, I
have to study the Old Testament—the big book.*

*In medical school I would discipline myself to study medicine,
but I missed the same principles concerning Bible study. I would
read only familiar biblical passages and did not hunger for new
knowledge. The goal principles I was setting down for my medical
life were not being put into practice in my spiritual life. I did not
stimulate myself to study in the Old Testament about David's great
men; how Saul and Jonathan died in the same battle; how the waters
parted not only for Moses, but also for Joshua, Elijah, and Elisha;
how Solomon did not heed his own words of wisdom and in the end
turned to folly.*

*Since I did not make myself study these less-familiar passages in
the Bible, I lived on a spiritual plateau. I did not excel in anything*

spiritually. I was a taker, with nothing to give in return. I needed to grow in the knowledge of God.

Because I know I am going into surgery, I start internal medicine rotation with less enthusiasm than I had started surgery rotation. I can find interest in medical problems that are in some way related to surgery, but find it very difficult to force myself to read about diseases I will never see or treat. I have to constantly remind myself that I should do the best I can if for no other reason than grades—all-important to being accepted to a good internship program.

Goals Already Accomplished

I think back to my college days, during which no course in particular seemed to be of significance in actually helping me to someday become a doctor. Yet each course was necessary for me to graduate from college and be acceptable for medical school. I can see a parallel in my study of medicine, which I wasn't all that excited about. I realize I must make my immediate-actions goal to learn all I can about internal medicine in order to finish medical school and be accepted to a surgical program. In this way I can look beyond the immediate difficulties and keep my eyes focused on the intermediate goal of completing medical school. I look at this as goal reasoning rather than tricking my mind. I reason one step ahead, keeping the major goal always in the back of my mind. Goal reasoning is the ability to look beyond the immediate actions at hand and to see ultimate results made possible by completing these actions.

Once again I feel this is worth writing in the goals book because it has helped me before and will help me now: "GOAL REASONING: The ability to look beyond, the ability to see the major goal accomplished in order to cope with the present situation." With this in mind, I return my actions and thoughts to internal medicine. We are required to work up three patients a week, doing a complete physical examination, making a diagnosis, reading literature concerning the particular disease, and then writing a long summation concerning the particular patient.

"I want you to learn how to work up a patient correctly," states Dr. Franks, the chief of the medicine service. An aging man of 65, he has a hatchet face with little expression other than a forced smile now and then. His beady, dark eyes are accented by his habit of staring at a single student while talking. Whether this staring has any significance depends entirely upon the conscience of the student at whom he is looking. Dr. Franks is nearing retirement age but is not slowing in his interest in teaching students. He expects a certain amount of work from us, and receives it—either from respect on the part of the student, or by humiliation from Dr. Franks. I take notes as he begins a lecture he has given to thousands of other students.

"I don't want any two-page workups like you did on surgery. I want ten pages, and I want you to write down all the negative findings as well as the positive. That's the only way you're ever going to remember to ask the patient all the questions you need in a complete examination. I also want correct spelling and I want to be able to read your writing—even if you have to print. You can get away with sloppy writing on the other services, but not on mine. There is a specific way I want patients worked up, and that is the way it will be done on this service. When you get on pediatrics, O.B., or surgery, you can work them up any way you want, but here you'll do it the way I tell you because I think this is the best way to learn to cover all aspects of the patient as well as the specific disease the patient has."

There are so many diversified diseases treated on the medical service that I soon build respect for the difficult cases. Diabetes, heart conditions, leukemia, renal failure—all of these have to be treated by specialists in each field. Vast knowledge has to be learned and applied with trials of different medications to successfully treat these patients. After two months on medicine, I have settled into a routine of almost a nine-to-five job except for the long nightly reading sessions required to keep up on this service.

Harriet and I have come to like our small three-room garage apartment and especially the nicety of the tin roof. On this particular night, as usual, she has gone to bed, leaving me sitting by myself reading a textbook on internal medicine. It begins to rain. Nothing quite compares with the sound of a good hard rain starting off with only a little drop here and then another one there. But not being able to keep up with the changing positions of the sounds, I let the book drop into my lap as my head falls back to rest on the cushioning of the chair. I always reward myself with the pleasure of listening to the rain pound on the tin.

My mind begins to wander: *What makes someone go into internal medicine? Why would anyone go into pediatrics and have to treat all*

*those screaming babies? Who would want to go into O.B. and have
to get up in the middle of the night to deliver a baby? That's when
they always seem to be born. Why doesn't everybody go into
surgery? Most of the patients are cured and back home a week after
the operation. The patients are grateful because they came in with
something wrong and a few days later it has been taken care of. And
above all, it is very satisfying to perform and accomplish something
with your hands.* These thoughts jog through my mind as I slouch
further down into the chair and allow my eyelids to relax. *I'm glad
not everyone wants to go into surgery...that would mean I might
have to go into internal medicine and do those long workups the
rest of my life....* I awake at four o'clock in the morning and realize
I have dozed for two hours. The sleep-inducing rain has stopped, but
I have no trouble crawling into bed and dropping back off to sleep.

Stop to Smell the Roses

I begin in the portion of the medicine rotation that is spent at the
city hospital. I keep noticing an elderly, wiry little gentleman in the
men's ward in the first bed on the right. He doesn't appear sick and
always speaks each time I pass his bed. On inquiring as to the diagnosis of the patient and why he has been in the hospital so long, I am
informed he has been in the same bed for over a year. Diagnosis?
"Nothing specific."

I decide to stop and talk, since I have a few minutes before the lecture begins. I introduce myself and soon am in a most intriguing conversation with an 87-year-old man without a single hair to cause his
head to itch, yet he frequently rubs it; without a single tooth in his
mouth, yet he constantly shows his gums with a broad smile. He was
a barber in his younger days—a "doctorin' barber then," as he puts it.

"I used to treat high blood pressure." He answers my ignorance
of ancient barbers. "I cut the jugular vein, let it run down into a little
curved basin that fit around this neck. Looked like a dinner plate
with a piece taken out of one side. When the basin was full, I'd just
hold pressure on the vein until it quit bleeding."

"Ever have one who wouldn't quit bleeding?" I ask, feeling that
I have just stumbled into Alley Oop's time machine and found
myself in ancient medicine.

"One," he answers honestly. I do not question him about it further.

I feel a certain satisfaction as I leave the old man in bed number
one. I invested ten minutes of free time and received, as a dividend,

a story out of the history book of medicine, told in first person. I treasure my ten minutes with him more than the hour lecture I am about to attend. I am sure I will remember his "lecture" years after I forget the formal medicine lecture of the day.

I continue my routine for another month and find that with the end of this rotation at hand and still so much reading to be done, it will be impossible to complete it all. I leave the service with the taste of neither honey nor lemon. I have not disliked it, but neither have I the desire to pursue such studies. The one thing I do come away with is the realization that some internists and some surgeons disagree on the treatment of some patients, and both let professional pride get in the way of deciding the proper, beneficial treatment. They don't mean to, and fortunately, only a few in each camp fall into this category. The goal-group phenomena that I learned in dog surgery definitely should be applied to these cases. The best possible care of the patient should be the goal, and the internists and surgeons should work together with that in mind. I have seen doctors work together as a group, with the results being exceptional care for the patient. I have also seen doctors work on the same patient but as individuals independent of one another, with much poorer results.

Internship at Hand

At the same time that I end the medicine rotation, the junior year of medical school is completed. There is a three-month break in the schedule between the junior and senior years, but it's not really a break. This supposed "free time" period allows the hospital to hire students for special projects. Also, it gives students the opportunity to get a job and make some much-needed money to live on, as well as to travel around the country and apply for internship programs. Once the senior year begins, it is difficult to get away to look at the different internship programs, so a wise student will put this block of time to good use.

I apply and am accepted as an "extern" in the surgery department for the upcoming three-month break. The job pays 200 dollars a month, which is a welcome treat to supplement the income that Harriet makes in her teaching job. My new job consists of working with the surgery interns and residents, working up patients, operating with the interns and residents, and doing some of the postoperative care. It's almost like being an intern except that I will not be responsible for the care of the patient and will consider it luck if any of the operations are passed down to me. Eight students are selected for the job, all of whom plan to go into surgery.

With the job problem taken care of, I look beyond my senior year and begin considering the different types of internships available. I can do a straight medicine internship, which would require 12 months of medicine with no surgery or pediatrics. Dr. Baxter, my student advisor, suggests that I seriously consider doing such an internship, since I will be doing surgery the rest of my life and will never again have the opportunity to study internal medicine for any length of time. This makes sense, but seems like a waste of a year I could be using in surgery.

A second choice is a "rotating" or "mixed" internship in which I can work in medicine, surgery, and pediatrics, spending four months on each service.

The final alternative is a straight surgery internship, spending the entire year in surgery. This is what I desire, but Dr. Baxter persists in recommending a straight medicine internship. He is a surgeon and he took a straight medicine internship; *he's not the best of surgeons, however.* Weighing each consideration through carefully, I decide on a mixed internship of medicine, surgery, and pediatrics even though I would rather spend the entire year in surgery.

This entails another major decision. Should I go to a "teaching" hospital, where there is a full-time staff paid to do research and teach, or should I go to a private city hospital, where I may get to do more surgery and make a lot more money as an intern, but not have the benefit of a full-time teacher? There are good and bad points to both systems, and many say it doesn't matter which program you enter because you get out of it what you put into it. Most of the teaching programs are available at state medical schools similar to this school. The nonteaching programs are offered at anything from small community hospitals to large county hospitals. I can make almost twice as much money in a nonteaching program, and this fact alone is enticing after four years of financial struggle in medical school.

The Major Goal Before You

Before I make my decision, I look one year beyond internship. I want to get a good surgery residency. The rest of my practicing years in surgery will be based on what I learn during residency, so I should probably try to get an internship in the same program at the same hospital. I will stand a better chance of getting a good residency if I am already in the program as an intern. Therefore I decide on a teaching hospital for my internship.

I narrow my choice to four hospitals and fill out the long applications to each. I make plans to take off the last week in August for an interview at each hospital. Not only will I have to choose which hospital I want, but I will have to be lucky enough for that particular hospital to choose me as well. I sign up for the "matching plan," which means that on a certain date I will list the hospitals I have applied to in order of preference. On the same date, each hospital across the country will submit a list of students they are willing to accept as interns, in order of preference. Both lists will be fed into a computer, and if the hospital I pick chooses me, there is a "match" and I will do my internship there. If my first-choice hospital does not pick me, then my name slips down to my second-choice hospital to see if there is a match; and if not, on down the line my name goes until I match with a hospital that has listed my name on its preference list.

Harriet and I decide to make the week of interviews double as our vacation, and she will join me in my travels. We borrow her parents' car, since our Volkswagen is pushing 80,000 miles, and I surely don't want to miss any important appointments due to car trouble.

Harriet has adjusted well in the transition from a college student (who was dependent on her parents for financial support) to chief breadwinner and wife of a husband who is rarely home. She keeps a neat apartment, is an excellent cook, and speaks frequently of having our first child. When I compare what she got when she married me to what I got when I married her, I realize that I overmarried. I got a better deal than she.

We discuss how important these internship interviews are as we head toward our first destination. I am nervous about the interviews, but Harriet is very supportive and encouraging. I know that with her support, everything will turn out all right.

I am interviewed at two university hospitals, both with great programs, but neither has that "something special" that compels me to want to go there. We head for the third interview, tired of traveling, tired of eating hamburgers, and tired of pushing to get to the next appointment by a specific date. Most of all, I am tired of being interviewed.

In this frame of mind we arrive at the third and final hospital on my list. It is a fairly new building, for the medical school is only five years old. However, I have heard so many good reports about its surgery program that I do not see how it can be so good and yet so young. We arrive late in the evening and pass by the hospital for a look at the outside. What an impressive sight! There is a lighted fountain in front, with a neatly kept lawn and shrubbery silhouetted against an array of floodlights. Over the entrance to the hospital is a huge marble mural of contrasting colored marble figures. The hospital looks great from the outside; if only the surgical program looks as great inside! I will have an opportunity to find out soon enough; my first interview is scheduled for eight o'clock in the morning.

Since I am applying for a "mixed internship," my first interview is with an internal medicine staff physician. He asks me where I am from, what I plan to go into after internship, and what my outside interests are. I mention working on a 1929 Model-A Ford Roadster intermittently for the past several years, whenever I had time. This is about as far as we go in the interview because he is also interested in old cars, so we spend the remaining 25 minutes talking about antique automobiles.

That was an enjoyable discussion, but I don't see how he can arrive at any conclusions about my ability to be an intern by talking about Model-A Fords. *Bad interview*, I think to myself as I look for the next office on my list. Dr. Peterson, pediatrics, Room H-202 at 9 A.M. I glance down the list of interviews and notice that I will meet an internist, a pediatrician, and an orthopedic surgeon. No general surgeons were on the list. General surgery is what I am most interested in, but I have no interview with a general surgeon.

Major Goals Never Vary

The remaining interviews go as most—questions, answers, smiles, and brief notes written by the interviewer. No one tries to sell me on coming to this hospital after I tell them I have decided on general surgery. The more I ask about the general surgery residency program, the more it seems apparent that the head of general surgery is only interested in "straight surgery" interns. Dr. Don Eler is the chairman of the Department of Surgery and is nationally known to run a tight ship. The only conclusion I reach is that I have to get an interview with him if I am to have a chance of getting into his residency program. Otherwise, as far as I am concerned, the entire morning has been a waste of time. If I am going to get into Dr. Eler's program, I must sell myself directly to him.

I drop by his office after finishing my last interview and ask his secretary if I can possibly have an appointment with him.

"You'll never get an appointment," she laughs. "He's in and out of here all day. You can take a seat and see if you can catch him for a minute between cases. He's too busy to be bothered by having to be here at a particular time, but he will always take time from his schedule if we can only catch him. I'll do all I can for you."

I sit down and, in my mind, begin going over what I am going to say to Dr. Eler to convince him to accept me in his program.

An intern walks into the office.

"Is Dr. Eler around?"

"No, he's still in surgery and I have no idea when he'll be out," the secretary replies, hardly looking up from her typing.

"I need to talk to him about a patient. Will you page me when he comes back to the office?"

"I will, but you know how he is. He will be gone again by the time you get down here. You had better try to catch him yourself."

As they talk, it occurs to me that I should pull this intern aside and get the real lowdown on the internship program, as well as his opinion of Dr. Eler.

"Excuse me, I'm here looking at the internship program and wonder if I could talk with you for a few moments." The intern nods and motions me into the hall and on into the residents' office.

"Hey, I'm Charlie Johnson. What would you like to know?" Charlie has a personality that makes me feel as if I had known him all my life. He is dressed in a gray scrub suit and cap, with a paper scrub mask hanging around his neck. He still has his operating shoes on, which were green at one time but now have so many bloodstains that they have turned a dark brown everywhere except on the heel portion. He has a natural smile and his ruffled, curly hair curls around his cap edges. He takes a seat and waits for me to speak.

"I am looking for an internship and at the same time a surgical residency. I figure to stand a better chance of getting accepted into a residency program if I were around for a year as an intern. I like to operate and heard this was the place to come to do a lot of cutting."

Charlie breaks in, "Well, you heard right. I came here from the University of Virginia as a mixed intern, but after two months on surgery I talked them into letting me switch to straight surgery. I've already done more hernias than you can shake a stick at and my resident is going to let me do a gallbladder next week. You know you aren't going to get to do that anywhere else—especially this early in the year."

"I know. You have to be a first- or second-year resident to get a gallbladder where I come from," I chime in.

"Most places are like that. The older schools pretty well have a tradition concerning which cases belong to the intern, which ones to the first-year resident, and on up the line. If you don't get to do a gallbladder until you are a second-year man, you sure aren't going to turn around and give it away to a man under you. That's what makes this place so nice. It's young enough that the chief resident is passing good cases down to the junior resident, and in turn he passes good cases down to the intern. You won't find another residency like it." Charlie is very enthusiastic about the program and, at least in his mind, is sure there is none better. "The boss—that's what everybody calls Dr. Eler—really pushes you, too. He believes if you are capable of doing a certain operation, you should be allowed to do it, no matter what year of training you happen to be in. If you are good, you can advance fast, and if you are not good, he will probably kick you out of the program.

"Look, I've got to get back over to the operating room. If you have time, stay a while and join me for my rounds this afternoon."

"When and where do you begin?"

"About 6:30 P.M. on the seventh floor." With that, Charlie smiles and heads back toward the O.R.

This is the place I have been looking for, I think as I walk back into Dr. Eler's reception room. *I've just got to get an internship here. If they will have me, I'm not looking any further.* I become more and more anxious as I wait. *What if he's too busy to see me?* I wonder. I don't feel like my interviews here were that good; nothing went wrong, but they weren't that good either. I'll have to see Dr. Eler even if it means staying over and coming back tomorrow. With no one to talk to, my mind has nothing to do but convince me of this decision.

First Impressions

Twelve o'clock. One o'clock. Two o'clock. At 2:15 a tall, lean surgeon in scrub clothes with a long white coat flapping behind bursts through the door, then hurries through the reception room and into his office. His door slams shut.

He didn't even see me. I hope he didn't see me; if he did, I don't think he wants to talk to me, slamming the door like that.

I am not sure what to say to the secretary.

"He probably didn't even see you. Let me call him on the intercom." She pushes the red button on her phone and I hear a buzzer sound in his office.

"There is a doctor here...concerning an internship. He has been waiting over three hours." She called me a doctor, but I am still a medical student. Sounds awkward, but good.

The door opens almost as abruptly as it had closed. He looks at me with a stern but friendly expression. "Come on in." Shaking my hand and leading me into his office, he glances back at the secretary. "Bring in his file." With that he slams the door behind him and takes a seat at his cluttered desk.

"What do you want to be when you grow up? A surgeon?" He doesn't give me time to answer. "Do you know what kind of internship program we have here? You are on call at the hospital every other night, but you work every night. On your nights off, you don't get home until ten or eleven, if you get home at all. Are you aware of that?"

"Yes, sir."

"You have five years to do an internship and residency. That's not enough time, so you either tack on an extra two years or you work day and night for five years. That's the way we run it here; you work hard but you also get to operate. Do you like to operate?"

"Yes, sir."

"Look at this." He reaches into a drawer and pulls out a small red paperback manual entitled *Surgery Handbook* and tosses it on his desk for me to pick up. "Look on page 34. You'll see a list of operations performed by three interns last year. You won't find a list with as many cases anywhere in the country." The secretary hands him a folder with my name printed on the front. In it are letters of recommendation and the transcript of my grades for the first three years of medical school. That small folder represents college and medical school. My whole past is laid out before him and my entire future rests on his evaluation of my medical life up to this very moment. There is no way to convince him to accept me by sitting in his office and talking to him unless my past record is favorable.

Never before have I felt the realization of the value of hard work over an extended period. All of the nights spent studying in medical school, any sacrifices I may have made, any hardships I have endured—all are wrapped up in the folder that Dr. Eler is holding. That folder is analogous to the silk sutures tied to the refrigerator door handle. It is a priceless symbol. There is no amount of money I would take in exchange for those few pieces of paper he is reading.

Last of the Dictatorships

Dr. Eler looks up from his desk. "Do you plan on general surgery or a specialty?"

"I plan to go into general surgery, but I'm also interested in chest surgery." I become a little less tense after the initial shock of actually saying a whole sentence to the man I have heard so much about.

"Did you apply for a straight surgery internship here?" he butts in.

"No, sir. I applied for a mixed program with six months of surgery and the rest split between medicine and pediatrics. I had my interview this morning."

"You want to do a surgical residency here?"

"Yes, sir, I certainly would like to plan in that direction."

"Then you want to do a straight surgical internship. I'll have to tear up your present application and have you fill out a new one for a straight surgery before you leave here today."

The next few minutes go rapidly, with a quick rundown of the residency program: what to expect; what to tell my wife to expect. It is evident that I will be working more than I ever thought possible, and will not have much of a home life for the next five years—if I am accepted here. Not once in the conversation does Dr. Eler mention that I can have a spot in his program as an intern. I know that the rules of the matching programs prohibit any agreements, written or verbal, prior to the matching of data, but I wish he could at least hint one way or the other. He is so straightforward and businesslike that I am unsure of what he thinks of me.

At the end of the interview we shake hands and I start writing out a new application. After looking at types of internships available, I check the box beside "straight surgery." With this application I know I am correct in my choice. After talking to Dr. Eler, there is no doubt about what I should do. Now if he will only accept me!

Accepting the Price

I decide to take a rain check on making rounds. I am too excited to wait to tell Harriet about my three "wasted" interviews and my "golden" one with Dr. Eler.

"Well, why do you think I won't like it if you say it's such a good program? It sounds just like what you've been looking for," she says.

I hesitate to explain. "You know all the other places we've looked. Do you remember the interns are on every third night? Every third night is not so bad because if I were up all night, then I could sleep the next and have the third night free to do what we want." I explain the situation as best I can to make her understand how hard it is going to be on her in case I get accepted for this program.

"I know you are leading up to something bad, but go ahead," she responds.

"Interns and residents are on every other night here. The bad part is that Dr. Eler says that even on our nights off we get home late, and if everyone is busy we may not get home at all."

Harriet makes a peculiar face, answering in disbelief: "How can they expect you to work like that? You can't operate without sleep. Anyone knows that."

"I'm sure we will get some sleep. Maybe not a lot, but at least enough to operate. Anyway, that's the way the program is run and it looks like exactly what I need. It's like Dr. Eler said—I could go somewhere else to a seven-year program and not have to work as hard, or even a five-year program, which is easier, but he thinks a surgeon ought to give every minute of those five years of his life to learning to become a surgeon. He feels it's that important, and I have to agree with him. The entire remaining years of practice are based on these next five years, and it is essential that I get a good base to work on."

I then look at Harriet and don't know if she is listening, or thinking, or just staring out the front window of the car, but our conversation ends for some time.

A Wife of Priceless Value

Finally she breaks the silence. "Why don't you try to get on here?"

I thought she would say something like that. She has always been supportive of my ventures. I suppose she realized what she was getting into when we married. "It will be better someday," I remind her, as I have so many times before.

As we head for home, I think back over the goal structure I see unfolding.

MAJOR GOAL: Complete surgical training.

INTERMEDIATE GOAL: Find a good surgical residency training program.

IMMEDIATE-ACTION GOAL: Find a good mixed internship.

I started out looking for a mixed internship. That was my immediate-action goal. However, ultimately, this goal was going to stand in the way of reaching my intermediate goal of a good surgical residency. So the immediate-action goal had to change to a straight surgery internship program in order to enhance my chances of getting into a surgery residency program. And bingo—the door of opportunity had opened for the surgery program, and I had to be flexible enough to change my immediate-action goal of a mixed internship to that of a straight-surgery internship for the sake of reaching the intermediate goal of getting into a good surgery resident program and finally becoming a surgeon. Why was the opportunity easy for me to see and decision easy for me to make to change to a straight surgical program? There was only one answer: The compelling desire for my major goal is so strong that anything related to the success of it comes easily. Sure, that's the secret. The stronger the desire for a goal, the easier it is to see the opportunities to enhance it and the easier the decision comes to change immediate-action goals.

I feel good about the certainty I felt regarding my decision to shoot for a straight surgery internship. My compelling desire to become a surgeon is so strong that any opportunity to enhance this goal becomes crystal clear, definite, without doubt.

We return home from our "vacation" and fill out the list for the matching program, indicating the order of my preference. I seal the envelope, drop it in the mail, and try to forget about my chances of getting my first choice. There was nothing to do now but wait until December, when the results are made known. In the meantime, I had to finish my summer job on surgery and prepare for the last year in medical school.

8

Senior-Year Preparation Pays Off

I HAD SPENT THREE YEARS PREPARING for graduation from medical school and admittance to a good internship program. With singleness of mind, I had carefully utilized both my time and my goal-structure techniques. I had been in constant preparation for my future, even though I did not know the precise details of that future. I did not know which internship program would accept me—whether a large teaching one or a small community one—but I was preparing, almost blindly, with the anticipation that I would indeed become an intern.

Again, I was setting goals for myself. I was deciding where I should go and I was doing everything possible to get myself there. My mind was set on that one goal of surgery, and it never wavered.

I wish someone had pointed out to me that God wants all of us to perform specific jobs in His kingdom's work, and that we are to prepare for those jobs, whatever they may be. There is an internship waiting for all of us on the Christian road, which is the way of discipleship. We do not know where His internship will take us— whether it will be something great in the eyes of man or something seemingly insignificant—but we should be preparing daily, hourly.

God's discipleship program is to be taken even more seriously than a medical internship program. Moses spent 80 years in preparation for the great task God had for him to do. When the time came, he was groomed and ready to devote himself single-mindedly to the task of leading the children of Israel out of Egypt.

Just as getting through medical school requires single-mindedness, so does serving the King of kings. To study what the Lord says for us to do, and then to obey His teachings without getting sidetracked, must be our highest priority. This should be done with the same fervor that got me to my senior year in medical school.

The first three months of the senior year pass quickly. This seems to be the easiest year so far because the pressure is off and I do not

87

feel as compelled to study every working hour. One thought keeps coming up: I wonder if I will get my choice of internship.

The big day arrives—December 6—and all the "matches" are fed into the computer. The senior class is called into the auditorium to receive the sealed envelopes from the matching program. The names are called in alphabetical order. Some open their envelope as soon as it is handed to them, while others place it in their pocket and walk out of the auditorium to solitude, where no one will know their results. There are shouts of joy from students who are matched with the hospitals of their choice; I see gloomy faces around, too. Evidently they either did not get matched at all or they got matched with their fourth or fifth choice.

I develop a case of butterflies in my stomach as my name is called. I return to my seat with the white envelope and tear the end of it off, blow nervously into it to separate the enclosed letter from the envelope edges, and lift the all-important statement out. *I know I can do the job if he will just let me try*, I keep thinking to myself about Dr. Eler as I go through the ritual of removing the letter. At first, I take just a quick glance; I can read the whole letter later, for I am sure my excited eyes can quickly find if I have been accepted by—yes! There it is! "The boss" is going to give me a chance to get into his program! I am one of 16 interns handpicked by him to work under his supervision. A lump comes to my throat. I can't laugh, can't talk, can't do anything except feel good all over. By the simple mathematics of the program having 16 interns and eight first-year residents, I know that only half of the interns he has accepted will end up in his residency program. But somehow I feel I can make the cut, if only given the chance. Now I have the chance.

Accomplishing Goals

I am so excited that I rush home to tell Harriet the good news. I can tell she is happy for me, but at the same time apprehensive about what lies ahead. However, neither of us has an inkling of what great excitement truly lies ahead of us in the next few months.

Time now seems to slow down, and it seems as if school will last forever. Then suddenly an event happens that really wakes us up.

It is a cold and rainy night, with the early March winds blowing the sheets of rain against the tin roof outside our bedroom window. Harriet and I are propped up in bed reading. She puts her magazine down and takes hold of my arm with both hands. "Do you know what I think?" She has a gleam in her eyes, and there is no earthly way I can guess what's on her mind.

"I give up," I respond as I set my book down on the bedspread, happy for an excuse to quit studying for awhile.

"I think I'm pregnant."

"You think what?"

"I think I'm pregnant. I made an appointment this afternoon to be checked Friday."

How can she be so calm about this? And tell me she thinks she's pregnant? Now it's my turn to be apprehensive.

"That's good. That's really good!" I hold her close as the rain continues to play its special symphony just for us—the three of us. Indeed, life is becoming more exciting, with the internship approaching, surgical residency to look forward to…and a family.

Senior year continues to be easy, consisting mostly of rotating on the subspecialties of surgery and medicine. It is while on these rotations that I become aware of the true correlation between medicine and surgery—how most subspecialties in surgery have a corresponding subspecialty in medicine. There is renal medicine/urology surgery; pediatric medicine/pediatric surgery; gastroenterology/general surgery on the intestinal tract; pulmonary medicine/chest surgery; cardiology medicine/cardiac surgery. Each of these pairs of specialties goes hand in hand in treating the patient.

There is perpetual talk between the residents in medicine and the residents in surgery about which is more important in treating the patient—medicine or surgery. The medical residents say surgeons are just a bunch of technicians and that trained monkeys could do their jobs. In turn, the surgical residents reply that medicine consists of giving pills, and when one pill doesn't work, another is tried till the patient either gets well on his own or has to be cured by the knife. Occasional talk in this vein was good fun for some of the residents, but with others it was no laughing matter. As I rotate from one subspecialty to another, I realize that neither group of residents is correct; it takes the difficult years of learning on both sides to be able to treat the different patients.

Other than the subspecialties of medicine and surgery, I rotate through a few weeks of pediatric clinics, neurology, psychiatry, and a few more one- to two-week rotations that are used only as an introduction to a particular branch of medicine.

By the end of May it is all over but the shouting. Graduation is near and no one is worrying about anything. We still have state board exams to take, but it has been years since anyone failed the exam; besides, we have been studying for four years, and a few hours of cramming at this time will not change our true medical knowledge.

As graduation draws closer, I discover that the class rings cost too much. "I'll get one later when we have more money," I tell Harriet. I wouldn't wear it anyway; my wedding ring is enough trouble to take off every time I have to scrub.

We are fitted for graduation gowns, and a few in the class even buy them. They are dashingly handsome with all the colors and velvet, but that remains low on the list of what I want to buy with the money I have. The gown is uncomfortable, but it does stir my excitement just trying it on.

I have to check with the administration office to ensure I'm not leaving any unattended matters, and I leave a forwarding address to which my grades can be sent. They hold little value anymore. Medical school is behind, and my acceptance into Dr. Eler's residency program now depends solely on how I do in my internship.

Everyone in the class passes the state board exam, and the night of graduation arrives. As I sit awaiting all the preliminaries, I reflect on some basic thoughts. The graduation ceremony is almost anticlimactic after four years of hard work. I am now a doctor, but why doesn't graduation mean more than it does? I look at the reality of the situation. I was partly a doctor the first day of medical school. I was more of a doctor when I started my first I.V. I was more of a doctor when I delivered my first baby and operated on a dog, and even more when I performed my first hernia operation. This fits with what I wrote years ago in my goals book: I am successful as long as I am working toward my major goal. That's the definition of success.

Inner Success

Many people would say I became successful the day I graduated from medical school. But I say I became successful the day I began to work toward medical school and remained a successful individual throughout the training period.

A new realization comes to light: The success of becoming a doctor is no more than the accumulation of a series of immediate-action goals. I haven't realized it until now, but the really important factors of success have been those day-to-day actions. I can look ahead to studying surgery with the proper importance placed on the daily immediate-action goals as I am confronted by them.

One does not have to wait until the attainment of a goal to be, feel, or appear successful. In fact, I am already getting a slight hint of what it will be like when I become a surgeon because, as of this date, I will apply myself 100 percent to becoming a surgeon.

I reflect back over the past four years. A lot has happened—I got married; I completed medical school. There is no way anyone could have told me what school would be like. There is no way to describe the odor of the cadavers that first year. No one could possibly have explained the emotional strain I'd feel upon taking the first examination. The first delivery will always remain a milestone toward actually becoming a physician. When it all began I decided to set goals, but there were hundreds of times that I had to act immediately in order to accomplish a certain project. It has not been as easy as setting a goal and doing it. One goal has built upon another in such a fashion that the process becomes a life pattern after a while—a second-nature sense about getting jobs done. I have come to know the meaning of the adage, "A job once begun is never complete until it's done." So many times I have wanted to quit without reading the last three pages of an assignment, or wanted to avoid reviewing some material the second or third time. It has been a real temptation to leave those loose ends dangling. But I have found that the last two or three percentage points of effort can make all the difference in setting you apart for achieving success, because most students will not expend that last effort. I also came to realize that even if that extra effort does not make much difference at the time, *sooner or later it will make a difference.* There is no way to pick and choose those times when it will make a difference.

So, I look forward to this coming year as an intern in a different way than I looked forward to the first year of medical school. I understand so much more now than I did back then. I realize that there will be many uncontrollables, many instances where I won't know what to do. But I also realize that I will somehow work them out. My goal structure has worked thus far, and I am certain it will continue to do so. My internship is a big unknown, and I know that my future training in surgery, and ultimately what type of surgeon I become, rests on my performance this next year.

I am going to give it my best.

PART II

INTERNSHIP

9
Internship—The Great Transition

As I begin the first day of internship, I realize what a dramatic transition I have just gone through. The day before, I was a medical student with no significant responsibility to any patients; now I have suddenly become an intern with numerous responsibilities.

An even greater transition, however, was the next one that came to my mind: A one-day-old surgical intern is very, very far from being a surgeon who walks out of the last day of his surgical training program. The chief of surgery has certain rules to be followed and certain techniques to be learned, all of which help the intern become the surgeon he is destined to be. That first day seemed so great at the time, yet in retrospect it was almost insignificant. When compared with the last day of surgical training, it was like lapping milk out of a saucer versus eating a 16-ounce rib-eye steak.

When I became a Christian I went through a similar transition. I started my growth as a baby Christian by lapping milk; by the time of my internship, I was consuming only spiritual milkshakes. Just as the chief of surgery had specific instructions and plans for my life over the next several years, God had plans for my spiritual life after I became a Christian. He had plans to work me up to the 16-ounce rib-eye, but I had not let Him. I had made that first transition from being a non-Christian to a Christian, but had not done very well in making the transition from a nominal Christian to a Spirit-controlled Christian. I did not understand the implications of having the Holy Spirit control me. I did not grasp what Paul was talking about when he explained the difference between being controlled by our old nature and being controlled by the Holy Spirit.

> The mind of sinful man is death, but the mind controlled by the Spirit is life and peace.…You, however are controlled not by your sinful nature but by the Spirit, if the Spirit of God lives in you. And if anyone does not have the Spirit of Christ, he does not belong to Christ (Romans 8:6,9).

Neither did I realize what a large and significant transition the maturing process was, or the difference between being spiritual and worldly. I did not see that Paul was reproving me as well as the nominal Christians in Corinth when he wrote:

> Brothers, I could not address you as spiritual but as worldly—mere infants in Christ. I gave you milk, not solid food, for you were not yet ready for it. Indeed, you are still not ready. You are still worldly (1 Corinthians 3:1-3).

I was living on milk—infant's milk. I did not have the desire to taste the meat that Paul described, nor was I ready for it. In fact, I wasn't growing at all and needed to be retaught even the initial principles of walking with Christ. I lacked maturity as a Christian but did not know it. All I was interested in at the time was maturing as a surgeon, setting personal goals, persisting, accomplishing. I was so captivated with the prospect of beginning internship, and actually being a medical doctor, that I thought about little else. I missed so much by not allowing the Holy Spirit to work in my life to conform me to His purposes.

Internships and residencies begin July 1 of each year, but I have been instructed to appear one week early for orientation. Harriet and I find an unfurnished apartment near the hospital and shop the used furniture stores, but buy only a bed and a table with four chairs. We officially move in, and I am ready to begin the year of internship.

The first few days are routine, learning where everything is located, reviewing the charts of patients we will be picking up as our own, and meeting the residents we will work with. As with any orientation, they could have told us in one day what they took five to do, but the big day finally arrives—July 1. The past interns gleefully become residents, and the night work they did for a year now becomes the work of the new interns.

The new residents seem so confident; I wonder if I can possibly be that way after just one year. I think about how much difference one year can make. Right now I'm not sure I can start an I.V., and the interns now becoming residents seem to have no trouble with completely caring for the patients. The job seems too big. I look at how much these last-day interns have learned through the year, and I know that my knowledge is miniscule by comparison. I feel like a bricklayer just beginning to lay bricks for a 15-story building.

One Step at a Time

As I think about a bricklayer, my mind eases and a relaxed half-smile comes to my lips. That's the secret; he completes the job one brick at a time. I won't look one year down the road. I'll look at today's brick and set all the other bricks one at a time. After all, that's how buildings are assembled.

Here at the medical center is a teaching-type conference each weekday, and two on Saturday. The ones during the week are hour-long sessions that include the joint efforts of the medicine department and the surgery department, but the two on Saturday are limited to surgery. Dr. Eler, as chief of surgery, is in complete charge; his true personality comes streaming forth as forcefully as a Colorado River rapid proving its supremacy to the rest of nature.

"Grand Rounds" is the title given to the first Saturday conference, and it is held in the hospital auditorium. As we enter the room a sheet of paper is given to each of us, and on it is the topic of the day: Carcinoma of the Colon. Twenty references are listed, each a journal article we can reference for review the next time we scrub on a colon case. The sheet represents another example of Dr. Eler's well-organized work habits.

The staff surgeons, as well as several private surgeons from town, line the front row in the auditorium. Dr. Eler stands at the podium and looks intently at some papers he is holding. He appears to be looking solely at the papers, but I notice that periodically he glances at the auditorium clock hanging on the wall. He is not looking at his papers at all—he is watching the time. At the very second that 9:00 A.M. arrives, Dr. Eler begins talking and the conference is started. Exactly one hour later he rises from his seat, interrupts the discussion, and announces: "The conference is over. The interns and residents will now go to the classrooms on the second floor for the 'Morbidity and Morality' conference. Students are *not* invited."

"Does he always run things this way?" I ask the resident beside me.

"Oh, yes. He even locks the doors to the lecture room at seven o'clock when he is lecturing to the students, and if any of them are one second late, they may as well have stayed home in bed because he won't let them in. You get used to being on time around here. In fact, we had better get over to the 'M & M' conference. That is one meeting to which you don't want to be late."

Confronting Mistakes

"M & M" conference is the term used to speak of the Morbidity and Morality conference, which consists of discussing all the complications and deaths that occurred during the week on surgery. This is noted to be the best teaching tool Dr. Eler uses in his residency program. Everyone has to list any complication or death that occurred on his patients during the preceding week and be prepared to discuss it with complete knowledge of the subject. A simple complication may require several hours of reading and reviewing the subject in surgical journals. It is well known, however, that no matter how well a resident prepares himself for the meeting, the last question asked by Dr. Eler will be unanswerable. He may ask only two questions before he surpasses the resident's knowledge of the subject, or it may take him 20 questions, but there will always be that end point where he proves the resident's incomplete knowledge of surgery.

The first M & M lasts until one-thirty Saturday afternoon. I quickly realize that Dr. Eler's compulsive punctuality plays no role in deciding when the M & M conference is concluded. It ends only when Dr. Eler asks the last unanswerable question of the last intern or resident.

The Errors of Others

After driving home, I think over the M & M conference. It has to be the epitome of the two best methods of learning: the "I have to go through it myself" experience and the "I don't have to go through it myself" experience. The more I can learn from the complications of another intern or resident, the less chance I have of encountering the same complications with a patient. I pull the *Goals Rule Book* from my pocket and look back at what I have written while on pediatrics as a student: There are two basic methods of learning—the "I have to go through it myself" experience and the "I don't have to go through it myself" experience. Learn as many "don't have tos" as possible.

The internship program is set up so that I'll develop experience in several types of surgery: urology, neurosurgery, gynecological surgery, orthopedics, emergency room, and general surgery. During the first month I am assigned to orthopedics.

The first night I am placed "on call." This entails completing the work to be done on the ward and sleeping by the phone in case there is any problem on the orthopedic service that the nurse may want me to handle. I find irony in that: This is my first night as an intern, and I am supposed to know how to handle any problem that may come up during the night on any of the 20 patients!

My pulse jumps to at least 140 each time the phone rings, and I remain so excited after each call that it takes me forever to get back to sleep. I hate to be called, but there is a sense of satisfaction in knowing that I now have had some responsibility as an M.D. and not just a student. I know absolutely no more now than I did as a senior medical student one month ago, but now my circumstances are different—I am an intern and expected to know how to handle problems that come up. I believe people are generally capable of doing what is expected of them, and I know it will simply be a matter of time before I begin to accomplish what is expected of every intern. I just feel awkward about answering the phone, and I hope my learning is not long in coming.

The First Operations

The third day on the service I am baptized into my first real surgical procedure since becoming an intern: I am given a patient who needs an amputation. Mr. Butler was previously admitted for an operation on his arteries to save his leg, but refused surgery at that time. It is now his fate to have the leg removed, and I am chosen to be the surgeon to perform the procedure. Dr. Bowen is head of the department of orthopedic surgery and will assist me in this, my first major operation.

I hurry to Mr. Butler's room as soon as I am notified of his admission to the hospital. He has a gangrenous right foot emitting an odor of dead flesh and infection. He is a gentle, easygoing man and does not reveal any pain he might be feeling from his dead foot. On the contrary, he only smiles and nods as I examine him.

"Why didn't you let them operate when you were in here before?" I ask sympathetically. I start my history-taking and physical examination in preparation for his amputation, which is scheduled for the next morning. His wife sits in the corner of the room and says nothing. Her clothes make it evident that the Butlers are not from an affluent background. She wears a thin cotton print dress with most of the buttons missing and held together with a combination of safety pins. Her shoes are all but worn out, the sides split down to large bunions on each big toe. A little trickle of tobacco juice leaks out the corner of her mouth, and the lower lip protrudes where she has stashed away a morning's supply of snuff. Mr. and Mrs. Butler are typical of the charity cases on which we operate. They are just plain old mountain folk, salt-of-the-earth types who have worked hard all their lives and very seldom sought medical help until they were almost dead, or in such a condition as Mr. Butler—nothing to do but amputate.

"Thought I could tough it out and get better, but it only got worse. Can you do anything for it, Doc?"

"Well, I'm afraid we can't do an operation to *save* your leg, but we can amputate to keep the infection from getting into your system and making you sick all over," I explain. He takes this at face value, asks no more questions, shows no remorse at not having had the operation on his arteries to save his leg two years before, and does not inquire as to what he should expect from his vascular disease in the future. Neither does his wife ask any questions or change her expression when I mention amputation. This is all new to them. They were never exposed to such medical facilities prior to the opening of this hospital. There were hospitals around, but they had never seen fit to enter the doors other than on an occasional visit to a sick friend. I don't know what else to say other than explain the operation and tell them what to expect after the surgery.

"You'ns ain't gonna bury his leg in the ground, aire ya?" His wife gives me the first indication of acceptance of me as a surgeon. "They cut Uncle Charlie's leg off and buried hit in the ground and the ants got to hit and Uncle Charlie said he could feel them things acrawlin' all over his leg, even though he didn't have hit no more."

The complaint of ants crawling on Uncle Charlie's leg is referred to medically as phantom pain. Many patients with amputations continue to "feel" the leg and to have different aches and pains related to that part which is no longer with them. The reason for this is that the nerve in the leg is an extension of the large nerve in the thigh. This nerve still sends sensations to the brain, and the brain interprets those as coming from the foot, or the leg, or from wherever the nerve impulse used to originate. The vague, tingling sensations occasionally feel like ants or bugs crawling around. I am doubtful Mrs. Butler will accept this explanation, and I don't know how to answer her question. I have never thought about what is done with the extremities after they are amputated. I assume they are just buried—in the ground. I surely can't tell her that, though.

"I'll make sure it isn't buried in the ground," I reassure her as I make a quick exit from the room. "We will be back this afternoon in case you think of any more questions concerning the operation." At least Dr. Bowen will be on rounds with me, and perhaps he can answer any questions better than I.

Amputation

I am off for the night at six and head for the library. I check out the large surgical atlas: *Techniques in Surgery, General and Abdominal.* "Amputation, supracondylar, right, 610–617." I find the operation in the index and flip to page 610. On one page are step-by-step illustrations of the procedure, and the adjacent page has a description and explanation of each drawing. I wade through the pages of drawings of muscles, arteries, veins, and nerves that I will encounter as I cut across the thigh. I haven't looked at them since my first month in medical school. I guess I had better learn all the branches of arteries that pass through the area; Dr. Bowen will probably ask that also. The more I study, the more I realize how much I have to relearn. Dr. Bowen made a special point to the residents on evening rounds that he was going to help me, since it was my first amputation, and they could watch. To me that means they can watch him drill me to the wall with questions about the procedure.

There is so much to learn. I decide that the best approach will be to write down the procedure step by step. Where do I cut through the skin? Write it down. What is the first muscle I will encounter? Write it down. What is the next instrument I will ask for? Write it down. There seems to be something almost magical about writing down the information. Soon I have the entire operation written down, from my first cut to the last stitch.

By 11:00 P.M. I can do the operation in my mind. I can see my hands working. I can see the anatomy. I know the next step. I know the next instrument I need and can ask for it. There is no doubt whatsoever—I can do the operation. I have already performed it three times tonight in my head.

We have an eight o'clock spot on the schedule, which means I am to be in the operating room at seven-thirty to get things rolling. Intravenous fluids have to be started, Mr. Butler's leg needs to be shaved, the operative site has to be scrubbed for ten minutes, and I have to scrub my hands for ten minutes before beginning the operation. At five to eight everything is going as planned. I am in the midst of scrubbing Mr. Butler's leg when Dr. Bowen enters the room. We are ready to begin the operation at 8:10.

"What kind of skin incisions are you going to make?" Dr. Bowen asks.

"I thought I would make the anterior flap from just above the patella to five centimeters above the femoral condyle."

"Okay, that sounds reasonable enough. Go to it."

The first pass of my knife goes through skin, the little bit of fat beneath the skin, and into the fascia covering the muscle.

"You cut through the fascia! That's too deep. You want to cut through the skin, then pull the skin up his leg and cut the fascia at a higher level, then pull both skin and fascia even higher and cut the muscle. Finally, pull the muscle up and saw the bone at an even higher level. You want to make an inverted cone out of the wound, so that the bone will be well-padded and not sticking out into the open when you finish. Now, cut the fascia a little higher, the correct way."

He has just gone through the whole operation in one sentence. I know all that. Just because I had a little adrenaline flowing, I cut too deeply. I know the steps of the operation but I did cut deep, so there is no use saying anything; just make another incision through the fascia a little higher and keep going.

"The first thing you want to do is find big red and big blue, isn't it?" Dr. Bowen appears to be having a good time, even though I am not particularly enjoying it. I feel he is toying with me just to put on a performance in front of the residents. However, he is one of the best teachers in the program, and I know I will learn from this experience.

"Big red and big blue," I think to myself. "Surely he can't be referring to the femoral artery and vein, with no respect to formal anatomy. I guess he is; that's the next step in the operation."

"Yes, sir," I reply.

"Well, dig them out and tie them off before you cut someone with that big knife you're flashing around."

I lay the knife down and ask for some scissors and pickups. I then dissect down between the muscles and find the femoral artery, vein, and nerve. I clean the tissues around each and ligate them with silk sutures. I place one suture high and one low, and then cut between so no blood will spill into the wound from either direction.

What's your next move? I think. *Looks like you're doing all right so far.*

I think back to the night before. Here it comes. I've got to name all the muscles as I cut through each one. I'm not sure I can remember well enough to name them without hesitating between some. "I am going to start by cutting the vastus medialis of the quadriceps femoris." I begin to spill back what I memorized last evening.

"Now wait a minute," Dr. Bowen breaks in, stops the entire operation, and leans forward just in front of my face. "You are not going to stand here and name each muscle of the thigh, are you? You don't think you will be able to identify each one of these as you cut through them, do you? If you did, we would be here all day. Now, what you are really going to do is cut all the *front* muscles and then cut all the *back* muscles and then saw the bone in two. Now, isn't that what you are really going to do?"

"Yes, sir…essentially that's all I'm going to do."

I can't help but feel a small amount of aggravation at this point. I think of all the reviewing I did last night. "Big red, big blue, front muscles, back muscles"; he's got to be kidding—this is an amputation on a human, not a frog. He makes it sound like I am a mechanic changing spark plugs. I keep those thoughts to myself but find it difficult to realize he is only trying to get a practical point across. On the other hand, the residents are enjoying his comments enormously.

I slice the muscle bundles down to the bone and begin to saw with the little handsaw that orthopedic surgeons use.

"Haven't you ever sawed a metal pipe in two before?" Dr. Bowen interrupts. "Act like you want to get through the bone today, not tomorrow. You would never make an orthopedic surgeon sawing like that."

I double my rhythm with the saw—just like cutting a metal pipe. I finish sawing and fill the marrow with wax, since it is soft and will continue to ooze blood if not plugged. I suture the front flap of muscles to the back flap and stick a rubber drain in the wound to allow any blood that may accumulate to escape out the drain instead of being trapped inside the wound.

As we put the dressing on, I ask Dr. Bowen, "What happens to the leg after we send it to pathology?"

"They burn it," he replies. "Why?"

"I was just wondering…just wondering."

Mixed Emotions

After writing postoperative orders on the chart and taking the patient to the recovery room, I now have time to be alone and rehash the events of the morning. There is a certain sense of accomplishment that we feel after we do something for the first time. But I have mixed feelings about accomplishing my first operation as an intern. It went well, but not as I had envisioned it the night before. Everything had gone perfectly in my mind while I thought through each step of the procedure as I lay in bed before going to sleep; I could see myself speeding through the operation and Dr. Bowen looking on with amazement at how well I knew the anatomy and how quick and sure my hands moved from one step to the next. I could see him telling me how well I had done at the completion of the procedure. Now that it's over, the point that stands out in my mind most is the fact that he didn't like the way I used a saw. Nevertheless, I have used my goal structure to its fullest. I have conquered my first surgical test successfully.

MAJOR GOAL: Become a surgeon.

INTERMEDIATE GOAL: Perform first case successfully.

IMMEDIATE-ACTION GOAL: Action. Study. Write it down. Do the operation in my mind. See my hands working. See the anatomy. Know the next step. Learn the right way to use a saw. Write it down until I can operate in my mind just as fast as I can write.

The *Goals Rule Book* is working.

10

Code 500—Life or Death

INTENSITY. I WAS INTENT ON BECOMING A SURGEON. I was studying, memorizing the operations in my mind before performing them. I was learning the proper way to handle specific surgical situations; I was maturing as a young surgeon. I did not see surgery as a little kitten to play with, but as a roaring lion to conquer. It was no timid matter; it was a serious battle. I knew what I was up against and was preparing to meet the lion head-on.

I have been to Africa and watched a lion roam the plains. He stalks his prey with cunning subtlety. The wildebeest, an animal the size of a zebra, goes on his merry way across the plains, unaware that the greatest of all beasts is hungrily watching him. Then, with the swiftness of a mighty wind, the lion pounces on the wildebeest, which is one of his favorite foods. In a matter of seconds, before the unassuming victim even knows what is happening, he is on the ground with flesh torn and breath fleeting.

Satan is like that lion. He is so subtle that we tend not to recognize his presence, or, if we do, we think of him as a tame kitten. Seldom do we consider the urgency of preparing to do battle with him.

The wildebeest knows that lions exist. He just thinks that he's too smart, that he will never get caught, that he can always find a way out. But he gets eaten. Christians know that Satan is real. We often think, though, that we are too smart to become his prey. We can be consumed, however, and too frequently we are.

Satan's temptations are like dominoes. We must stop the first one from falling, or it will knock over the second and the third. We need to heed Paul's advice to the Ephesians:

> Our struggle is not against flesh and blood, but against the rulers, against the authorities, against the powers of this dark world and against the spiritual forces of evil in the heavenly realms. Therefore put on the full armor of God, so that when the day of evil comes, you may be able to stand your ground (Ephesians 6:12,13).

We toy with temptation because we expect a kitten, not a lion. But the Scriptures admonish us to be serious about growing to maturity in Christ. That leaves no room for flippancy about sin. We must study the Word as if our marriage, our family's well-being, our very lives depend upon it. They do.

One lion that I knew was waiting in the high grass was called "Code 500." It was perhaps the one I feared the most.

Early in my internship, I realize I will have to accept the fact that I will have to jump the hurdle of "firsts" many more times through the internship year. And the one jump I have dreaded is now being announced over the hospital intercom: "Code 500, seven I.C.U. Code 500, seven I.C.U." This is the code used in the hospital to notify all doctors of a cardiac arrest at a specific location. Whenever announced, all available doctors are to rush to the scene to begin resuscitation—to revive the patient. This time the call is for the intensive care unit.

I take off for the stairwell and begin the long run to the seventh floor. The elevator takes too long, and besides, there is no way to hurry an elevator stopping at each floor. As I take two steps at a time, rushing as fast as I can, I become aware that my mind is doing two things: It is making my body move to the scene as rapidly as possible, but it is also hoping I don't get there before anyone else. What would I do if I were the first to arrive? There would be four or five nurses already with the patient; within seconds, the "crash cart" with all the necessary drugs and items needed would be rolled in by two technicians; the eletrocardiogram cart would be wheeled in by yet another technician, and two other nurses would plug in the defibrillator paddles and stand ready in case the heart needed an electrical shock to stimulate it into action. All these individuals begin working on the patient until the arrival of one person who takes charge when he comes into the room—the first doctor to arrive at the scene.

Success Requires Doing

I don't want to be the first to arrive. But if I do only the things I want to do, I will never reach my major goal. I am sure no other intern wants to be the first to arrive either, but I must push myself to do things I don't particularly like to do in order to reach my goals. It is the immediate-action goals that I don't like, but I realize the necessity of fulfilling them.

I know the reason I don't want to be the first to arrive. It's because I don't know exactly what to do. I know some of the things that have to be done initially, but there are many different diverging paths that may need to be taken on any given patient, and I haven't yet gained the experience it takes to run the show from beginning to end. I know it is only a matter of time before I do arrive first and will be called on to handle the situation, but I do not want that time to be now. I want to learn some more before I have to handle a Code 500.

I burst into the I.C.U., my mind ready to work at 100 percent capacity if needed. The chief resident is present and already working on reviving the patient. I am relieved for the moment. Now I must observe *everything* he does and commit it to memory—not the kind of memory I used in college to memorize an organic chemistry formula for a test, but the kind of memory that is stored in the mind for quick, practical recall at a crucial time. I have to start learning each of the many diverging paths of treatment one must take with a patient, and the sooner I learn them, the more confidence I will have and the better off the patient will be.

I take notice of each drug the chief resident uses, when he uses it, and the dosage. I watch him feel for the pulse, eye the electrocardiogram, inject medication into the vein, then into the heart. I listen as he tells the nurse how much to charge the defibrillating paddles, as he tells another nurse to inject some I.V. medications. I watch, I listen. I am aware only of what the chief resident is saying and doing. I block out all other conversation coming from the nurses, junior resident, technicians. This is a procedure that I must learn how to do firsthand. There is no book written that can tell a doctor how to handle a Code 500. Only observation...experience...*doing* can ever teach me this portion of becoming a doctor. This definitely falls into an "I have to go through it myself" experience. I again realize I must do things that others don't particularly like to do in order to reach my goals.

The patient is revived, and the anticlimax of routine patient care prevails once again. I leave the unit and make ready for morning chores.

Another day of internship passes. Another, and another. Dr. Bowen is the best teacher of surgery I have ever worked with and I would like to spend more time with him, but my schedule calls for me to spend the next month on pediatric surgery.

One Stitch at a Time

There is so much to learn that in no way can my mind conceive of doing big surgery when it does not even know how to do an appendectomy; it boggles the mind to even think about acquiring that much knowledge. There is only one solution to the problem: Proceed one stitch at a time. First I will learn the basis of cutting and sewing, then start putting them together in the form of an amputation, a hernia, an appendectomy, a gallbladder, a stomach, a lung, a heart. That will be the system—one stitch at a time.

The service is small—just a first-year resident, Len Stewart, and me. I want to learn to do two types of cases while on this rotation—hernias and appendectomies. There are always plenty of hernias scheduled during the month, but the appendectomies seem to come in spurts; entire months have gone by without a single "appie" coming in.

Two weeks pass. I have performed seven hernia operations, but I begin worrying about not having the experience of the "first appendix" under my belt. It is supposed to be an easy operation, but until I do one I have no way of measuring the difficulty of the task. As with so many aspects of life, there is no good gauge with which to measure the difficulty of a particular operation. On an arbitrary scale of one to ten, one surgeon may list an appendectomy as a "one." Another surgeon may be technically poor, and after having several difficult appendix operations, may list it as a "five." This same surgeon may develop competency as his years of surgery progress, and he may change the rating back down to a "two." Again, some surgeons tend to overestimate the difficulty of a procedure, while others underestimate it. The only true rating I can place on any given operation can come only after I have performed it. Thus, the fact that I have not yet done an appendectomy dangles in the forefront of my mind daily.

More "Habits"

Two possible appendix cases come into the emergency room by week's end, but both prove to be intestinal flu. I am scheduled to be off for the weekend but instruct Len to give me a ring if an appendix case turns up.

The phone rings at one-thirty Sunday morning. I am sleeping so soundly that Harriet has to wake me to answer it.

"Len here."

"Yes, Len; what's up?"

"Your appendix case came in about half an hour ago. Still want to do it?"

"It will take about 15 minutes for me to get there, but don't start cutting without me."

Harriet looks at me in disbelief. "You aren't on call. How can they expect you to come in when you aren't even on call?"

I am sure there is no way to explain this to her. "Look, this will only take an hour or so and I'll be back home before you get back to sleep." In the few short weeks of my internship I have quickly come to realize that no matter how much a wife may love her husband, no matter how much she tries to think like him, no matter how much she tries to want what he wants, the feelings of the intern and wife are different. Harriet wants me to obtain the surgical training I desire, wants me to work hard at it, and wants me to attain the goals I have set for myself; however, she also wants me at home some of the time and awake at least part of the time I am there. There is no way for me to convey my reasoning to her. I, too, like to come home and would rather be awake than asleep, but the desire to become a surgeon keeps reminding me that I must take advantage of every opportunity that comes my way.

What creates this desire? What makes desire a compulsion? Why is my compulsion so strong that I will get up in the middle of the night and go operate? I don't know. But it is there, and it's growing stronger as I feed it with completed immediate-action goals.

Harriet turns over in bed. She is upset, though not because I am going to work the rest of the night; she will still get a good night's sleep. The problem is that tomorrow is the only day out of two weeks that I'll have time to spend with my pregnant wife, and I'll probably end up using that time to catch up on my sleep. This is not fair to her, and she knows it. It is not fair to our marriage. Internship is a strong competition for my time. There is really nothing for me to say. I realize what she is thinking and why she is reacting the way she is. I know I should say something, but I don't. I dress with the light off. Maybe that will say something. I ease out of the bedroom as if she has fallen back to sleep and quietly close the door to the apartment and head for the hospital.

Life's Priority List

The patient is still in the emergency room when I arrive. They are finishing a case on general, and we have the operating room next.

Len is in the chart room sipping coffee. "The patient is in room three. Go see what you think; didn't do a rectal, saved that for you," Len laughs and returns to his coffee.

There is a little boy and his mother in the room. He appears to be about eight years old. He lies very still on the examining table with his knees pulled under him, cheeks flushed with fever. His face remains expressionless as he rolls his eyes up to meet mine.

"When did the pain start?" I ask his mother as I gently roll him over onto his back and pull his shirt up to his chest.

"Started last night about this time," she replies. "Thought it was something he ate, so I gave him some stomach medicine, which helped for a while, but this morning he started vomiting. He got worse, so I thought I'd better bring him in."

I look back into the boy's face. "What's your name?"

"Billy," he says quietly. He is shy. He has never been in a hospital, never been so dependent on a stranger like me.

He points to the exact spot that is typical for pain that comes from appendicitis, located in the right lower quadrant of the abdomen.

"Now, Billy, I am going to push over here on your left side, and when I lift my hand up, you tell me where it hurts."

I push on the lower left portion of his abdomen, let up, and Billy grimaces immediately. "It hurts in the same place," he says, pointing to the spot on his right side.

"I want to do one more thing, Billy, and then I'll leave you alone. I want to put my finger in your rectum and feel around." I push my finger into his rectum and point toward the left side. "I know that's uncomfortable, but is there much pain when I push on that side?"

Billy only shakes his head no.

"What about now?" I push on the right side and Billy lets out a little whimper of pain.

"That makes it hurt again," he says in a quivering voice.

I withdraw my finger, turn to his mother, and explain that I think he does have appendicitis and will need surgery as soon as we can get a room.

"Should I have brought him in sooner, doctor?"

"I think you got him here soon enough. He'll be sick for a few days, but he will do all right." Of course, it really would have been better if she had brought him in 24 hours sooner, but how was she to know? Besides, she has enough concern on her mind for the time being, and doesn't need me to reprimand her for bringing him in late.

Appendectomy

I walk back to the chart room. "Looks like you found me a classic one, Len."

"I thought that would be nice for your first one." He gives a big smile. "Give me a call when you get him in the room and ready to be put to sleep. I'm going to catch a few winks in the residents' office while we wait."

A good half hour passes before the O.R. calls for the patient, and another half hour goes by before the anesthesiologist is ready to put Billy to sleep. I wake Len at about quarter to four and tell him we are ready to begin.

This is the first time I have ever entered the abdominal cavity on a patient; only in dog surgery have I operated inside the abdomen. I cut through the skin and subcutaneous tissue down to muscle, start dissecting out the different layers, and Len interrupts me. "Don't take all night just getting down to the appendix. You don't need to open each muscle separately; just push a clamp down to the peritoneum and spread."

I give it a try and am surprised at how quick and easy it is to go through the muscles. Len places two retractors into the wound and pulls the muscles apart, giving me an area about the size of my fist to work in. As I cut through the peritoneal lining of the abdominal cavity, pus extrudes into the wound. He has a ruptured appendix! He waited too long to come to the hospital, and now the operation will be prolonged and much more difficult to perform. After much digging around, I locate the appendix and remove it, wash out the abdomen with saline, and place a drain into the area where all the pus was. I close the wound around the drain and tape the dressing in place.

We roll the patient to his room and make sure he is waking from anesthesia before talking with his mother about the operation.

It is six o'clock before I crawl back into bed at home. Harriet looks lonely sleeping on her side of the bed. I stare into the faintly lighted room as a new day is breaking. I resolve to stay awake today and spend time with Harriet; I will make myself stay awake. But for the moment I drift off to sleep, having the satisfaction of not only taking out my first appendix, but of taking out a ruptured appendix, a much more difficult case.

The routine of being an intern begins again Monday morning at five-thirty. Harriet cooks breakfast for me and makes a lunch. I am barely awake; I didn't nap at all during my day with Harriet.

"Always Doing It That Way"

Three nights later I am awakened by the nurse from the pediatric intensive care unit. She tells me that the patient Len operated on earlier today has a temperature of 103 degrees. I drag myself up to the unit to do a "fever check." I am not sure of the rationale behind all I do during the fever check, but it is a combination of tasks that all interns do a when a patient develops a fever check. I order a urinalysis to check for kidney infection—normal; draw blood for a complete blood count to see if the white count is elevated, indicating the body is fighting an acute infection—negative; make the patient spit up some sputum to look at under the microscope to see if I can find any bacteria. I spend one-and-a-half hours doing the fever check and still don't know what's causing it. I order an aspirin suppository and return to my room. I hate doing work like that. Just like a machine: Get up, draw blood, check urine, look at sputum, give aspirin, and go back to bed. I haven't found anything positive in a fever check, but it is expected anytime a patient's temperature exceeds 101 degrees.

During the next morning on rounds, I discuss the patient with Len and tell him of my dilemma with routine checks.

"Who told you to do fever checks? I didn't." Len surprises me with his sarcastic reply.

"It's something all the interns do."

"I didn't when I was an intern," Len replies authoritatively.

"How can you ever find the cause of the fever if you don't do fever checks?" I shot back. Two minutes ago I was ready to argue against doing such checks, but now that Len lets me know he doesn't do them, I turn and take the defensive for doing the checks. I need to know the reasoning against doing them if I am ever to learn a good argument.

"Simple. If a patient develops a fever the night after a surgery, it is coming from his lungs. If you spend five minutes making the patient cough instead of an hour getting a fever check done, his temperature will be down to normal by morning. Ninety-nine percent of surgical fevers come the first night after surgery, and if you remember to make them cough, you have half the battle licked. The second time period a post-op patient gets a fever is five days after surgery. You don't need to do a fever check—you need to look for an abscess. It will probably be in the wound, and if it is not there, it is wherever you operated. It is as simple as that. A first-day fever needs coughing and a fifth-day fever needs draining. Don't waste your time waiting for blood cultures. Go ahead and treat what's causing the fever." Len acts almost disgusted with my hour-and-a-half effort last night.

Double Benefits

However, I benefit doubly from this experience. First, I have learned how to treat post-op fevers; second, I will no longer waste my time doing "routine" anythings. If I don't understand why I am doing something, I will ask until I find out the reasoning behind doing it. I will either find out the whys of postoperative care or find a better way to provide the care. My biggest gain from this encounter with Len is the fact that from now on I will avoid practicing medicine the way everybody else does simply for the reason that "everybody else does it that way."

By the end of the rotation, I have three more appendectomies to place on my "gauge" as well as nine hernias. It has been a rewarding month; I feel more like a surgeon every day.

As the weeks pass, I begin to notice Melvin Slusher, a third-year resident whom I consider the most intelligent resident in the program. As a result of reading every chance he gets, he knows most of the numbers and facts about the different surgical diseases. I respect his knowledge and admire him for it. We have not rotated on the same service together yet, but for some reason he picks me out of the rest of the interns to feed advice on how to "make it" in a competitive program.

Just after starting the third month of internship, Melvin and I start an informal discussion while having a cup of coffee at two in the morning. He had just finished an emergency laparotomy, and I had finished all my scut work for the night.

"Internship and residency are one big game played by yourself and your cohorts," Melvin says as he stretches out on the sofa in the residents' office. "There are 16 interns in your group and only three chief resident spots in the program. Face it. Only three of you are going to make it to the top spot, and you have to figure a way to be a little better than anyone else at your level if you really want to make it in a competitive program. Every morning, every intern makes rounds at six-thirty with his resident, doesn't he? Half the interns in the program come running down to the operating room late just because they have work to be done on the ward before they make rounds. My advice is for you to get up half an hour earlier and get that scut work done and out of the way before the resident ever gets there. Then you can make it to the operating room on time, or even early, and get the patient ready for surgery. You will stand out head and shoulders above the rest of the group."

Getting Ahead

Then Melvin adds, "Everyone needs some 'getting ahead' time, some time that one spends getting ahead of everyone else. Usually this time is best found before everyone else gets up in the mornings. You remember that. Do more than just what is expected of you."

I thank him for his advice and check my notebook to make sure I haven't left any work undone.

"All done," I slam the book shut and bid Melvin good night.

"Wait a minute," he says, looking at me. "Let me see that scut book."

He glances over my work list. "I can't believe it. How do you ever get your work done? No wonder you are still up at two in the morning. I am going to give you some advice that will be worth a month's paycheck to you—probably two months on your pay scale. You wrote that work list this morning as it came to mind, didn't you? Then you didn't change it at all, did you? And you carried out each task and checked it off your list in haphazard order, didn't you?"

All I can do is nod affirmatively. I don't see anything wrong so far.

"Okay, here it is—the best advice you will ever get from me. After you write your list every morning, rewrite it and place the items in order of importance, starting with the most important. Do these tasks while you are still fresh. By the end of the day, all the important work is done and you are left with the less important tasks that don't drain you mentally. You can complete them quickly and get to bed. This will save you at least an hour a day. Use half of that time to get up early and you still come out with 30 minutes' extra sleep."

If Melvin considers this the best advice he will ever give me, I'll do it. I thank him and head for bed, although I am not particularly sleepy. Before turning out the light, I add two more rules to the goals book: 1. Get ahead of others—do more than is expected of me. 2. Write daily chores down in order of importance."

I turn out the light, lie back, stare at the now-black ceiling, and steal a few minutes of quiet time from Dr. Eler and his regime before dropping off to sleep. He will never know that I reserve a time I can think about anything I want. I think of nonsurgery, of the outdoors, of that which I have temporarily been robbed, of mountain climbing, running a river, a hike in the Grand Canyon, a swim in the ocean— anything but surgery. I must make full use of my little secret closet of time because most nights, only a few seconds pass between the time I lie down and the time I fall asleep, even as I fight to stay awake and travel with my thoughts.

I have just fallen sound asleep when I hear the phone ringing. "Good morning, it's five-thirty...don't go back to sleep now." The operator then gives me humorous advice that I can do without at five-thirty in the morning.

I hang up the phone and force myself to slide my feet to the floor and sit on the side of the bed. *I can't do it,* I think to myself. *I can't possibly start getting up 30 minutes earlier every morning.* I continue to sit and contemplate my possible future and try to figure out exactly how important Melvin said it was to get up and get started before anyone else.

I shuffle to the bathroom, flip on the light, and stare at a blank face in the mirror as I rest against the sink. I do not know how long I stand looking in the mirror, but I do experience the same sensation in my eyelids that I have just before going to sleep...once closed, seconds pass before I can reopen them. Each blink, a miniature nap.

"Okay, I'll go along with you." I speak to the image in the mirror, agreeing to make the early rising a practice, plus organizing my list of work for the day. After all, my life is just one big habit of internship, so I might as well add more habits to it, especially after making my number-one rule as an intern: Whenever a *positive* decision is made, never consider changing it; whenever a *negative* decision is reached, reconsider it after a full night's sleep.

Write It Down!

I try this new system of starting earlier and organizing my work list and am astonished at how much better the whole day goes if I know I have not left something undone on the ward while being tied up all day in the operating room. With this new outlook, I begin to like internship more every day. Melvin was right. For the first time, I feel I am moving ahead of many of the interns. But best of all, I am finishing the scut work earlier and earlier. I become much more proficient at my chores of restarting I.V.'s, changing dressings, drawing blood, writing a history and physical on the charts of the new patients admitted, making sure blood is in the blood bank for patients who have surgery the following morning, getting the pre-op patients to sign their operative permits, checking the chest X rays on patients scheduled for surgery, removing sutures from patients who are to be discharged the following day, making postoperative patients cough after surgery by injecting saline into their tracheas, and attempting to read about the operations we will be scrubbing on the next day. I can't thank Melvin enough for his sound advice.

As time passes, I find myself referring more and more to the *Goals Rule Book*. Internship becomes a true reality, although my family life has suffered. Time at home is almost nil. I look forward to the time I can be at home more. Harriet is about to give birth; I am ready psychologically to have a child. I don't care whether it's a boy or girl, just so long as the child is healthy, unlike the Pinewood children I met while on pediatrics in med school. But in terms of time, I am not sure I am ready to have a child. I will not get to spend any time with him or her for the next five years. Is it right to go ahead and start a family when there is so much demand on my time? How will it affect my children to have basically only one parent for five years? There is no other way to do it; Harriet is going to have to carry the load completely. I have to depend on her for this. Right now she looks like she is going to split wide open if she doesn't deliver soon.

At five o'clock in the morning Harriet phones the on-call room at the hospital. She is having labor pains. Eighteen hours pass and she delivers—a boy, seven pounds, four ounces. I celebrate by going to bed and sleeping four straight hours without being called. I plan to live at the hospital in the on-call room until Harriet and the baby are released from the hospital. I couldn't take time off because I would start neurosurgery in three days. But this is such an exciting time! Our baby is such a small thing. We name him Ben; both my grandfathers were named Ben. It is difficult to believe that we are parents now. Harriet lets me hold him, but I feel awkward and am afraid he will bend in the wrong places. I've held babies before, but this one is so different. I hate the fact that I'll have to start neurosurgery soon because it is so time-consuming. But I have no other option, and must get back to work.

Time always allows the inevitable to happen, and before the newness of being a father wears off, the three days pass, and I am once more divorced from my wife and married to a new surgery rotation. The first few days of any rotation are unbelievable, but this one is especially difficult. I must learn quickly what the neurosurgeons expect of me. I must learn about 20 patients who are already on the service and work up the three new patients just admitted—a challenge, for I am the sole intern on neurosurgery. I will be on call every night. It appears impossible, but I feel confident that time will prove its point once more, and I will develop new "time plans" to save valuable seconds, minutes, and even hours during the working day. I will face this new rotation one stitch at a time, and I will survive.

11

The Rebekah Principle

> She quickly lowered her jar from her shoulder and said,
> "Drink, and I'll water your camels too." So I drank, and she
> watered the camels also (Genesis 24:46).

*ALL 16 OF US INTERNS WERE GOOD WORKERS; we were all doing well in
the program. We were all doing exactly what was expected of us. I
was investing large amounts of time being as good an intern as I
could be, but so was everyone else.*

*I had just learned a most important principle about how to get
ahead in a competitive situation. I had learned how to multiply tenfold my chances of being accepted as a resident. All I had to do was
to get up 30 minutes earlier every morning. All I needed was to
decide voluntarily to do a little more than was expected of me.*

*If all the advice I've ever received or given were added together,
this would be the sum: Do more than is expected, and advancement
will surely come. If I stopped here, however, this principle would
merely be worldly advice; it would lack spiritual significance. In
studying the Scriptures, I see this advice given over and over, but for
a different reason than getting ahead.*

*The first time I see it mentioned is in Genesis 24. Abraham sent
his servant to find a wife for Isaac. The servant talked to God about
how to select just the right woman. He wanted someone above the
ordinary; he wanted the best, the one God had prepared for Isaac.
Being a servant, he came up with a principle that has stood the test
of time—the Rebekah Principle. He determined before God that the
girl who did more than was expected of her would be the one for
Isaac. The woman appointed for Isaac, he decided, would be the
one who exerted extra effort. When he said, "Please let down your
jar that I may have a drink," he envisioned that she would say,
"Drink, and I'll water your camels too" (verse 14).*

*Rebekah not only drew water for the servant to drink, but she
also drew water for all ten of his camels without being asked.
Because she did more than was expected, she became the wife of a
very wealthy man. She received an inheritance that far exceeded her
trouble of drawing the extra water. God surely blessed her life.*

Jesus upholds the Rebekah Principle in Matthew 5:41 when He says, "If someone forces you to go one mile, go with him two miles." In Luke 6:29 He further states, "If someone takes your cloak, do not stop him from taking your tunic." Jesus is saying we should be willing to do more than only our duty, to do more than is expected of us.

The Rebekah Principle is Christ-centered. The motive behind this principle is love for Christ—a love that energizes us to go the second mile, to give of our tunic also, and to water the camels also. The Rebekah Principle does every deed in the name of the Lord Jesus Christ: "Whatever you do, whether in word or deed, do it all in the name of the Lord Jesus Christ" (Colossians 3:17).

❖   ❖   ❖

During the first week we operate on several brain tumors and place several shunts in hydrocephalic babies. The cerebrospinal fluid, which continuously flows through the cavities of the brain and around the spinal cord, is blocked in these babies, and as the fluid builds up inside the brain, pressure increases and the head begins to enlarge. The neurosurgeons place tubing from the cavity in the brain to the atrium of the heart to allow the extra fluid to flow out of the brain, through the tube, and into the circulation. It amazes me that something so mechanical can be placed in a human and actually function.

Two-and-a-half weeks go by. I think I am going to make it through the month, although I have slept less than at any time I can remember in my entire life.

I continue to work: My major goal is still to become a surgeon. My intermediate goal is to become a surgical resident under Dr. Eler, and I pursue that goal with all my ability. The immediate-action goals become numerous. It is a daily battle to get through this rotation. I have to dig deep in the goals book to keep everything in proper perspective.

Halfway through the fifth month I am told that the staff is meeting to choose the residents for next year. There are 16 interns eligible for eight first-year resident positions. I earnestly believe I am as good as the best of the interns, but what I think does not carry any weight in that staff meeting. I still have not been on Dr. Eler's service, so he doesn't personally know whether I am a favorable or unfavorable intern. My one ace in the hole is Dr. Bowen, chief of orthopedics. I had a good month with him and if there is any question about my being accepted for residency, I think he will stick up for me.

After the meeting, we are informed that Dr. Eler will contact us individually the next day.

I spot Dr. Bowen leaving the hospital and go over to him, meeting him just outside the front entrance.

"Could I speak with you a minute, Dr. Bowen?" I catch up and stride along with him on his way to the parking lot. He doesn't slow down.

"If you are here trying to get me to tell you whether you were accepted into the residency program, you are wasting your time. You will get the news tomorrow from the boss himself."

He won't tell me. I shouldn't put him on the spot like this.

"I had better go back in and finish my scut work. See you tomorrow, Dr. Bowen." Dejectedly I slow my pace and turn toward the side entrance of the hospital.

"Say!" Dr. Bowen calls to me after an eternity of three seconds. "Congratulations."

I turn back toward him but do not get to reply; he has already resumed his half-walk, half-run pace toward the parking lot.

I made it! I hurry back to the hospital entrance. So much adrenaline is flowing through my body that I could work a week without sleep or food. I am exuberant about knowing that I got the nod to stay on as a resident. I will hurry and finish my scut work so I can tell Harriet the news.

Sweet Dividends

The immediate-action goals all paid off. The intermediate goal of being accepted to the residency program is accomplished. Now all that stands between me and the major goal is a multitude of immediate actions. I am finally on the last leg. The end is in sight at last.

The next day Dr. Eler makes official my acceptance into his residency program, calling me into his office and telling me face to face. It is a good feeling, especially since I am about ready to start work, still as an intern, on his service. I still have seven months to go as an intern, but will be working with the boss.

General surgery is divided into services made up of two separate teams, called the "gray service" and the "blue service." Dr. Eler heads the gray team, while Dr. Jeter heads the blue team. Each team has its own chief resident, first-year resident, and two interns. I am on the gray team with Paul Throm as the other intern. He also has a baby son born a month before mine, so we have lots to talk and brag

about that the other interns don't understand. Paul is a very determined worker and doesn't mind staying at the hospital on his nights
off until the scut work is done. I repay his kindness by doing the
same. The result is less time at home on our nights off but more
sleep at the hospital on our nights on.

Details

"Dr. Eler is going to help me do my hernia case tomorrow," Paul
comes rushing up to tell me on the fifth day we are on the service.
Dr. Eler tries to scrub with the interns on their first operation on his
service, and it usually turns out to be an experience never forgotten;
I am not sure whether he tries to make it that way or if it just always
turns out to be so. Paul spends the rest of the afternoon going over
the anatomy of the inguinal region, the area just above the groin
where the hernia occurs, until he is sure of every detail of the operation. He has reviewed the procedure in the surgical atlas numerous
times and has done several hernias at the V.A. hospital, but that isn't
quite the same as doing the operation with Dr. Eler.

The following morning, Paul enters the operating room at seven-
fifteen, a quarter of an hour sooner than Dr. Eler requires the interns
to be there, but Paul does not want to chance anything going wrong
on this case. I, along with several other interns who have come to
"watch the show," appear around seven forty-five. Paul is already
scrubbed and is "prepping" the patient, washing the inguinal area for
a ten-minute period.

"I'm as ready as I'll ever be. Look, you all don't have to hang
around for my benefit. I'm sure I can do just as well without you."
Paul is nervous but covers it up with his subtle joking.

Five minutes to eight, Paul is getting gowned and gloved and
plans to have all the drapes on the patient when Dr. Eler walks in. We
know he will come bounding through the O.R. doors right at eight
o'clock and expect everything to be in order and ready to go. Paul
has done a superb job of getting the patient ready for surgery before
that crucial moment of eight o'clock.

Disappointments

Dr. Eler walks in, looks at our small group of interns, looks around
the room, and then at Paul standing in all his splendor. "Where is this
patient's chest X ray?"

Paul's shoulders drop. He knows how the boss feels about having an X ray on the view box in the operating room. We all know it, but no one thought about it until just now; and now everyone is ready to kick himself for not thinking of it earlier. We remember the story told to us so many times about the patient who had his hernia operated on and at the same time had a small cancer of the lung which could be seen on the chest X ray. But no one looked at the X ray prior to the surgery, and three months later the patient was readmitted to the hospital—dying of that cancer. I do not know if the story is true, but it is passed around as coming from Dr. Eler. True or false, it makes a point for always looking at the X ray prior to operating, and the only way Dr. Eler can be certain we have looked at the film is to have it showing on the X-ray view box in the operating room.

To "explain" why the X ray isn't there is an impossibility. The truth is the way out for Paul.

"I forgot to put it up, sir."

"Out."

"Do you want me to get the X ray, sir?"

"I said out!"

"But, sir..."

Dr. Eler walks to the scrub sink and begins scrubbing his hands. Paul takes off his gown, removes his gloves, and walks out of the room. The rest of us follow. Dr. Eler performs the hernia operation—by himself.

Computing the Facts

Dr. Eler had meted out a severe punishment for Paul's crime. I wonder what drives Dr. Eler to do something like that. The incident upsets me almost as much as Paul; that could just as easily have been me. I go to the on-call room and take time to insert some "fact" cards into the computer (actually my mind). I have developed a mental picture of my mind as resembling a computer.

Actually, that is the way the mind works if we let it. Facts are fed in, and through a process called "thinking," a conclusion is reached, the sequence being called a "thought process." I have become almost obsessed with this idea that the mind is just one big computer, and I catch myself using it as such. Reasoning in such a way, emotions are exempt.

The fact cards read, with no emotions:

1. There were several interns present in the operating room to watch Paul and Dr. Eler do the operation.

2. Dr. Eler had previously expressed his views on the necessity of looking at the chest X rays prior to every operation.

3. Dr. Eler had previously instructed all interns and residents to put the film on the view box so there would be no doubt that the film had been looked at.

4. Paul had not put up the X ray, and that act was in direct defiance of Dr. Eler's instructions.

Conclusion card:

In Dr. Eler's world, Paul was either correct or incorrect. In this instance, Paul was incorrect, so he did not get to continue with the game, since he broke the rules.

According to my computer, I cannot become upset at Dr. Eler for throwing Paul out of the operating room. It was Paul's fault. Whether I would have done the same had I been in Dr. Eler's shoes is not even to be considered. Each of us has asked to be in his program and, accordingly, has agreed to play by his rules.

The incident is as easily explained as that. He is the rule-maker and the referee, and all we have to do is follow the rules. I am sure of one thing: No one in our group will ever start another case without the pertinent X ray on the view box.

12

Is It Worth the Price?

WHEN PAUL DID NOT OBEY THE RULES, Dr. Eler said, "Out!" God's way, however, is different from Dr. Eler's. God's plan still applies after we have been thrown out of the operating room. The difference is described by two words: grace and redemption.

We all fail to live up to God's expectation. The apostle Paul told the Christians in Rome, "All have sinned, and come short of the glory of God" (Romans 3:23). So many times we forget to "put the X ray on the view box." We may wrong a business partner or go through a divorce. Whatever our transgression, we soon find we cannot unscramble the eggs we have scrambled. We ourselves cannot make sufficient amends for our sins. We are separated from God, "thrown out of the operating room," because we have not played by the rules. We need grace.

In surgery, whenever we did something that displeased Dr. Eler, the simple fact was that we had done wrong. That was the end of the matter. It was a mark against us, and that was final.

God deals with us differently, however. He shows us grace: "It is by grace you have been saved, through faith—and this not from yourselves, it is the gift of God" (Ephesians 2:8).

God's love does not end with forgiving us when we repent of our wrongdoing; His grace overwhelms us. Our obedience, in turn, is not the way by which we remain in His favor; rather, it is a response of gratitude to the grace that He has already shown us.

I am now well into the internship year, and the burden is building. I am accumulating more sleepless nights than I care to talk about. Harriet seems almost a stranger to me. Life has become all work, my mind running at near-full capacity. One morning I stare at myself in the mirror and ask a question I had never thought I would ask: "Is it worth the price?"

The weeks pass rapidly. I do more and more operating, but the work is time-consuming. I am never home and am getting to the point that little thoughts about looking for an easier place to train begin to play around in my mind. I was up all last night and will have to stay late again tonight to help out. This is my night off, but it's too late to bother going home. I drag myself to the sleeping room. I am alone; my two roommates must still be working on the floor. I sit on the edge of the bed without turning on the lights. I'm not sure it is worth it. I am officially on call tomorrow night—my third consecutive night away from home. Interns don't have to work this hard at other places, and those programs still put out good surgeons. No one can derive enjoyment from pushing his body beyond the physiological breaking point of competence; yet it becomes a necessary evil built into a surgical program like this. Maybe I ought to go back to my old med school and finish surgical training. The night call is only every third night. However, I would not get to do as many surgeries as I do now.

Mind Control

Confusing and conflicting thoughts run through my mind as I sit on the side of the bed staring at the motionless dark of the room, not knowing whether I can physically keep up this pace for several more years. For the first time in my life I am faced with a decision of desire. My intermediate goal has been reached; I have been accepted as a resident in Dr. Eler's surgical program. I am now confronted with the truth of the matter. Do I desire to stick it out here, confront numerous immediate-action goals, and forfeit almost all my free time? Or should I apply to another program, where life may be a little easier and I'll have more time to spend with my young family? On the final day at the end of the training I will become a surgeon, no matter where I train. Harriet has already gone through so much and has given up so many of the things we used to talk about having and doing; it is almost unfair to ask her to continue through more years of what the last few months have been like.

I lie back on the bed. I cannot continue to let these thoughts fester in my mind. I must make a decision. If I am to stay, I must remove all thoughts of leaving and never let them reappear. If I am to leave, I must begin writing applications for a surgery residency elsewhere.

I think back to the rule I made at my desk the day before I started medical school—whenever a positive decision is made, never consider changing it; whenever a negative decision is reached, reconsider it after a full night's sleep. Right now, negative thoughts are drifting through my mind.

Up to now, I've found it rather simple to make decisions: I list all the facts in my computer mind, and almost as soon as I do, the answer comes forth. This decision is different. The facts point away from my being here in the first place, much less staying. Why would I pick such an internship to start with? The room grows darker and quieter, and my mind begins to dull. The computer quits working. The power of concentration weakens until I give up my attempts at decision-making and drift off to sleep.

I wake in the morning, quickly rehash the thoughts from last night, and come to a conclusion. I will stay here in this surgical program if Dr. Eler will keep me. I will never consider changing it. That is all there is to it.

What's more, I will protect that decision. Whenever a thought about leaving enters my mind, I will immediately deliver it a knockout punch and replace it with a positive thought about staying. That will be the secret to controlling my mind. Once again, I add to the *Goals Rule Book:* "CONTROL MY MIND: Replace negative thoughts with positive thoughts."

Over the remaining days of my internship, I come to realize the power of controlling one's mind and thoughts. After reaching the decision to remain in Dr. Eler's program, thoughts about leaving have never again become a problem to cope with. The remaining two months are spent maturing as an intern, readying myself for residency. July 1 makes me officially a resident in surgery.

I compare this past year of my life with that of a patient who underwent major surgery and had postoperative complication upon complication. There were many times when the patient almost didn't survive; there were times when his family thought he would never make it back home; and at one point the patient himself almost gave up hope of recovery. But now he is eating regularly, he is up walking around the room, he smiles occasionally, the drains are out, the wounds are healed, and he is recovering nicely. He still has a long way to go for complete recovery, but at least he knows he is going to survive and walk out of the hospital a healthy man.

The Value of My Goals

Two weeks ago I successfully took charge of a Code 500. It has taken me a year to fill in the many divergent paths of treatment with knowledge, but I have met the challenge. I have successfully taken care of the sickest of all patients, one who was minutes away from dying of a cardiac arrest.

I also have learned a lot about the achievement of the goals in my life. I study back over my goals book and find that the rules are actually working. I am still sticking to the major goal and am still considering myself successful. As long as I continue working toward my major goal, I am a success.

I see new interns coming on service and remember back to my first day with all its uncertainties. If they will only persist for one year, if they will only persist for one day, if they will only persist for one more operation, one stitch at a time will prove them successful.

Harriet and I reminisce about the year we have just completed.

Internship was supposed to have been the worst year of the surgical program. I reassure Harriet, as I have so many times in the past, that our lives together are going to get better.

"I hope you are right," Harriet says. "But as long as Dr. Eler is around, I can assure you that you are going to be busy." She knows too well the facts of the game called surgical residency. She knows that the rotations are the same as in internship, but with responsibility. She knows that she won't see much of me for the next few years. She knows too well. She won't even play the game of "it will be better" with me. All I know to do is to keep trying.

What can help insure our marriage? I wonder. The divorce rate among residents is way over 50 percent. In a magazine article I read this: "While the divorce rate is soaring, there is a solution to the problem. Statistics show that in the homes where there is Bible reading and prayer and where families go to church together every *week,* there is only one divorce in 400 marriages." That is not bad marriage insurance! I think I will take out that policy even though I know there is no way we can possibly attend church the every-other Sunday that I am on call. Harriet agrees that it is worth trying.

So our young family begins the surgical residency program with at least a plan. "It's going to get better. Just wait and see," I assure Harriet as I leave for the hospital for that exciting first day as an honest-to-goodness surgical resident.

PART III

JUNIOR RESIDENCY

13

Tests and Crises

EVERY DAY IN THE LIFE OF A RESIDENT brings new crises with new problems and new issues. These mean pressure. It is almost a promise to the surgical resident: He can count on a new crisis sometime during each day.

Going from an intern to a resident meant greater pressure for me. I had confidence, though, that I could meet any crisis that residency presented. I had structured, practiced, memorized, and adhered to my goals. I knew I could face the new rotations in the same way I had prepared myself so many times before: one stitch at a time. I knew I would survive and end up accomplishing my goal of completing the surgical program.

I did not realize it then as I do now, but every day in the life of a Christian is full of tests and crises. Some are small and some are large, but all must be faced directly. As I matured as a Christian, a strange realization seized me. I once thought I would face fewer and fewer crises as I followed the will of God more closely in my life. I was mistaken. Crises continued to come, but now I had divine help in handling them.

Jesus foretold in John 16:33 that we would have troubles:

> I have told you these things, so that in me you may have peace. In this world you will have trouble. But take heart! I have overcome the world.

I have not found God eliminating crises so much as I have found Him giving me direction in them. In the same way that I prepared myself for the surgical crises—one stitch at a time—I am learning to prepare for the crises of my world—one stitch at a time. With each crisis that develops, specific scripture becomes a stitch; as crisis after crisis mounts and I add stitch after stitch, I continue to mature. Also as a Christian, I can claim the promise in Romans 8:28:

> We know that all things work together for good to them that love God, to them who are called according to his purpose (KJV).

God has a way of taking situations in our lives and weaving His thread through each troubled spot to make us more of what He wants us to be.

As I started that first day of surgical residency I knew I would face many new crises. I wish I had known the peace of God through all of them. I could have—if only I had asked.

❖ ❖ ❖

I feel confident after a year as an intern, and I start this year with as positive an attitude as I started my first day of internship. I glance over the new schedule telling where I will be assigned this year, and I discover that most of the rotations during the first year of residency are going to be on the subspecialties: pediatric surgery, orthopedics, cardiothoracic, neurosurgery, and urology. I had hoped to get most of the year in general surgery rather than the subspecialties, but I guess it will be good to go ahead and get these services out of the way. If I don't do them this year, I will have to give up general surgery next year in order to get them done.

Most of my new rotations will be similar to the ones I had as an intern, but the difference will be that I now rotate as a resident, not as a lowly intern. I will gain experience as the responsibilities increase. The necessary scut work will be done by an intern under me. I will get much more sleep at night, getting up only for emergency operations or postoperative patients with complications. This becomes a reward only because the demands of internship were worse. To most people, life as a resident would be so undesirable they would question the worth of going through something so terrible. I have the advantage of having lived a year as an intern and am able to lengthen my gauge, which spans the scale from easy to difficult living; it is all relative.

The True Value of Time

I would not want to go through internship again, but my enjoyment and appreciation of the little things in life have been enhanced tremendously as a result of serving an intern. I will never be able to sit down for an hour and do nothing but watch whatever happens to come on television, but I will be able to enjoy time I can call my own. I will be grateful for any one-hour period in which I'm allowed to do anything I want, whether it is reading, studying, cutting the

grass, or sitting at home and talking with Harriet. It has been difficult to live with my entire life's saving of time stolen by the surgery
department, but it has taught me something far more important than
how to change dressings on an infected wound, or how to restart an
I.V. in the middle of the night: I have learned the true value of time.
Not just weeks and days, but hours and minutes and even seconds.
I have learned that seconds are wasted waiting for an elevator, seconds are wasted at the operating table hundreds of times during a
single procedure, that seconds have a unique way of adding up to
minutes, and a mere 60 minutes a day may be the deciding factor
between a good intern and a poor intern.

I take these hard-earned trophies and begin my first rotation as a
resident in pediatric surgery. I begin a new page in the *Goals Rule
Book*. The anatomy of the goal structure has been easy to dissect
after so many years of goal-setting. I quickly jot down the following:

MAJOR GOAL: Complete general surgery and become a surgeon.

INTERMEDIATE GOAL: Complete pediatric surgery rotation.

IMMEDIATE-ACTION GOAL: See what pediatric cases are
scheduled and begin reading about them—right now!

Advancement

I have one intern under me. Only a year ago I was the intern on pediatric surgery, scrambling to get to do half the hernias and appendectomies. My policy is going to be different; hernias and
appendectomies belong to the intern. I will help him on every case,
but he will be the first surgeon. I will get to do some chest cases
while on this rotation and will spend most of my time studying and
reading about the chest-related problems of the pediatric age group.
I occasionally think about continuing training after general surgery
and doing a residency in chest surgery. That is several years away; I
don't need to make a decision now. But at least I can devote some
study to it and see how much interest it holds for me.

In one month's time I perform several bronchoscopies and open
two chests. Today I admit one of the cutest four-year-old girls I have
ever seen. Her problem is serious; she has a completely destroyed left
lung due to tuberculosis. I am scheduled to remove this worthless lung.

Dr. Bell, the chief of the cardiothoracic department, is going to
assist me in the procedure. We meet at six for evening rounds.

"Do you know," Dr. Bell says as he places her X rays on the view box, "who the patient is?"

"Rhonda Thornton is her name. Other than that I don't know what you are getting at."

"Have you talked with her parents?"

"No, sir, there hasn't been anyone here with her."

"Do you mean to say you are going to take out a four-year-old girl's lung and not even discuss the operation with her parents?"

"I always talk with the parents before surgery, but I didn't see anybody with her. I'll check back later tonight."

An Orphan's Operation

"She is an orphan; that's why her parents aren't here," Dr. Bell informs me. "She is going to be adopted by Jim Teller, one of the senior medical students. He and his wife will probably be coming around sometime tonight to see her; they know you are going to be performing the operation, so go ahead and explain what you are going to do. I've talked to them once about it, but you may as well give them your two cents' worth."

I get the message Dr. Bell is giving me. If I am to do the surgery, I should also talk to the parents. The fact that Jim is adopting her will make the conversation much more difficult, for he knows I am a resident and have very little experience in chest work. However, this is part of the learning experience. I will tell them what I plan to do, and hope it is the same procedure that Dr. Bell described to them earlier.

I begin the case listed as first surgeon, but it is Dr. Bell who shows me where to cut, what to tie, when to slow down, when it is safe to speed up. There is no way I could possibly complete this operation without his standing on the other side of the table "leading me by the hand." He explores the chest cavity thoroughly, then asks me to put my hands in and feel around. He shows me where to start my dissection on the lung—where to use scissors and where to use a blunt "pusher." He assists me through the entire procedure, even to the point of placing some of the closing skin sutures.

As we finish, the circulating nurse asks, "Dr. Bell, who do I list as first surgeon?"

He nods my way: "There is your first surgeon. I only assisted him."

I note a hint of sarcasm in the nurse's question, but that's okay; I just did my first pneumonectomy whether she realizes it or not, and before I finish here, I will be doing so many pneumonectomies that she won't have to ask who the first surgeon is; she will know without a doubt. *One stitch at a time,* I remind myself. I'll be doing radical pneumonectomies one day, but today's stitch is good enough for now; I know my time will come.

Rhonda does fine. A week post-op she is running around as if she had never been operated on. She is happy when I tell her she can go home today. Looking at her sparkling eyes, I can only imagine the excitement and happiness that awaits her six weeks from now, when Jim goes to the orphanage to take her home for real.

I continue to learn different surgical procedures, a whole new realm of surgery. There are many things that happen to infants and children that we don't see in adults. For example, there is Jimmie Turner, a nine-year-old boy who hasn't had a normal bowel movement since he can remember. Each time he defecates, his rectum actually turns inside out and protrudes about six to eight inches outside his body. Every time he uses the bathroom, he has to manually push his bowel back inside. In spite of this handicap, he appears to be normal psychologically.

"I sure hope you can help me, doctor," Jimmie says sincerely. "The worst time is at school when I have to take so long to go to the bathroom." He is mature in the way that he talks about his problem, accepting it as just that—a problem and not a stumbling block. He and his mother live alone, and by the way that they dress and talk, I assume he has had problems growing up, which make his physical condition seem minor.

I assure him I will try my best to make him "good as new" within the next few days, and his eyes related the excitement of even a possibility of being able to alleviate the situation.

On the day of the surgery I do a suspension-type operation in which the colon is actually suspended from above after it has been pulled back inside as far as possible. Jimmie does well post-op and is discharged in a week. Since I first entered surgery, I have not had a more grateful patient, adult or child.

The rotation passes too quickly, like anything else you enjoy doing. On my last night as resident on pediatric surgery, I go to the residents' office to make a list of cases I performed while on the service. I do this at the end of each rotation, since I will need to know the diagnosis, operation, and outcome of the procedures when I apply for my surgical board examination. I try to keep track of the cases as I go along so I won't have to do all this bookwork at the end of residency.

The Cost of Future Gains

I hate to see this rotation end and dread starting cardiothoracic surgery, or "C-T" as it is called, as it is supposed to be the most time-consuming rotation of all. I made it through this rotation in my internship year, and I know I will just have to buckle down and stick with it. There are three to four scheduled open-heart cases a week plus any emergency heart patients that come along, which are often the most difficult operations because these patients usually are in very poor condition. They seldom come off the heart-lung machine without several trials, all of which means more time on the operating table. Then even with the best of postoperative care, the heart may still end up continuing to pump poorly for a few days and then quit.

Lung cases are done on Mondays and Fridays. Wednesday is reserved as a clinic day to see pre- and postoperative patients. Looking over this calendar of events, I see that Wednesday afternoons are free. It can't be all that bad if we have an afternoon off to catch up on ward work, I gleefully reason to myself, only to find that Wednesday afternoons have turned into the time reserved for implanting cardiac pacemakers—a task that sometimes is very time-consuming.

My primary job is to make certain the postoperative heart patients get proper care. I watch these patients more closely than those on any other service, since minor changes in a heart patient's condition can mean death. There are all types of gadgets, wires, tubes, and monitors to help keep a close eye on these patients. Three small polyethylene tubes are placed in the heart at the end of a surgical procedure and brought out through the skin and connected to a monitor. One tube measures the right atrial pressure, one the pulmonary artery pressure, and one the left ventricular pressure. Three wires connected to the chest wall transmit a continual cardiogram to a small TV-like screen. The first night, the endotracheal tube is usually left in place, and the patient breathes with the help of a respirator that has to be regulated to bring in just the right amount of oxygen and to blow off just the right amount of carbon dioxide. This necessitates drawing "blood gases" on the patient to determine at what level these gases are circulating.

Two larger tubes, about the size of a small garden hose, are brought out the side of the chest to drain any blood that may accumulate. The blood is drained into bottles, which must be closely watched to check the amount of blood loss. Still another tube is placed into the bladder to measure the urine produced, and an hourly check is made of the amount.

I remember only vaguely how to keep check on all the necessary statistics from my month as an intern. The chief resident above me will certainly help get me organized to alleviate me from having to rely on him for each detail.

We perform many heart operations on this service, and we remove several carcinomas of the lung. The worst of the operations is that performed for carcinomas of the esophagus. By using the word *worst,* I do not mean the technical procedure is not a good operation. What I mean is that the overall outcome for patients who have to undergo this operation is extremely poor. Nevertheless, if I had carcinoma of the esophagus that could be surgically removed, even though it is one of the least curable of malignancies, I would still undergo the operation.

The Worst Trip Traveled

One surgical procedure for the tumor is to resect the esophagus and replace it with a section of colon, sewing one end to the back of the throat in the neck and the other end to the stomach. In this way food can travel from the mouth into the colon substitute and on to the stomach for normal digestion. We have such a patient, Mr. Johnson, admitted for surgery. Joe, the chief resident, begins resecting the esophagus in the chest and I resect the right half of the colon in preparation for "swinging" it up into the chest for suturing. The operation goes well, but on the fourth postoperative day it becomes evident the suture line holding together the esophagus and colon in the throat is breaking down. Mr. Johnson develops signs of infection in the neck areas and starts draining saliva and mucus out of the neck wound. His chances of surviving such a major complication are two—slim and none. Still, we discuss what measures to take in an attempt to save him. There is reluctance to perform more surgery at this time other than to try to divert the stream of saliva from the original operative area in the hope that the site will heal. All the while the infection worsens and the patient goes rapidly downhill.

On the eighteenth postoperative day the inevitable happens. The infection creeps around the left carotid artery in Mr. Johnson's neck and "eats" its way into the wall of the vessel, then through the wound, then "blows the carotid." By this I mean that blood begins to squirt all over the bed, floor, and patient. The only person on the ward at the time is a medical student, who, instead of grabbing the artery with his fingers to compress the source of bleeding, runs for help. By the time any of us return with him, Mr. Johnson is dead. He has bled out lying in bed. The pool of blood has "puddled" around him and is beginning to form into a soft jell. This is a terrible sight to see, especially knowing that he was aware of what was happening until the time when there was not enough blood to keep his brain functioning properly.

This particular incident bothers me emotionally. I can almost feel my mind changing the computer cards around so that I will have a single card telling me I dislike treating cancer patients who have a poor chance of survival. The five-year survival rate for this cancer is only around five to eight percent, and what we did to Mr. Johnson seemed like a "mighty long run for such a short slide." I find it hard to accept such a low survival rate on these tumors, but find it equally difficult to accept that nothing can be done. If I were given a five percent chance of living, I would go to the extremes to "cash in" on that percentage; I assume these patients must feel the same way. Nevertheless, Mr. Johnson didn't make it.

After two months on the service, I find myself fairly proficient in taking care of the patients as well as keeping up with them. There is so much information on each that I develop a system whereby I put all important data on an index card, a single card reserved for each patient. I refamiliarize myself with Mr. Harrison, an aneurysm patient, by looking at his card just prior to making rounds with Dr. Bell. It's almost like cheating to have such an impressive record of what happened day by day on a particular patient.

Saving Time

Making the best of the time required for making rounds requires that a resident be organized. As long as all the "numbers" are collected and presented everything runs smoothly, allowing Dr. Bell some extra time to teach us rather than have us look up information on the chart. It is remarkable how much time can be saved when a little time is spent in organizing the patient's records.

I work at being an organized resident, learning how to take care of critically ill patients in an efficient manner. Each morning I make my list of things to be done in the order of their importance. I gain extra minutes during the day by saving seconds. My immediate-action goals keep me moving right now to get something done. *Procrastination* is a word I hardly recognize. Right now, right now, right now has become my lifestyle. It is all becoming automatic, the goal structure is finally forming automatic goal-oriented habits.

By the end of the rotation, I have mixed feelings about cardio-thoracic surgery. It is the ultimate in the field of surgery. The residents and staff are placing new valves in hearts, cutting out lung tumors, and handling life-and-death situations daily—all very exciting, but the price to pay for this training is dear. Timewise, the lifestyle of the cardiothoracic resident is very similar to the intern; the chief resident is on call around the clock, seven days a week. I am attracted to chest surgery, but at this time cannot convince myself of the added value of the extra training. I can put off the problem of deciding whether to go into C-T for a few years because I have to complete my year as chief resident on general surgery before I can be accepted to the C-T program. I will talk with Dr. Bell sometime about the possibilities. Right now, I have to start a new rotation—orthopedics. Again, I will be rotated as a resident instead of an intern. Every now and then I thank the good Lord that I am not an intern; I will never have to relive that year.

Steve Webb is the senior resident on the "bone" service. I will be working with him for the next three months. The plan is for me to cover the emergency room for orthopedics every other night, and he will back me.

More Than Expected

After one week, however, I realize I am missing out on half of the cases—the ones that come in during my night off—so I discuss the situation with Steve. I am wasting some easy "getting ahead" time with this setup.

"How about letting me take first call every night, and if I get anything I can't handle I'll give you a call." I don't have to stay at the hospital on orthopedic call, so I will at least get home for a few hours almost every night and still do a lot of bone setting and minor orthopedic surgery, as well as scrub on the larger cases. Steve agrees and the arrangement works out well.

My suggestion harkens back to the "do more than is expected of you" concept that Melvin taught me as an intern. I was doing this not to compete with the other residents, but to get ahead in my knowledge of orthopedics. With the new arrangement, every other night will be "getting-ahead time" because I will be doing more than what is expected from the other residents in the program. I have successfully learned to do more than what is expected of my job, to do more than my share of the work. The *Goals Rule Book* is holding true to form.

Harriet is beginning to wonder if we will ever have any time together. She keeps asking me if it is really going to get better once I get through residency. Will life ever be normal again? Will I ever have any time to spend with her? Will our children ever get to know me as a father who plays ball with them and takes them places? Am I sure that surgery won't always be a thief of my time? Certain doubts begin to grow in her mind. I know what she is thinking—she may have lost me to surgery. I can tell her differently, but she sees the mold already being formed, and I am slowly being poured into it. I reassure her, and reassure myself. I must guard against falling into that mold, that trap called "surgery in place of family." Yet I must not let up now. I have too much more to learn, too many more operations to master to back off right now.

"Someday it will be better. You'll see. It will get better." I give Harriet all the sincere assurance I can muster. I now must put these thoughts behind me and look toward that major goal of becoming a surgeon. I must keep my eye on the finish line until the race is won.

Dead Tired

Another day of surgery is finished. This evening I feel dead tired. I was up all last night with little piddly things in the E.R. I make it home for a late supper but am called right back to the hospital to see a victim of an automobile accident. I call Steve and tell him we are going back to the O.R. We finish operating on the patient's arm and hand at 1:00 A.M., but there are still multiple fractures to work on in his legs. By the time we finish operating and casting, it is 5:00 A.M. I decide there is no sense in going to bed, so I go up to the residents' office for coffee. We are very giddy at this time of morning, and the fact that we have gone two nights without sleep seems unimportant. We make rounds, eat breakfast, and go to the clinic to see follow-up postoperative patients. After an hour of unstimulating clinic work I begin to get sleepy and disinterested. I look a few hours ahead and plan to skip lunch and slip up to the on-call room to catch a few hours' sleep, since I will be on call again tonight.

"Come on in here." Steve interrupts my thoughts as he motions me into one of the examining rooms. "There's an old patient of mine I want you to see." I sit down beside the patient as Steve sits in a slightly cushioned chair. I vaguely hear Steve telling me about the operation he performed on this patient two months previously.

I suddenly hear laughter in the room. "Hold it right there," a surgery resident says as he snaps our picture. I open my eyes and see the room full of residents and interns. Steve is just opening his eyes and looks sheepishly over at me. We both had fallen asleep and left the patient sitting there; he left the room and told another resident what had happened.

The resident taking pictures explains: "He said you two were sitting there talking to him, and eventually you stopped making sense, and the next thing he knew, you were both slouched down in your chairs asleep. When I walked in I thought I ought to capture the scene on film. I also thought I ought to bring in as many of the house staff as I could find." Steve and I remain frozen to our spots as everyone throws in his jab.

"If you can't take it, admit it," one intern jokes.

"Some of us have it, others don't," another chimes in.

"Real tough. Lose a few hours' sleep, and look what happens."

"Hope the picture turns out. Living proof."

I can't think of anything appropriate to say. I look at Steve, but he looks back with an expressionless face. Everyone thinks it is funny except us; we don't care whether or not this is funny. All we want is a few hours of sleep—without interruption.

We catch up on our sleep, and six hours later we fall back into the routine of being a resident. It is very different rotating on a subspecialty service as a resident rather than as an intern. Back then, everything was new and different. I paced myself at 100 percent no matter what service I was on. Now as a resident I relate my time and surgical experience back to general surgery and to what I think will be important to me after I get into private practice. I cannot feign interest in the reconstructive portion of orthopedics, since I know I will never be doing this type of surgery. I can no more fake interest than a salesman can fake enthusiasm for an undesirable product he is selling. I elect to spend my time on this rotation with the more practical portion of bone setting and cast applying.

Orthopedics comes to an end for me. This moment means more than just finishing a subspecialty rotation; it marks the completion of two-thirds of my first year in residency. These rotations have provided excellent experience, but I can't help being eager to complete them so I can begin my "first love"—general surgery. I still believe that general is the most diversified field in surgery because it covers such a wide range of diseases and operations, each day presenting new situations and new challenges. I must wait for that, though. I still have the neurosurgery and urology rotatations to do.

14

Tragedy Strikes a Football Player

Thou shalt have no other gods before me (Exodus 20:3 KJV).

In all thy ways acknowledge him, and he shall direct thy paths (Proverbs 3:6 KJV).

MOST OF US DO NOT WORSHIP WOODEN AND STONE GODS today, as many people did in Old Testament times. What misery the Israelites made for themselves by worshiping false gods! God commanded them to have no other gods before Him, but they would not listen. When they served other gods, they invariably got into trouble. Their lives fell apart and they failed to experience all of God's wonderful promises to them.

As I began to mature as a Christian, I realized that what happened to the Israelites then can happen to Christians today. The only difference is that our gods are more subtle, more sophisticated. Some worship the god named leisure, others worship success or prestige or wealth. It is easy for me to see now that I had allowed surgery to become my god. It was my main god and first love in life.

The deceiving characteristic of my idol was that it was so admirable. It accomplished good, not evil. I am not saying I should not have been in surgical training; I just shouldn't have let it take precedence in my life. I had many chances to ask God for direction and wisdom; so many times, though, I did not. I left Him out more times than I included Him. I did not see my mistake at the time, but I excluded God from some of my largest goals in life.

Today I must be constantly on guard against anything that may become a god to me. I don't want to miss out on any part of the fulfilling life that God has planned for me. Simply, I want God for my God.

Neurosurgery rotation for a general surgery resident is only slightly more prestigious than it is for an intern. A resident doesn't do any surgery, and he is responsible for the ward work the interns don't get around to. I think back to last year, when Dr. Carter made a resident scrub when he had lost so much sleep. I simply cannot see how anyone can spend his life in the field of neurosurgery. After only two days, it is developing into the most depressing rotation I have ever encountered.

I receive a call in the afternoon about a football player we are admitting from the practice field. He supposedly has sustained a spinal cord injury and is paralyzed from his neck down. Neurosurgery is expected to make him "well" again. It is difficult to remain positive on this service, but I realize that my life will be miserable if I don't control the negatives by replacing them with positives.

Robert Mills, a defensive lineman for the university, had a good freshman year last year and was trying to sew up a spot on the varsity squad during spring training. He had been warned about "spearheading" tackles before; today he neared a runner, lowered his head, and rammed into the runner's abdomen in order to knock him off his feet. He made a beautiful stop but lay motionless after the play was completed. He was conscious, but could not move his legs or arms.

I meet Dr. Carter, chief of neurosurgery, in the emergency room to examine Robert. He has the muscular build that is typical of a college football player. He does not realize the full significance of his injury and complains of missing the rest of spring practice and the probability of losing the starting position he has worked so hard for. He knows he cannot move, but speaks as if his paralysis is only temporary. He believes he will be able to walk and run and even play ball again. "Just you wait and see," he tells the coach who accompanied him to the hospital.

We operate, hoping that all we'll find is a swelling of the spinal cord which would mean hope for Robert. Dr. Carter talks of possibly being able to decompress the area and give the cord enough room to swell without compressing itself to death.

Only God Can Heal

The operation is done to no avail. There is no change in any of the numerous neurological exams we perform on Robert in the following days. Weeks and finally a month passes with all hope fading for his recovery. The team gives him the game ball of the spring encounter and all the players sign it encouragingly. His attractive girlfriend stays with him almost constantly the first week, then begins to make appearances less often. By the fourth week, she is breaking her date with Robert—"just for this weekend," she promises him. I have come to know him fairly well and begin to see the inevitable changes come, both physically and mentally. I knew it would be only a matter of time before Robert's girlfriend realized that his situation was not going to change. Any thoughts about getting married have disappeared by now. The football team, seeing no change, stops coming by so often. They have their own lives to live, tests to study for, dates to plan for on Saturday. Their world gradually leaves Robert out. He cannot participate in any of the activities their lives revolve around.

Robert finally begins to painfully accept reality. I do not know when he first admits to himself that he is completely paralyzed; he doesn't speak of the negative aspect of his predicament—not being able to walk, run, or roll over in bed. But he does stop speaking about the positive aspects of his once-active life. He quits asking when he will be playing ball again, quits talking about marrying the beautiful girl (although he still remembers the details of their last date before his injury), and doesn't speak of his teammates. His change of conversation doesn't gradually evolve from that of running, to trotting, to walking, to standing, to sitting, to lying flat on his back; it stops just after running. He never mentions that he is permanently useless from his neck down. I do not know how to discuss the problem with him. We were never taught what to say to a patient in this type of situation. No professor ever lectured on the art of discussing the future of a college football player turned puppet. The textbooks are silent on the subject. All I can offer him are my prayers and blundered conversations.

Robert loses weight quickly. The pounds melt away; not pounds of fat, but of muscle. By the end of six weeks I cannot recognize him as the hunk of an individual who was brought to the hospital wearing a grass-stained football uniform. Robert has shown only one attribute that has allowed him to come as far as he has: the determination to continue a productive life. He keeps his smile and begins to talk of what he may be able to do in a wheelchair, of what he may be able to do with the little bit of shoulder muscles that are left, never speaking in terms of self-pity or regrets.

Unused Potential

What makes an individual continue to strive for high goals in situations like this is beyond my comprehension. Some of the residents comment that Robert's injury is one accident they would not want to survive. Initially, I tended to agree with them, but after talking with Robert one day, I had to disagree that his life is worse than death. On the contrary, he seems to value what little bit of physical being he has left more than some of us value a full, healthy body. Every few nights I catch myself playing the "assuming game," in which I assume that I have the very same injury and then try to decide what my feelings would be. I am unable to cope with such games and always end the session by overthrowing the rules committee and declaring "reality." I do not have the injury; I can never know for sure what my reactions would be like because I am not in that situation.

I toy with the frayed edges of the *Goals Rule Book*. I have placed so much importance on making goals and trying to accomplish them. Now it seems almost insignificant compared to the goals and rules that Robert will have to make for his broken body.

A physician, I have been told, is not supposed to spend much time concentrating on the emotions of his patients. He should never become greatly involved in this aspect of his patients—only diagnose and treat them. I have heard these comments, but I feel they are lies. I am a physician. Physicians are human. It is human to have some empathy for patients, whether or not it is actually expressed.

Robert Mills is not the only depressing case on the service. Case after case of head injuries appear. Some people die, some remain only vegetables, some survive. Brain tumors in young and old alike come, many ending in death or a state of being that would have better ended in death. We help too low a percentage of patients that come to the hospital; yet no group of doctors works harder in trying to help.

I am glad that time has run out for me on this service. I am scheduled to move to another subspecialty—urology. I am not glad in the sense that I disliked the service or the people in it, but in the sense that I kept coming up on the losing side of patients admitted to the neurosurgery service—a bullet in the head, a smashed skull, a brain tumor. I haven't particularly enjoyed working this rotation, but it was necessary, according to the *Goals Rule Book*. In order to achieve a major goal, I must be willing to do what I don't like to do.

As I leave the service, I know that this is one field of surgery I can never enter. It takes a special, objective type of individual to be able to cope with such depressing problems, and I definitely do not fit into that category. Therefore I make a pleasing transition from the neurosurgery rotation to urology.

Urology proves to be more relaxing and enjoyable, with less complicated aspects of patient care. Dr. Delbert Webb, the chief of urology, is new to the department. He appears anxious to make a good impression on the house staff working with him. The teaching aspect of the rotation is primarily derived from following Dr. Webb in the clinic to pick up as much practical advice as possible.

"One thing you have to learn is how to communicate with these older people we get as patients." He impresses upon me the fact that there is more to being a surgeon than operating. One must learn to "know" the patients, to speak their language, and to understand their ways.

Young in Spirit

It seems that every male over 60 who comes to the clinic has an enlarged prostate gland, and this, in turn, causes them to have to strain to pass their urine and further causes them to dribble at the end of voiding. As the prostate gland enlarges, it blocks the outflow tract of the bladder, resulting in the patient having to get up more and more often during the night to try to empty out as much of the bladder as possible. This is the story I hear repeatedly from the male patients, the history always being the same. I even wonder why the urologist bothers to take the history, for the cases are always the same.

Today is clinic day, and I follow Dr. Webb from one room to another as he examines the patients, teaching and explaining as he goes. The third patient is wearing overalls, has a felt hat cocked on the back of his head, and has as friendly a smile on his face as you would ever want to see.

"Good morning," Dr. Webb speaks first. "How are you getting along?"

"Just fine, thank you."

This man is the type of individual who knows no stranger, and he acts as if we were both his next-door neighbors. He is friendly but not overbearing, and sits forward in his chair with his hands on his knees, 100 percent of his attention directed toward Dr. Webb.

"I understand you are having trouble passing your water."

The old man's smile fades as he stares at Dr. Webb with awe. "Why, yes, I do have a little trouble with my water," he replies.

"You have to strain a lot to get it started?"

"I sure do, I sure do." He repeats himself and looks at Dr. Webb as if he cannot believe the questions being asked.

"You have a little dribbling when you finish?"

"Why, yes! How did you know that?" His eyes widen and a slight grin appears.

"Do you get up several times at night to go to the bathroom?"

At this question the old man slaps his knee with his farm-worn hand and begins to laugh. "You're too much. How in the world do you know all that about me?" I am sure he thinks he is in the presence of a magician of the first rank.

Dr. Webb assures him that many men his age have the same symptoms, and that all his difficulties can be relieved by a simple operation.

"Oh no! No, no. I don't need no operation." He no longer leans forward to listen to Dr. Webb, but leans back and stretches his neck a few times, looking first one direction and then another. He alternates glances between Dr. Webb and me. "You see, I just bring my wife to see you about her bladder trouble. She'll be back in a minute; she just stepped out to the bathroom."

Even Dr. Webb cannot keep from laughing out loud. The incident is only a reminder of the very few females we see on urology. We continue the clinic, with a fresh smile coming on our faces every time we think back on the old man.

The routine of urology rotation continues. Surgery continues, and occasionally death intervenes. We learn from some deaths and question others. Death is something the residents never like to discuss, but every Saturday morning we know that one thing is certain: Dr. Eler will be asking, "Why did the patient die?"

Urology rotation ends. Dr. Webb gives me the usual routine about coming back to his service any time I can and spending more time with him. I have enjoyed the work, but the time has come for me to set aside all the subspecialties of surgery and devote my remaining time to general surgery, which was my reason for being here.

I actually have a whole night off between the urology rotation and the beginning of general surgery rotation. Harriet and I have time to eat dinner together and relax without having to worry about being called back to the hospital.

"Don't you think it's about time we have another one?" I tilt my head and look in Harriet's eyes, waiting through a long pause for her response. I can almost see her mind working: another what?

Then it registers. She leans forward on the sofa and looks directly back into my eyes, saying, "Another what?"

She knows, I know, and we both agree that our family ought to grow some more. Here I was, beginning general surgery rotations and beginning a larger family. How much more exciting can life get?

The weeks of general surgery rotations turn into months, and I am repeatedly scrubbing on new operations that I have not yet been allowed to perform. I decide I must come up with some rapid learner's course on how to learn the techniques of surgery if I am ever to get ahead in this game called "residency."

I review the *Goals Rule Book* as a starter. I notice that many of the residents above me are lax in attitude when they are assisting in an operation, whereas the same resident is very aggressive and attentive when he is first surgeon. As residents, we are assistants approximately half the time, and therefore half the time spent in operations, for most residents, is either wasted or adds very little to the learning process.

After some careful thought I reach a conclusion, recalling the practice I made as an intern learning to perform my first amputation. I wrote the procedure down on paper and performed the operation in my mind before I ever stepped up to the operating table. Why not carry that one step further? Why not look at myself as the main surgeon on every case I assist on? I can get twice the usefulness out of my surgical experience if I pretend I am the first surgeon on every case I scrub on.

Rehearsal in the Mind

I begin to apply this principle. In this way, when a patient comes into the emergency room with an injury of the magnitude that places him categorically as a chief resident's case, I try to run my mind one step ahead of the chief resident, having to make quicker decisions than the chief in order to see if he makes the same decision. Instead of passively learning from the chief resident, I actively learn by treating the patient in my mind even before the chief resident treats him. I look at myself as already being the surgeon in charge, of already achieving my major goal. I decide whether or not to operate on a particular patient; decide which emergency X rays should be ordered; make a diagnosis and a format for treating the patient; then check my score by merely observing what the chief resident does. I can grade myself.

I then decide to take the scheme one step further. When I am posted as first assistant on a case, I replace the "assistant" computer card in my brain with a "first surgeon" card and prepare for the case as if I were to be the operating surgeon. This means hitting the books the night before the operation, making myself read at least two journal articles on the diseases involved, and spending however many hours it takes to memorize the step-by-step process of the operation. I don't let my game end when I actually step up to the operating table as first assistant. No, the game only begins at that time. I have to think fast. I have to think one step ahead of the surgeon and anticipate every advancement in the procedure. It is a mentally lost point if we come to a portion of the operation and I do not know exactly what to do next before the surgeon makes his move. I begin to see myself as first surgeon, see myself as already having achieved my major goal. These thoughts become more and more significant, to the point that I make another entry in the *Goals Rule Book:* "Once the major goal comes within reach, begin to see yourself as already having reached the goal. Begin to live and act as if you have actually achieved the goal. Believe you have reached your goal already."

Reaching the Goal

I close the book and place it back in my coat pocket. Surgery is fun; life is fun; I am happy in this field, especially when I am operating.

I continue life as a general surgery resident, spending most of my time in the operating room and on the wards taking care of the postoperative patients. Life becomes one long routine—getting to the hospital at 6:30 A.M., working all day, staying late every other night, not going home at all every other night, not letting myself think about how much longer it will be before I will enter the real world of private practice.

The day that I am to start my year of chief residency finally arrives. I look back to the first day I began surgery training as an intern, and realize how much knowledge and skill I have accumulated in such a short span of time. I plan to at least double my knowledge of surgery within the next year. Much responsibility is placed on the shoulders of the chief resident, and much attention must be given to organization, and above all, 24 hours a day has to be devoted to surgery. What makes this 24 hours a day different from any other 24-hour period I have spent as a resident is the fact that as a chief resident I have more responsibility than ever before in my life. While I know that I am well trained and I'm well prepared for whatever might come, still, there is a small shadow of uncertainty that keeps arising in my mind. I feel confident that I can handle the big cases expected of me, but I also know that the coming year will pose the greatest challenge ever. I pull out my *Goals Rule Book*. The last rule I wrote stands out: "Begin to see myself as already having reached my goal."

I look further back on the list: Proceed one stitch at a time.

I will combine these two rules to help me make it through the chief residency year. One stitch at a time got me through internship, and I am sure it will work again.

I marvel at the fact that I am now the chief resident in general surgery. It is an exciting time to be near the top of the pyramid. The view is much better up here looking down on all that I have been through. Internship and junior residency look rough, having already been through them. I am not sure I could go back and do those years again. No, that's something that the body and mind can go through only once.

However, there is one dark cloud in the midst of all the excitement. Harriet is still not pregnant. What is wrong? Over two years have passed, and still every month brings hope—and then disappointment. She has been pregnant once before. Why can't we conceive again? I carry this burden with me as I enter the big year ahead of me.

PART IV

CHIEF RESIDENCY

15

The Examination

As I neared the end of my residency training program, I made ready for the mock board examinations. I reviewed articles and lists of cases. I presented myself to the chief, who asked, "What have you done that makes you think you deserve being allowed into the examination?"

I made my presentation, telling him that I have completed medical school, taken a demanding surgical internship, and was now nearing the end of one of the most difficult surgical residency programs in the United States. I mentioned the number of surgical cases I had assisted in and the number in which I was the first surgeon. I had studied the surgical material intensively and attended the daily conferences religiously. In short, I felt I deserved to be admitted to the board examination because I had earned that right through hard work.

All the good works I did in surgery were crucial in helping me to pass the test. But one day a fellow Christian asked me a question about a different kind of test.

"If you stood before God at the gates of heaven," he queried, "what would you tell Him if He asked, 'What have you done to deserve entrance?'"

I then realized that all the good works I had ever done would, by themselves, count for nothing. My friend's question caused me to realize that the only way to eternal life is purely and simply by God's grace through the sacrifice of Jesus Christ. I can become deserving enough to take the surgical boards, but I can never earn my way into heaven.

> It is by grace you have been saved, through faith—and this not from yourselves, it is the gift of God—not by works, so that no one can boast (Ephesians 2:8,9).

Real salvation comes by putting Christ at the center of our hearts and allowing Him to begin controlling our lives. I was asked by my chief of surgery as I began my examination, "What have you done

*that makes you think you should be allowed into the examination?"
My answer was, "I deserve it." If I were to face a similar question
at the gates of heaven—"What have you done that makes you think
you ought to be allowed into heaven?"—my only response could be,
"Nothing, nothing at all! Only Christ's death and resurrection enti-
tles me to enter. I have sinned and repented of those sins. You have
provided the only way, which I gratefully accept."*

> I am the way and the truth and the life. No one comes to the
> Father except through me (John 14:6).

I'm excited as July 1 arrives and I become a chief resident. Under
me is a third-year resident, a second-year resident, a first-year resident, and two interns. I accept the challenge. No one oversees me
except the attending staff. I call my own shots, make my own decisions, and act accordingly. The staff will come to my aid if I ask them
and will assist me on any of the more difficult cases, but as of today
I begin acting as a full-fledged surgeon. I have much to learn within
the coming 12 months, but now there is one big difference—I not
only have the responsibility of the patients on whom I operate, but
also on every patient operated on by every resident and intern under
me. I will have to decide which cases the junior resident is ready to
perform, and which cases I will need to do myself in order to gain the
experience I need to become a fully trained, qualified surgeon.

The Greater the Prize, the Greater the Price

What price will I have to pay for this? One year of being on call
every night, one year of seeing my wife and family only at short
intervals, one year to bring together all the surgical knowledge I have
acquired since that first one-hour lecture in the introductory course
of surgery in medical school. This price must be paid to bring it all
together into one workable unit called a surgeon. I have to learn to
take care of the most complicated cases possible, learn to deal with
the residents and interns under me, and come tumbling out at the
end of the wash a proficient surgeon 12 months from now. Numerous
intermediate goals will have to be met and carried out. The *Goals
Rule Book* will be put to the ultimate test. In this one year, it all has
to be pulled together.

My first act as chief resident is to call together the residents and interns under me to discuss what I expect of them. "I have only two basic rules for you to follow. There are a thousand lesser rules, but only two basic ones. The most important is to call me anytime, day or night, whether I am in the operating room or at home, if there is even the slightest question in your mind about a patient's condition. I don't want to hear the following morning that you thought about calling but decided to wait until I got to the hospital to tell me about it. If something goes wrong, I want to know about it *right now.*

"The second rule applies mainly to the interns. Carry a pen and some paper on your rounds and write down what I want done on each patient. There is no way you can remember all the things we will talk about on each patient. The only way to be sure everything is covered is to write it down. Then, don't go to bed until everything written down is checked off. I will not accept *excuses.* I will accept *reasons* why something was impossible to do on a patient, but never will an excuse suffice. I will leave it up to you to figure out the difference between an excuse and a reason.

"Now, what I'm about to say next is not a rule; it's just some sound advice that has worked for me. After you write your scut work list in the morning, rewrite it in the order of importance of the work to be done, and do the work in that order. That way, even the worst intern will complete the most important jobs. Plus, you will be using your time much more efficiently." That advice, of course, comes straight from the *Goals Rule Book.*

I have accepted the fact that I cannot run my services properly and strive for friendship with those working under me, but I do hope to at least gain their respect.

Shortly after beginning "the year of the ultimate," I am performing operations I have dreamed of doing for the past three years: taking out colons, bypassing blocked arteries, and resecting stomachs (and most anything else in the abdominal cavity that has a diseased segment). The scheduled cases are intriguing and are educations within themselves, but it is the emergency cases—the unannounced, the unexpected—that prove to be the real test of a surgeon.

The Emergencies of Life

I answer a call to the emergency room to see a 17-year-old boy who has been shot in the stomach. Clarence Adams lies with clenched fists, fright and pain on his face as a small trickle of blood runs down his abdomen. The emergency room intern has already started an I.V. and sent blood to the lab for typing and cross-matching. The nurse has called an X-ray technician to come take emergency films.

"Where do you hurt, Clarence?" I begin my examination.

"My back, Doc. I think I hit my back." He lies straight as a board, afraid that any movement on his part may renew the initial pain of that bullet entering his internal organs.

I roll him over to look for an exit wound. The bullet had entered his abdomen just under his right ribs, but I see no exit wound. "The bullet is still somewhere inside you. We'll have to get an X ray to find out where. Can you move your legs?"

"Yes."

"Can you feel me pulling the hairs on your legs?"

"Yes."

"Have you ever been operated on before?"

"No."

"Any stomach problems or kidney trouble?"

"No."

"Allergic to anything?"

"I don't know. Doc, am I going to be all right? Am I hurt bad? I'm not going to die, am I?"

"You're okay. Hold still a minute." I examine him as I talk. I place a stethoscope on his chest. His lungs sound clear; I can hear his heart sounds, and they seem normal enough. I feel his abdomen—no distention. I am sure there will be some blood in it, but as soft and flat as it is, there can't be too much bleeding going on in there. I again place the stethoscope in my ears and hear no sound of his intestines moving around. I glance directly at the wound—no powder on the skin. He was shot from a distance. I place my hand on his groin and feel a bounding pulse in his artery. His blood pressure is good—stable for the time being.

"Let's get those films and take him to the O.R." I motion for the X-ray technician to get a move on it. I suspect Clarence has a few holes in his bowel that will need sewing up, and maybe a hole in his liver. We'll know as soon as we open him up.

Bob First, my junior resident, injects some dye into Clarence's bloodstream so that the kidneys will show up when the X ray is taken. We will know whether the kidneys are injured before we open his abdomen.

Above All Rules and Regulations

The operating room is on emergency status—one working O.R. and one set of scrub nurses. I call the operating room and inform them I'm bringing up a patient. I am told there is another case going on and it will be at least two hours before they finish and can free the scrub nurses to do the work.

"You put the instruments in the room and call some more nurses," I find myself gripping the phone tighter as I speak to the O.R. night supervisor. "We'll do it without nurses if we have to. I can't wait two hours to find out what's going on inside a gunshot wound." I instruct the nurse, trying not to sound too overbearing. I realize from past experience that getting the patient on the table—just getting the body into the room—is half the operation time and sometimes the most important half. "I'll have him there in 15 minutes. See what you can do for me."

Bob and I look at the developed X ray. "Looks like it's just below his diaphragm." I quickly glance at the X ray and notice a bullet lodged in the vertebra; it looks like a .22. Whenever a gunshot wound comes into the emergency room I have learned to look at the X ray to see where the bullet has lodged, then make a mental note of what lies in the path of the bullet between the wound entrance and where it lies on the X ray. This technique isn't 100 percent accurate, but it gives me an idea of what to expect. Looking at this X ray, however, I cannot tell whether the bullet is lying below or above the diaphragm. This is important because if it is below the diaphragm, I can make an incision in the abdomen and not be concerned about going into the chest. But above the diaphragm is yet another matter, for it involves the heart, lungs, esophagus, and vena cava. This would require an incision extending from the abdomen on into the chest— a much larger operation.

After studying the X ray carefully, I decide to prep both the patient's abdomen and chest. In case I do have to go into the chest, I'll have him prepped and draped already. I make an initial incision in the abdomen. There's some blood, but not enough to account for the bullet going through the liver. I expect to see a gaping tear in the liver and am surprised to find such a small amount of blood in the abdomen. I slide my hand over the top of the liver and find it intact. Once more I put my hand over the liver and can feel the undersurface of the diaphragm just above. There is a small hole in it with something soft plugging it. The bullet must have just grazed the top of the liver, then gone through the diaphragm and into the vertebra. How can anyone be so lucky to have a bullet go through his body and not even touch a vital organ? An inch lower and it would have blown a hole in his liver. Two inches higher and it would have entered his heart and meant instant death.

As I remove my finger from the hole in the diaphragm, the entire abdomen begins to fill with blood. Evidently I have knocked off a clot which had "plugged the dike" and allowed this boy to live long enough to get to the hospital. Within seconds at least five pints of blood flow through the hole that I can no longer feel and do not have time to find again. The bullet has indeed gone above the diaphragm and traversed some vital organ that has the ability to bleed out this much blood so rapidly. There has to be a hole in the heart; I have never seen a patient bleed so much, so quickly. Evidently Clarence's initial bleeding had formed enough of a clot to plug the hole. Now I have undone what nature did, and this boy is going to die unless I can do something *right now*.

"No blood pressure at all up here!" the anesthesiologist calls out from the head of the operating table. He begins frantically pumping blood in through the I.V.s and yells for his intern to bring all the blood he can find in the blood bank.

The Ultimate Test of Character

I quickly place a lap sponge through the pool of blood and into the area of the hole in the diaphragm. I have been in situations similar to this before—there is no time to think about what the next step should be, whatever I do has to come automatically. What I do next cannot be redone nor changed. Without hesitation I must come up with the one correct narrow road to take immediately or the patient will be dead before I have a chance to consider other possible alternatives.

I take a knife and slash the chest open. A heavy pair of scissors cuts through the cartilage between the ribs and sternum, opening his lower right chest. Almost frantically I manually spread the wound open, only to see a pool of blood in the chest. I expose Clarence's heart and find it beating ineffectively. It looks smaller than normal. I open the pericardium, the thin sac surrounding the heart, and begin massaging while looking for the site the bullet went through. The bullet must have gone through the back side of the heart because I can't find a hole on the front. I know that I'll never get the back side of the heart exposed well enough to close a hole; I continue massaging the heart.

There's no blood coming into the heart! I think to myself. I squeeze and then release my grip to allow the heart to refill, but it remains empty. After a few seconds it gradually refills and I again squeeze. I am not pumping enough blood out of his heart to keep a toenail alive, much less enough to keep his brain oxygenated.

I still assume the bullet has gone through the heart, just above the diaphragm, but feeling through the pool of blood which has now completely filled his right chest, I cannot find a hole. My mind rushes for something to do. *Where else could so much blood be coming from?* I ask my computer mind again for an answer; no reply. I squeeze the heart again, but it is only a time-wasting measure on my part while my mind looks for a hole my eye cannot see through the pool of blood.

The inferior vena cava! That's it! The large vein that carries blood from the lower portion of the body, comes through the liver, then through the diaphragm, and empties the blood into the heart. There is a very short segment of the cava that lies between the diaphragm and the heart, a space no bigger than the width of my fingers.

"I've found the hole!" I shout.

I can feel a hole in the front and a separate one in the back side. The bullet has gone through the center of the cava. There is little room to work and even less time to do it in. This boy is dying and I have to decide how to repair the holes in the big vein and keep his heart and brain alive while I do it.

Reaching Deep

How am I going to get to the back side of the cava to sew it? I think to myself. *It is so short, there is no way to rotate it around and sew the back hole.* Time is passing. I place a vascular clamp above and below the holes in the cava. This stops the bleeding. That much I accomplish, but there is no way for blood from the lower half of the body to return to the heart. I have bought very little time to work with.

"Keep pumping in the blood!" I glanced at the head of the table as I again massage the heart.

"What do you think I'm doing?" the anesthesiologist snaps back. "I've pumped in eight units already but you suck it right back out." Everyone is on edge, and for the first time I begin wondering if we are going to be able to pull this off. It is getting easier to massage the heart, since it fills quicker with blood from the top half of the body, but I soon realize I am not gaining much time by standing there squeezing the heart. The hole is still in the cava and needs repairing before the heart can ever pump on its own. I stop massaging the heart.

"Pott's scissors." The scrub nurse passes them quickly. I extend the hole in front of the cava as much as possible by incising the full length of the exposed vital vein, allowing me to see the hole in the back of the cava from the inside. Now I am able to sew the back hole quickly without removing any of the cava. I'm left with a larger front hole to close, but I can see and reach it much more easily than the back hole. I close the back hole and begin working on the front. Bob massages the heart while I work and is able to pump blood intermittently to the brain.

"Let's see if he will come back." I finish the sutures on the front hole and remove all the clamps. Now all we can do is massage the heart and hope and pray it will start pumping on its own. We look at the heart, but it is doing absolutely nothing. It lies flaccid in my hand, with not a trace of muscle activity.

"Give me the adrenaline." The nurse passes a syringe and needle and I inject the adrenaline directly into the left ventricle. The flabby, previously unresponsive heart begins to contract. It is remarkable. The heart begins to beat forcefully and the anesthesiologist reports that he can now hear a blood pressure. The heart continues to regain its strength and, within a few minutes, we know it is going to hold its own.

My eyes focus on the heart. "That's about as close to dead as I'd ever want to be," I say to Bob. The tension is off and we talk, feeling a bit more relaxed about the situation. "This fellow will never know how close he came to being called 'out' by the Big Umpire—that is, if he makes it postoperatively."

After spending over an hour closing the chest and abdomen, I go to the dressing room to change out of my blood-soaked scrub suit. I remove the scrub pants, and all of a sudden it becomes real to me exactly how much blood Clarence lost. The entire front of my undershorts are completely soaked with blood. I wiggle my toes in my shoes and can feel that my socks are soaked. I feel as though I had walked through a mud puddle. Never before have I thought about *blood* as now. I know that blood is necessary to sustain life, but have thought no further than that. Up to now, I hadn't been all that compelled to think about blood. After all, we don't go outside and spend an hour thinking about the air we breathe, do we? If we were to become trapped in a mine and come within minutes of running out of air before we are rescued, then we would suddenly develop an acute awareness of the air around us.

Two things have transpired as a result of this incident. Clarence can still enjoy the sunshine, and I have acquired a wisdom about blood that cannot be written in a textbook. I am beginning to feel the pulsations of the life of a surgeon. It is indescribable but pleasant.

Clarence does make it. He is discharged after seven days without even the simplest of postoperative complications. I try to explain to him what happened seven days ago on the operating table, but am sure he will never fully realize the extent to which he had knocked on Death's door, only to be fortunate that no one had answered.

16

The Book That Changes Lives

I HAD SPENT MANY HUNDREDS OF HOURS STUDYING in medical school. I had read case after case about different diseases. I had read book after book on anatomy, histology, pharmacology, physiology, and pathology; all had enriched my knowledge toward becoming a doctor. Many times I had read late into the night, pondering fact after fact, seeking to learn more. I had heard my professors read from these books of knowledge, then quote from them. I had listened intently to lectures and noted meticulously what the professors were saying. As I moved closer to becoming a doctor, I found my life changing in response to the medical facts I was absorbing.

My life is drastically different now as a surgeon in private practice than it would have been had I studied for any other job or profession. I wear the mark of a surgeon. I am introduced as a doctor. People smile and ask me medically related questions. But somehow those changes are all external. What has affected my soul, the real me deep inside?

Only one Book has reached down to this level. Only one Book has altered the way I treat my wife and family. Only one Book has taught me how to grow through times of trial, how to trust the only One who will never let me down, how to obey the One who has a right way to do everything. The one Book that has genuinely changed my life is not a medical book, it is God's living Word—the Holy Bible. Nothing has impacted me like the Scriptures. It is different from all the other books ever written. None of the medical books I read in school were inspired by God. Only the Bible comes directly from Him.

Second Timothy 3:16 says: "All Scripture is God-breathed and is useful for teaching, rebuking, correcting and training in righteousness."

As a doctor, I have seen bodies that have almost bled to death. The heart is present; the liver is there; so are the spleen, kidneys, colon, and gallbladder. All the parts necessary for life are intact, but only blood can animate those organs. Blood is the essence of life. It is more than just another organ, like the brain or heart; it is living and makes the entire body alive.

God's Word is similarly transforming. It makes our earthly beings come alive. It reaches into the depths of our souls and gives us the substance that nothing else can provide. As Christians, God's Word is our life's blood.

> The word of God is living and active. Sharper than any double-edged sword, it penetrates even to dividing soul and spirit, joints and marrow; it judges the thoughts and attitudes of the heart (Hebrews 4:12).

One evening after only two months as chief resident, I take some time to reflect back on what residency has all been about and how it has affected my way of thinking. It is not all work and no play, but it is a "way." I have slowly been pulled into this "way of life" in which the loss of sleep is welcomed—if I get to operate. The loss of time from my family, the loss of free time to play golf or tennis, the loss of outside activities on which I had once placed such a high value, the loss of everything that most people consider essential to happiness—becomes insignificant in the world of surgical residency. If I am not operating, I consider my time wasted. I feel that I should do all the surgery possible in order to prepare for private practice.

On top of this is added the education of when not to operate. It is equally important to know when *not* to operate as it is to know when to operate. This portion of training only increases time spent at the hospital working up the patient to see if he actually needs an operation. The essence of the residency program boils down to the philosophy: "If a patient needs an operation, operate now; if he does not need an operation, don't make matters worse by operating."

In the Hole

As residency has progressed, I sense I have been sucked into a hole, and how far down into it I will go before realizing there is more to life, I don't know. Rick, Bill, and Robert, the interns and junior residents, are all in the same hole with me. Someday I'll decide how deep I must go in order to become a good surgeon and then come out, but right now all I can do is get just as deep as I possibly can while I have the desire to get there.

With these thoughts, I rationalize my whole existence as chief resident. It doesn't seem sane, but I choose to live it and pay the price to become a surgeon. I find it hard to believe I am physically able to cope, and am astonished to realize what punishment the body and mind can endure and continue to function properly. Very few are the times a resident loses a day's work due to illness, even though he goes without sleep for two or three days at a time. Many days go by when both breakfast and lunch are missed, and dinner may not come until late. Few weeks pass that he doesn't feel he has pushed his body to its breaking point and then have to stay up a few more hours. Usually, just before the actual breaking point, an hour or two of sleep is obtained by missing a conference or grabbing a quick nap when there is a lull in the action. Sleep and food become two priceless commodities, but given a choice between 30 minutes to get something to eat and 30 minutes to lie down and sleep, the decision to sleep always wins.

Controlling Your Thoughts

I forgo philosophy for reality; time to get back to work. I force myself not to think of the time when all my residency problems will be over. I must force such thoughts out of my mind until the last day on the service or I will not be able to survive. I have learned to control my thoughts to a great extent through these years of surgical training. If I have a thought that works against my major goal, I immediately knock it out and replace it with a thought that will enhance that goal. I have labeled this the "bad apple" rule in my book. I imagine that I have a bushel of apples, and if I see a bad apple, I just toss it out and replace it with a good, fresh one. I find this to be a simple way to control my mind.

Time passes quickly, and I begin to talk with Dr. Bell, the chief of cardiothoracic surgery. I have decided to do chest surgery when I enter private practice—not to perform open-heart operations, but to operate on people's lungs. This decision has been long in coming. At first it was only an occasional thought as I watched some chest surgery, but I developed a real interest in learning how to operate in the chest, and within the past month the door of opportunity has cracked open just a little bit. Dr. Bell has offered me a residency in his program. This crack of opportunity has to be evaluated. There is no way to become a certified thoracic surgeon without taking training in both heart and chest work. I reason with Dr. Bell that I will be wasting my time if I operate on hearts, and I do mean time because the resident who works under Dr. Bell is on call all the time, and post-op heart cases take more time to maintain than any other type of surgical patient. Dr. Bell replies that my reasoning is ridiculous, pointing out that time spent taking care of heart patients and operating on hearts will be invaluable no matter what field of surgery I end up in.

Never Make a Lateral Move

Just before Harriet and I go to sleep, I bring up this matter of going into cardiothoracic training.

"You said yourself it would be like internship all over again. Why would you want to punish yourself like that?" Harriet had survived a year of being an intern's wife, and by the tone of her question I am not sure she wants to go through that experience again. It is not exactly like being a widow, but it leaves a similar flavor in your mouth.

"If I don't do it now, I never will. I am psychologically prepared for it now. What do you think I ought to do?"

"What do you want to do? What do you think you should do?"

"I don't know…I don't know." I stare at the interface between the floor and wall. Actually, I do know. Why am I telling her I don't know? She knows what I want to do, and she knows what I think I ought to do. Why is she asking those questions? Why are we playing this game?

"Suit you if I go ahead and sign up for the program?"

"You are the one who has to go through it."

"You do too, in a way."

"Whatever you think is best, I'll go along with."

"I think I'll do it."

The matter is settled. We prepare for bed and for a new day, knowing that we will soon be a cardiothoracic resident and a cardiothoracic resident's wife.

True Commitment

Early in the morning, I stop by Dr. Bell's office and make a verbal agreement with him. Beginning next July 1, I will enter his program as a resident on cardiothoracic surgery. It seems I am always biting off more than I can chew, then left with the burden of chewing it. Nevertheless, I am committed.

I refer back to my *Goals Rule Book*: "Whenever a *positive* decision is made, never consider changing it; whenever at *negative* decision is made, reconsider it after a full night's sleep."

I had made a positive decision: to go into cardiothoracic surgery. I will use the bad-apple rule to control this decision. If thoughts against my going into this program come up, I will throw them away and replace them with thoughts that favor going into the program. The negative thoughts had their say-so before I decided to take up the new program, and they lost. They will get no second chance.

So, at the completion of this year, I will begin a new era in my residency training. In one way I look forward to that day because it will mean the end of general surgery training and the completion of an entire chapter in my goal of becoming a surgeon. My major goal now moves up a notch. I realize how easy I have it right now compared to how difficult it will be once I begin C-T. Why do I choose to follow that path? I don't know now, and probably never will. Dr. Bell opened a door of opportunity, and I am compelled to walk through it.

The Wrong Alternative

For the present time I must deal with the problems confronting me in general surgery. A 29-year-old man tries to kill himself by putting a .22 caliber pistol to his abdomen and pulling the trigger. The bullet goes through his colon and spleen, not killing him, but necessitating an operation with fairly minor consequences. I simply cannot understand why anyone would attempt suicide. I have often wondered what goes on in such a person's mind after he has tried to commit suicide and some surgeon comes along and keeps him from dying. I am certain if this case were taken to the Supreme Court, they would rule that the surgeon was infringing on the patient's individual rights. Nevertheless, this never-ending game continues to be played between the suicide patient and the surgeon. *Very seldom* does the patient win unless he blows his brains out with a hollow-nose, high-velocity bullet.

In this particular case, the suicide patient is quite "normal" and rational in discussing why he shot himself. He was not trying to commit suicide but was only making a point. He thought his wife was running around, so he decided to shoot himself, reasoning that this would make his wife realize how he felt about her unfaithfulness. He thought this would make her stop going out with another man. It is all very rational—to him.

His father, mother, and two sisters have stayed in his room almost constantly since the operation. They are shocked when I mention getting a psychiatric consultation for him. His father will not allow it, alluding to the fact that both of the patient's sisters have shot themselves previously and the mother tried to shoot herself on one occasion, but the gun misfired. To this particular family, shooting one's self was a normal way to handle a problem, and they were not going to let me call any "head-shrinker" in on the case and give them a bad name back home.

I find it difficult to believe what I have just heard. All I can think to do is explain to them that if enough of the family shoot themselves enough times, sooner or later one of them is going to wind up dead regardless of the point he is trying to make. And what would the people back home say then? I am sure they do not believe me. After all, they have two sisters, a mother, and now a brother who all have shot themselves, and every one of them is still alive, which makes me glad I am in surgery rather than psychiatry. As a surgeon, I don't have to explain or understand their reasoning.

I discuss the matter with the students in one of the afternoon teaching sessions. "Suicide is one problem I do not understand, and alcoholism is another. Habitual drinking is a dreadful thing to contend with from both the patient's and the surgeon's viewpoint."

Bad "Habits"

"I say 'habit' rather than 'disease' because I feel it is not a disease process that a person can 'catch' or 'come down with' or discover he has. I look at it as a habit, just as smoking is a habit. Some individuals are more prone to be controlled by a habit than others, and these individuals become what is known as alcoholics." I enjoy lecturing to the students working under me. Our sessions are informal, with good interaction and no quizzes.

"One of the end results of drinking is cirrhosis of the liver. It is an intriguing subject to study because it results in both psychological and anatomical changes in the body. The liver becomes scarred and loses its ability to function properly. The venous blood from the intestines and spleen normally flows through the liver and on to the heart. However, when cirrhosis develops, this blood pathway through the liver is 'dammed' or blocked. Pressure builds up behind the dam and the blood has to find another route to the heart. One possible route is through the veins in the esophagus. By using these veins, the blood can bypass the liver and empty into other veins leading to the heart. As with any compromise that takes place in the body, a price must be paid. The only way this route will suffice is for the pressure in the veins to increase enough to 'push' the blood through the esophageal veins and around the liver. These veins in the esophagus are not accustomed to a high blood pressure, and once all the blood quits going through the liver and begins using this route as a bypass, trouble develops. The veins in the esophagus become engorged with blood, dilate, and become tortuous, giving the gross appearance of long worms wiggling their way up the esophagus. Such distended veins are call 'esophageal varicies,' similar to the varicose veins found in the legs. They are fragile and frequently bleed, resulting in a massive amount of blood flowing into the stomach, only to be forcefully regurgitated back up the esophagus and into the mouth. Each time the patient vomits, there appears to be a quart of blood, and the patient and doctor alike think the patient will surely die.

"If you take the overall number of cirrhotics who bleed from varicies, 70 percent will die within one year and 60 percent who have bled once will rebleed within a year. These numbers are fairly consistent whether the patient is operated on or not. For this reason, many internists and surgeons do not believe such a patient should be operated on, since they do not feel it can help increase the person's chances of survival. However, there is no doubt that some of these individuals are indeed saved by the knife. Such patients are bleeding to death. Every nonsurgical method of controlling the bleeding has been exhausted, and there is no hope for the patient other than surgical attempts to shunt the blood away from the esophageal veins, thus relieving the pressure in them and stopping the bleeding."

I complete the minilecture to the students and realize that with only two months left in my chief residency program, I still have not performed one of these shunt operations. The alcoholic patients I have consulted with up to now have either died a rapidly bleeding death, or quit bleeding and refused surgery.

A Slow and Painful Death

Within two weeks, two patients come in for shunts. The second has just arrived in the emergency room. Her name is Jeannie Franco. When I arrive, she is vomiting huge quantities of bright red blood into a plastic blue-green basin that a nurse has handed her. I am one of the first to see her and insert a long tube into her stomach. There is an outer balloon around the tube, and by inflating it, it will "hold pressure" against the bleeding veins temporarily. I inflate the balloon and Jeannie's bleeding stops. The situation is under control for the time being; the only problem is that the balloon cannot be left inflated indefinitely. I will leave the balloon inflated for an eight-hour trial period. At the end of that time the balloon will be deflated and the situation reevaluated. The veins will either begin rebleeding massively, or there is a chance they will not rebleed, and this will give us time to get her to surgery before the "finger in the dike" lets go again. There is no way to predict whether an individual patient will rebleed or not. We just wait the eight hours, deflate the balloon, and see.

Both Jeannie and her husband are in their late forties, both alcoholics who could "never seem to stop drinking," as her husband puts it. He is about as scared as an individual can be from all this bleeding. He has blood on his shirt and pants from Jeannie's vomiting; he has assessed the situation correctly—Jeannie may die.

The time passes and the balloon is deflated. Blood fills her mouth and flows over her chin and onto her gown; it starts to soak the sheets. I quickly reinflate and the faucet is turned off once again.

Jeannie looks at me with pitiful, sorrowful eyes. It is amazing what eyes alone can relate. Her eyes repeatedly try to connect with mine as I busy myself getting the tube fixed. She is afraid of dying. It is real to her. She wants help but can only beg for life with her eyes, knowing the seriousness of the situation. She is helpless, totally dependent on someone else. She keeps looking at me, never moving her eyes from mine.

The internist is present and the care of the patient is partially his. His advice has to be honored in this situation, as there is no absolute answer. He asks for another 24-hour trial and concedes to surgical intervention if she rebleeds at that time.

Medical management is not going to work in this case. I will perform the shunt operation to relieve the pressure on the veins, and she will die post-op. It is the story I have heard so many times about these patients.

Twenty-four hours pass, and I alert the operating room that I will most likely be bringing a patient down for a "shunt." I check the blood bank to make sure they have set up the six units I ordered for the possible operation.

I again deflate the balloon. Jeannie bleeds massively. I reinflate the balloon and order her directly to the operating room. I take a few minutes to talk with her husband before going into surgery.

"She's in bad shape, John," I begin. "Her chances of pulling through any type of surgery, especially an operation of this magnitude, are not good. Even if she does, I will guarantee she will be dead within a year if she doesn't completely quit drinking."

"Oh, I'll make her stop drinking," John replies in all sincerity. "I'll see to that."

"I don't believe you," I tell him. John appears hurt by my statement. "The reason is that for her to quit drinking, you have to quit."

He is angry and his voice cracks as he speaks. "I can do anything for my wife. If she lives through this, you'll see." He heads for the waiting room without waiting for a reply.

I complete the shunt operation with some difficulty, but the bleeding comes under control. There is no more bleeding after the operation and Jeannie remains in the hospital for three weeks. The day finally comes when she is ready for discharge...alive.

"Jeannie, I hope you and John have talked things over about this drinking problem. Your liver will never be normal and you have undoubtedly cut off many good years of your life. However, you will cut them off completely if you don't start taking care of yourself." My sermon over, I wonder how much good it has done. She would not understand my *Goals Rule Book*, but she had better learn fast how to set one particular goal and make it: to quit drinking.

I see Jeannie and John at the clinic two weeks following discharge. They are all smiles and reassure me they have both quit alcohol and have not touched a drop since her operation. I express interest, but retain serious doubts that their good intentions will survive. In this particular case the operation saved Jeannie Franco for the present, and she has benefited both physically and mentally from her encounter with near death. Will she be a "lucky one"? Will I ever again operate on a "lucky one," or will they all fall into the calculated "death numbers" that the internists and surgeons discuss so much? I don't know whether I will ever know about the others, but Jeannie and John don't particularly care about them. She has beat the "numbers"—for the time being.

I make it home tonight at a decent time. For a change, Harriet and I are able to eat at the same time. I begin telling her about my discussion with the students, about how bad a patient with cirrhosis can bleed and about Jeannie and her husband, John, and how I hope they quit drinking. As I talk and eat and talk some more, I gradually realize that Harriet is not listening to me. She is acting like she is listening, but I know she isn't.

"Do you agree?" I ask her.

"Yes, I agree," she responds.

"You agree with what? You don't even know what I was talking about. There was nothing to agree with." I begin eating again.

"You want another boy or would you rather have a girl?"

"You're pregnant?! I can't believe it."

"I've already been checked."

"This is great! Boy or girl—whatever you want to have will be just great with me."

The excitement of another child keeps me awake—especially considering that we have been trying for so long.

The next day picks up where yesterday left off—surgery in the morning, and clinic in the afternoon. I stop in the residents' office after completing clinic and notice a small typewritten note in my mailbox. It is from Dr. Eler.

"Can't" Doesn't Exist

Private patient coming Sat. afternoon. Mr. James Clement. Needs E.C.G., chest film, liver studies, sigmoidosocopy on admittance. You will get above done.

YES   NO   (CIRCLE ONE)

Typical. I have come to know Dr. Eler doesn't like "words." He sends notes to be checked *yes* or *no*. He doesn't care whether I have a good reason for not doing something; he only cares whether the job will be done. If I were going to be out of town for a meeting Saturday, there would be no reason to bother explaining that to him. My only option would be to circle the word *no*, or cancel the trip and circle the word *yes* and be here when his patient arrives.

As I analyze Dr. Eler's system of doing things, I begin to appreciate the core of his thinking process. He doesn't know what the word *can't* means. To his way of thinking, anyone can do anything he sets his mind to. I agree; that is basically true. We all do what we want to by a process called *excuses*. I can be asked to do something completely within my power and come up with the "correct" excuses not to do it.

Dr. Eler wants only the basic answer to all his written questions and requests. He does not allow for any excuses, and therefore an honest answer is the result. Furthermore, he doesn't have time to listen to the explanations or excuses of all the people under him. At that, I circle *yes* and place the note in the "out" tray on the secretary's desk.

As I near the end of my chief residency on general surgery, I can look back on it with pleasure. True, it has been a rough year with many disappointments, but I have also gotten many rewards. I've learned that I cannot completely control what happens to every patient on whom I operate. Some develop problems and complications I cannot explain, and some whom I think will surely die somehow manage to recover for reasons I cannot explain.

Respecter of Time

I have learned to appreciate and respect *time* like never before. This past year I have had no nights off, no weekends to call my own. Anytime I have been away from the hospital I have carried a two-way radio in order to be available, since there is only one chief resident for each service and there is no one to cover for me. In February, my parents came to visit for a week, and I can count on one hand the hours I had been able to spend with them. I remember the occasional weekend nights that Harriet and I would visit with friends only for me to fall asleep on the sofa or be called back to the hospital. It does no good to explain to anyone what it is like being poor. I do not speak of money, but of free time. It has been like going for an entire year with no money in your pocket and with no glimpse of better days. A man can work two days and nights consecutively without sleep if he knows he will be off at the end of that time. But how terrible it is to start into that second night without knowing whether or not one will have to go in a third night without sleep or a period of respite.

I take consolation in the fact that eventually the day will come when I will finish residency. No job in the world can be this time-consuming. I am already forgetting many of the sleepless nights I have spent in the O.R. and wonder how much time will pass after residency before I forget how difficult it really has been. I want to forget the bad times, but I think I should remember some of them so I have a gauge by which to measure my life experiences.

As long as I keep some of this in my memory bank, I will always appreciate any opportunity I get to relax for five minutes without having anything at all to do. I will be able to enjoy sitting on a hillside surrounded by nature more than a person who has never known such busyness. A vacation will always be a treat I will forever be thankful for; each weekend of leisure will be a million-dollar treasure that can never be sold. I will never waste time unless I preplan it as a time for needed rest; I will never watch television unless I choose to waste the time. In these short years of training I have learned the true value of time, and anyone who threatens this cherished portion of life will be looked upon as a thief and an enemy. Time has become all-precious to me.

With only one week left as chief resident, I do not schedule any surgeries, but plan only to assist the junior resident on any cases he would like to perform. The only case he can find for my finale is a woman with a breast lump that looks suspiciously like cancer. She noticed the lump four months ago but sought medical advice only recently. I don't understand how a woman can let something like this go unchecked. I realize there is a natural fear of malignancy, but the only thing that will ultimately bring death is a cancer that is inoperable or is unresponsive to radiation or chemotherapy.

A Step at a Time

The remainder of the week glides by easily for me. The junior residents, who will become chief residents in a few days, have already taken over; I wander on up to the cardiothoracic section to see what is in store for the remainder of my residency. The one thing I notice immediately upon making rounds on C-T is that these patients are sick and that many will die if hour-by-hour tabulations are not kept current. I thought time was of essence this past year, but I begin to wonder if I haven't just come off a vacation, and I'm now getting ready to start some real work. I don't see how there is enough time in a day to do everything expected of me. However, this is the same feeling I had when I started my internship, my junior residency, and my chief residency in general surgery, and I feel confident that this will be no different. Twenty-four hours will come and go every day; I will make it through each day the same as I have done before. The *Goals Rule Book* is becoming worn, proving itself true as I begin the last mile of my goal journey...one stitch at a time.

PART V

Cardiothoracic Residency

17

The Beginning of the End

LIFE IS MUCH MORE FIERCE THAN A SURGICAL PROGRAM. I do not understand why I did not approach my entire life as I did surgical training. Looking back, I now see the correlation between spiritual living and surgical residency.

As Christians, God has given us rules to live by, just as our surgical chief gave us rules for surgery. God has given us specific instructions concerning who we should marry ("be not unequally yoked"); how to treat our spouses ("husbands love your wives"); how to face every situation ("in all your ways acknowledge Him").

He also promises tremendous blessings if we obey His commands. He promises us abundant life here on earth ("I have come that they may have life, that they may have it more abundantly") and life with Him after death. To succeed, we need only to obey our Commander—what He says, we must do. Even when we do not understand all the reasons, still we must obey our Lord and Savior, Jesus Christ.

At long last, I was starting the last leg of a lengthy journey through surgical training. I was about to begin one of the most advanced surgical programs one could go through, learning how to operate on the heart and lungs. I had accomplished more than I ever imagined I could. I had set goals and reached them. I was at a point where I could go out into the field of surgery and have a private practice.

How had I reached this pinnacle in my life? The answer was very clear to me. Dr. Eler had been my commander and had told me day to day what to read, what to study, how to hold a knife, how to use the scissors, how to ligate an artery. He had given me the assurance that if I were to do all he told me, he would guarantee my coming out at the end of the training program as a competent general surgeon. The only reason I had conquered such a fierce battle was because I had obeyed my commander, and he had kept his promises.

I had obeyed my commander in surgery—Dr. Eler. I needed now to begin obeying the commander of my life—the Lord Jesus Christ.

This is an unusual transition period for me, having completed general surgery training and starting a completely different type of surgical training program. By the end of my year as chief resident on general, I felt competent to perform any operation that came my way. I could go out into the "real world" and start practice as a general surgeon; however, I could not say the same about entering the chest cavity. That's why today, I am once again like an intern starting the first day on the surgical service. Of course, in terms of patient care, my overall responsibility, and the need for me to be organized, I am not like an intern.

Dr. Bell is my new boss. He is the one I have to answer to, and he has instructed me how to answer. If he asks a question concerning a patient, he wants one of two answers without hesitation: a direct answer, or "I don't know." He taught me this in one short episode over a year ago when he asked a question related to a patient he had referred to general surgery. I hesitated only momentarily when he blurted, "You either know the answer or you don't. If you don't, just say so." Ever since, I have felt free to be perfectly honest with him in my answers, and I believe he has more respect for my answers because I have conformed to his desire for everyone to be completely honest with each other.

Be a Good Learner

Dr. Eler is past tense, and although he taught me most of what I learned in general surgery, I now have to gather the knowledge of surgery of the chest from the head of the cardiothoracic department—Dr. Bell. He has chosen me to be his number-one resident. I have control over three individuals and am solely responsible to him for every action any of them makes. I am assigned one junior resident who is on call 24 hours a day while he is in the cardiothoracic service. I am the only one who can tell him when he can go home, when he has to stay up all night with a patient, or when he can sleep; about the only thing he will be allowed to do on his own is breathe. I have never had such responsibility before, and must learn to act fairly or lose the ever-important respect of the trainees working under me. I cannot let the junior resident pass the breaking point— the point where he becomes so inefficient that he becomes useless. I will have to share my sleep ration with him and still acquire enough sleep myself to remain physically capable of standing at the operating table for the full length of an open-heart procedure.

I am given two interns, and both remain on the service for a one-month period. It will be the most difficult month of their internship, and they have to accept it as that. They alternate night call and are expected to remain at the hospital watching the postoperative patients in the same way that a new mother would watch her newborn on his or her first night at home. There is no on-call room for the interns on C-T—very seldom will they be allowed to sleep. There is no reason to have a room assigned that will never be used. Nor is there any way I can be fair to the interns about the little amount of sleep they will get during their one-month period on the C-T service. There is no way I can relieve them from some of their duties. I will be up at night often enough as it is and then be expected to operate hours on end the following day. The interns have to survive only a month. I have to survive many months after they have rotated off C-T, so I must pace myself for the duration of the time. They will dislike me, but I have no alternative. I had experienced the exact same demands on my life when I was an intern on C-T.

No Man Is an Island

These three individuals and I make up the service. I am supposed to be the most highly trained resident in the hospital and am expected to exhibit stately leadership to those under me. Yet I make rounds the first day on the service with all the uneasiness of an intern making his first rounds. No one knows this because I hide my feelings well. Part of my ability to lead this group is based upon their respect for my leadership, and I have to sustain the respect I earned from being their chief resident on general surgery. Nothing in the goals book can help me here; this is a new experience.

I have proven myself in medical school, internship, and the general surgery residency. Now I have to start anew and learn how to remove a lung, close holes in infant hearts, replace valves in adult hearts, study the arteries in the heart, know where to sew vein bypass grafts around blockages, deal with emergencies of the chest in situations where I will face the problems alone, and reason only with myself concerning what to do. In addition, I will learn how to insert cardiac pacemakers in hearts that do not beat at a normal rate. I have all this to learn in the months ahead, and cannot help but feel some apprehension as I begin this final but most difficult portion of training. I look forward to the day I can look back on surgical residency as the end of a chapter of my surgical career. Then I will be competent. There will be no fear to hide, no apprehension to cover up, no false leadership required. But enough of that thinking; I must first live this final chapter without letting up.

I plan to enter this first month with caution. I don't want to start the year off poorly. I will be assisting Dr. Bell on the heart cases for the first few months in order to learn how to put a patient on the heart-lung machine and see how most of the operations are performed before I get to become first surgeon.

Persistence to the End

The first month proves interesting. I assist on several open-heart cases and am putting patients "on the pump" after only two weeks. I learn to split the sternum or breastbone, to insert tubes into the veins going into the heart, and to connect those tubes to the heart bypass pump in order to drain all the blood going toward the heart into the pump. Another tube is passed from the pump and inserted into the aorta, the large artery coming out of the heart. In this way the heart can be completely bypassed, opened, operated on, and closed again, and all the while a mechanical pump is keeping blood flowing through the body. Putting a patient on the pump is very minor relative to the actual cardiac procedure, but it is a big step in the direction of actually getting to operate on the heart. I perform this part of the operation as if it were the most important step in the procedure. To me it is. If I do not learn to do it well, I cannot expect Dr. Bell to let me move on to the actual open-heart portion of the operation. I remember my rule book again: I must proceed one stitch at a time.

I feel elated, astonished that the first ten procedures are all successful, without any major complications. It is difficult to believe that a human heart can actually be cut open and sewn back together, and then still function as before. Open-heart surgery is the biggest single advance in the field of surgery since the beginning of anesthesia. Countless people have benefited from operations that have been truly lifesaving. Numerous others are able to live active and useful lives only because a heart valve can be replaced, or an abnormal opening in the heart sutured, or a vein used to bypass a blocked artery. However, these great benefits are not obtained without a price. Also, new techniques are not always successful; no new operation can carry a guarantee of success— only of hope.

Aim High

There are few "second chances" with heart surgery. Operating on a diseased heart is a game of perfection for the perfectionist. A single mistake may lead to catastrophe. A shortcut on the operating table may result in the heart never beating on its own again. A wrong decision at a critical moment in the procedure may bring death.

These facts are superfluous to me at the present. Their meaning cannot be appreciated until I am placed in the position of actually operating on the heart. Being told these statements is like reading sentences out of a surgical manual, like reading a menu but never eating the meal. I will have to experience cases that do not turn out as expected—cases that will make an imprint on my mind in such a way that I will never be able to forget them. This will be my learning process, just as it has been through internship and general surgery residency. In reference to the *Goals Rule Book,* I now need both "I have to go through it myself" and "I don't have to go through it myself" experiences. Right now I dread some of the former.

I finally get to perform my first heart operation—the simplest of them, but a giant step in the right direction. It is called a *mitral valvulotomy.* One of the valves in the heart is scarred as a result of rheumatic fever and has closed the opening between two chambers of the heart to such a degree that the blood flow through it is greatly impeded. I place the patient on "bypass," then open the heart and make two small incisions in the scarred valve, opening it to near its original size.

Practice in Your Mind

The patient does well post-op, and I make ready for larger operations. It's a significant matter to work as a first assistant on a case that I know I will handle as the first surgeon within a few weeks. I mentally check back into the *Goals Rule Book:* I picture myself as already having achieved my goal; I picture myself already performing valve surgery. Even though Dr. Bell is doing it with *his* hands, I am doing it in *my* mind. As I assist him, I make numerous mental notes concerning the minute details of the case: how Dr. Bell holds the tissue forceps when in a critical area of the heart; how many knots are necessary for each suture when sewing in the valve; what size suture he uses; how he makes sure all the air is out of the heart when the procedure is completed. I want to be able to do it all without having to rely on him for the next step. I want to be proficient enough on the first artificial valve I put in so that I do not have to ask a single question related to the technique. I have even forfeited my secret "closet of time" just prior to going to sleep, and now any time I lie down during the night, I think myself to sleep by mentally going over the operation step by step. I always drop off to sleep before finishing the procedure, but I know I am ready to put in a valve.

I wander into the intensive care unit before going to bed to make a last check on the patients. The unit has seven beds, supposedly split between cardiothoracic surgery and general surgery. As I begin rounds I realize that C-T has all seven beds filled with the sickest people in the hospital. I pick up a chart and sit down in the large easy chair in the corner and flip the cover of the chart open. Instead of reading the page of intern's notes before me, I only stare at the chart and reflect on the preceding week, the most difficult I have lived through. We ended up doing four hearts, a thoracic aortic aneurysm, and an esophageal lye burn (which destroyed the esophagus, stomach, and first portion of the duodenum). The burn patient died, and we had to take two of the heart patients back to the operating room because of rebleeding. One of the rebleeds occurred while I was operating on the esophageal burn, and I had to get someone else to finish the case while I took the heart patient back to the operating room.

When at the Bottom

I continue staring at the chart. I cannot run any faster. It's been like trying to drink a waterfall. I can't handle any more. Hearts rebleeding, people swallowing lye trying to kill themselves, seven patients in I.C.U. requiring personal attention. The only thing I have going for me tonight is that there are only 24 hours in a day and then another day begins. I am tired and sleepy. It has to look better after a few hours of sleep.

I force myself through the check of patients in the unit and settle down to study the chart of the next patient scheduled for open-heart surgery. It looks like the most difficult case we have encountered this year. The patient is a 63-year-old female who survived a heart attack several years ago but was left with an aneurysm of the heart (a ballooning-out portion of the heart that robs the rest of the heart of its efficiency). This area needs to be removed before the heart completely gives out.

I complete my workup on Mrs. Krozier and return to the residents' library to begin a review of aneurysms of the heart. I make myself read everything I can find about each case I scrub on, a rule I made as an intern that I still stick to. I already know in a general way what the pathology of the case is and what operation will be needed, but I must now learn the details of the disease process and operation. I must learn more than I will ever have to know about each particular operation because so many of the details will be forgotten over time. After beginning to read about the aneurysm that is causing Mrs. Krozier's heart failure, I see that following a heart attack, the wall of the left ventricle of the heart may begin to bulge, much like an inner tube sticking out through the side of a tire. The problem at stake is not so much the possibility of a rupture, but the fact that this portion of the heart is not doing its share of the work. As the aneurysm (the ballooning-out portion) enlarges, more and more blood in the heart stagnates in that area and is not pumped into the body. Mrs. Krozier is in heart failure due to the aneurysm and cannot do much more than go from her bed to the table without sheer exhaustion. The purpose of the operation is to remove this portion of the heart and let the remaining heart muscle carry on the needed pumping action.

Two days later we get ready for the operation. Dr. Bell will perform the surgery, and I will assist. We start at the usual 7:00 A.M. operating time. Everything goes well. Dr. Bell places Mrs. Krozier on bypass and excises the ballooned-out area of the left ventricle. A piece of muscle about four inches in diameter has to be removed in order to excise the aneurysm in its entirety. Looking at the heart, I can easily see why this portion of muscle is not able to pump. It is less than a quarter of an inch thick and shows no sign of activity at all. The area is cut free, leaving a large hole to be brought together by placing sutures through the remaining edges. The muscle looks and feels like soft fish flesh rather than the normal firm cardiac muscle. Every other stitch Dr. Bell places pulls out and has to be replaced, but he finally places the last stitch and no leakage of blood comes through the newly placed suture row. He has done a superb job of closing the defect left after removing the aneurysm.

We take Mrs. Krozier to the recovery room and keep a close watch on her for four hours. Very little blood is coming through the chest tubes. She is stable. We next take her to the intensive care unit, hoping that the critical period has passed and that we have been able to pull her through without a major complication.

Everything is going so well with Mrs. Krozier that I take some time to explain to the medical students the purpose of the chest tubes following open-heart surgery.

Teaching Those Below

"A blood thinner is used during the operation to keep the blood from sticking to the heart-lung machine, preventing clots in the system. At the end of surgery the thinner is neutralized to a certain extent, but there is always a continuous oozing of blood for a few hours. The blood accumulates in the chest and is allowed to escape to the out-side through these pliable plastic tubes placed through the chest wall and connected to the bottle on the floor. The bottle has markings that allow us to measure how much blood is lost each hour. Eighty to 100 cubic centimeters is the upper limit per hour. If too much blood comes through the chest tubes, this indicates the bleeding inside is more than just ooze from the operative site and the patient has to be reoperated on to find and control the hemorrhage."

The students listen intently, but they will never be able to appreciate what I am saying unless they someday operate on a heart, stick in chest tubes, watch how much blood comes through, and make a final decision on whether or not to take the patient back and open him up to find the site of the bleeding. I conclude the minilecture and relax.

It is 10:00 P.M. and there's not a trace of trouble. I enjoy taking care of a patient who does well after surgery. Mrs. Krozier still has an endotracheal tube in her windpipe and is connected to a respirator. Essentially all I have to do is regulate the machine to keep her breathing normally. I go over a few more of the basic mechanics of post-op care with the students, but few appear interested enough to stay past bedtime to ask questions. I dismiss all but two who will remain with Mrs. Krozier all night to observe the actual postoperative care on an open-heart patient. She is putting out about 80 cc's of blood an hour, and I am content to accept this amount of loss through her chest tubes.

Reality

All of a sudden I notice blood pooling under my feet. My mind rushes for an explanation. I want a simple solution. This is the first time I have been confronted with a postoperative complication that I have not been able to reason out almost as soon as the problem unfolded. "There is a unit of blood running into her I.V. It must be disconnected and leaking onto the floor," I think quickly to myself.

This reasoning proves to be false as I glance at the I.V. tubing and find it intact. Blood is now completely covering the floor under the bed. I kneel to look for the source under the bed and see the chest tube bottle, which collects the blood draining out of the chest through the plastic chest tubes. The bottle is sitting in place on the floor at the other side of the bed. It is completely full of blood and blood is even spouting out the small hole at the top! I cannot imagine what is going on. All I can think of is getting her back to the operating room where we can do something about it—whatever it is. I yell at the intern to grab the chest tube bottle while I disconnect the respirator and start using the oxygen bag to help Mrs. Krozier breathe. The intensive care nurse excitedly tells me she is notifying the operating room that we are on the way with a patient.

I wait anxiously for the elevator. Why doesn't the elevator come so we can get her to the operating room? Everything is so pressing! Time is so important!

We wheel Mrs. Krozier into the operating room and I quickly open the chest. By now I realize the only thing that can cause this much blood to show so quickly through the chest tubes is a rupture in the suture line where we had such a difficult time getting the muscle to hold together. Sure enough, the lower end of the sutures has pulled out of the heart muscle and blood is pouring through the opening. I grab a gauze tampon and place it over the hole to stop the bleeding, then look up and see Dr. Bell making his appearance in the O.R. The intensive care unit nurse had presence of mind enough to call him at home and tell him of the problem.

"What happened?" He begins getting gowned and gloved. I have never been more glad to see anyone in the whole world as I am to see Dr. Bell.

"Part of the suture line tore loose in I.C.U. Blood started pouring out her chest tubes all over the floor. It scared me; I couldn't figure out what had happened. It looks like about half the sutures have pulled through."

"I thought we had gotten her through, but this is a mess." Dr. Bell is now at the table assessing the situation. "Nothing to do but try again."

We begin pumping blood back into her and finally start to obtain a decent blood pressure. Dr. Bell begins the tedious process of trying to place stitches into the muscle that has proven to be so fragile. He places the last suture into place and ties down. No more leaks. The drama is over. He has successfully reclosed the tear, and we must now repeat the postoperative care that we started so many hours before.

I look at my watch and see 3:15 A.M. staring at me. I had completely lost track of the time. All is quiet, and by some miracle Mrs. Krozier is not only alive but is stable once again. I decide to get some sleep, leaving the intern by the bed to keep a watch on things.

At 4:30 I am awakened by the intern yelling at me to come back to the intensive care unit. I run in. There is blood all over the floor under the bed. Mrs. Krozier's heart has ruptured again! My brain computer takes only a split second to reach the conclusion this time, only five-and-a-half hours after it initially strained so hard to reach the same conclusion.

This time we are not so lucky. As each stitch is replaced through the heart, it pulls through. At 5:30 Mrs. Krozier is bleeding to death on the table with all of us standing silently, unable to pull it off again.

"Closing the hole the first time was difficult; closing it the second time was unbelievable; closing it the third time is impossible. She's dead." Dr. Bell backs away from the table and walks out of the room.

Unwanted Experience

I remain with blood still dripping from the operating table onto the floor, the front of my scrub suit soaked, and with so much blood in my canvas operating shoes that I feel that now-familiar squish when I move my feet. I begin closing the chest with one layer of heavy suture material—no use doing a plastic closure now. This is one wound that will never heal. I begin having far-reaching thoughts as I stand alone at the table closing the chest of a dead patient. *So this is the way I learn,* I think to myself. *This is the "I have to go through it myself" experiences necessary to acquire the knowledge of a chest surgeon. Learn by doing. Learn by seeing. I would rather not have to learn this.* We started the initial operation almost 24 hours ago and gave our all, yet Mrs. Krozier is dead and there is nothing we can do about it. No one is paying much attention to the fact that there is still a patient in the room. The scrub nurses are busy cleaning their tables and discussing what cases they are going to scrub on this morning. The anesthesiologist is cleaning his cart and replacing the drugs he has used. I hear an occasional laugh and a few complaints about the loss of sleep tonight just because of the chest doctors. I continue to sew, speaking only to my mind.

She didn't have much of a chance either way, I think. *All chances are gone now. If we hadn't operated, she would be alive this very minute...but if she were alive, she couldn't do anything but get out of bed for a few minutes a day.* My brain argues with itself as I finish closing the chest. I place the last stitch. Time to forget Mrs. Krozier. A new day is here. This morning I am scheduled to put my first mitral prosthesis in a good-risk patient. I must pull all my thoughts into that operation. I have to see if everything is in order for the procedure, need to make rounds on the patients still in I.C.U., and need to give instructions to the two patients to be discharged this morning.

Only as I remove my breakfast of cheese crackers from the snack machine and start toward the Coke machine do I realize that I have not eaten for almost 24 hours. Even now I am not hungry, only shaky from low blood sugar. Excitement can momentarily stave off hunger, but it has no nourishment. There is no time for me to go through the cafeteria line.

One hour passes and I am busy with the normal workings of being chief resident. The incident that happened only hours ago seems weeks away—forgotten because there are too many things going on to think about that now. *Forget the dead and concentrate on the living,* I tell myself. *I am experiencing—and learning.* Perhaps this is the only way to get through my year as chief resident—concentrate on the living.

The mitral valve operation goes well. I put in my first artificial valve but have no feeling of elation. I am numb to my surroundings. Mrs. Krozier died. Forgotten? Not quite. I performed a successful operation. This almost seems to balance out the emotions. A plus and a minus within a 24-hour period, and I find it difficult to cope with my mixed feelings.

I decide to go home for a while during the evening lull, but don't feel like telling Harriet I put in my first valve today. What's the use? Why keep going at this pace? What good is helping one person if the next one dies? I need some sleep to clear my mind enough to get back in there swinging. I decide not to eat supper, but rather to lie down on the sofa and snooze until the junior resident calls the latest lab results to me.

Tomorrow will be better. I flip through my worn goals book. I would hate to relive each experience that has led to an entry in the book. In some ways I have lived a rough existence. In other ways life has been simply great: operating, operating, operating. It has been tremendous to be given the opportunity to train to become a surgeon, to experience all the situations that have made the *Goals Rule Book* possible.

I close the notebook and relax.

18

Responsibility to Those Below You

EVERY SURGICAL TRAINING PROGRAM INVOLVES A PLAN for maturing, which begins with the first day of internship. An intern is a total "taker." For one solid year he gleans wisdom from the resident above him, but teaches others almost nothing. The first-year resident, who is only one year ahead of the intern, has the responsibility of teaching the intern everything he himself learned the previous year. Simultaneously, he learns from those more advanced than himself. Then each year thereafter, as he progresses up the ladder and accumulates more surgical knowledge, his responsibilities expand. This is the basic principle for maturing as a surgical resident. The more one learns, the more responsibility one has to those below him.

> From everyone who has been given much, much will be demanded; and from the one who has been entrusted with much, much more will be asked (Luke 12:48).

As I finished my cardiothoracic residency, I was feeding all my insights into surgery to those below me in the program. Spiritually, though, others were feeding me. Many individuals taught me scriptural truths about letting the Holy Spirit work in my life, and for several years I was a "taker." I will always be indebted to those who were ahead of me in my spiritual walk, who led me on the right path.

Once I settled into private practice, I began to see many areas in my life that needed measuring against the standard of Scripture. Then, when I volunteered through an organization called World Medical Mission to work in a mission hospital in India, I gained insights from God's Word that I thought others might need also. I began to realize the importance of passing on to others what the Lord was teaching me. It wasn't that I was now mature; it was more like I had begun my first-year residency and could help some interns under me. I realized that no matter what level of spiritual maturity I had, the Lord could use me to disciple someone who might be only a short distance behind me.

The next day is brighter. Bob First, who worked under me as a resident on general surgery, starts his rotation on C-T as the junior resident. He has decided to go into cardiothoracic and will stay on the service for the remainder of the year as my junior resident. He has already proven to be a hard, conscientious worker I can rely on, and his presence on the service makes C-T a whole new world to work in. I am glad he decided on C-T, for he will be an asset to the inner workings of the program.

Bob and I decide we need a room near the I.C.U. that we can call home for a while. We find a storage closet that is easily converted and dress it up a little. We talk the secretary into typing up a list of Murphy's Laws to place on the wall of our new hangout. They seem so appropriate to our troubles:

1. In any field of scientific endeavor, anything that can go wrong will go wrong.

2. Left to themselves, things always go from bad to worse.

3. If there is a possibility of several things going wrong, the one that will go wrong is the one that will do the most damage.

4. Nature always sides with the hidden flaw.

5. If everything seems to be going well, you have obviously overlooked something.

The original plan for the interns and residents seems to be working. The intern on call will still remain in the I.C.U. throughout the night while Bob and I will be next door in our new on-call room. If a problem arises, the intern can get the appropriate resident. Bob will handle most problems and will usually be called first. If he is unsure of what to do, he will call me. But there is only one problem—we don't have any beds. We borrow one from the pediatric on-call room, since they have an extra, and we also find an old two-cushion sofa that can pass for a place to curl up. We are set.

It is strange that such a small thing as a room next to I.C.U. could make such a difference, but the entire service becomes more relaxed. Even the interns are satisfied, because now they don't have to fight

Bob anymore for the red easy chair in I.C.U.—a favorite place for all for a quick nap.

Good Does Not Last Forever

The past few days have been relatively easy, with only scheduled surgery being performed. The number of emergency operations have dropped off. When we are tied up with many emergencies our schedule can easily be turned upside down. If an emergency comes in at two in the morning, that is the time the person has to be worked up and operated on. Without a doubt, there are numerous times an emergency operation is required to save a life. Death has no timetable, unless perhaps it is favorable to night, when residents are trying to sleep.

I am awakened to the dreaded ringing of the phone and told there was a baby born yesterday afternoon with aortic stenosis, and she has just been transferred to the pediatric service nearly dead. We take her to the operating room immediately in an attempt to open the valve to relieve the pressure being built up within the heart. I am to be first surgeon. I don't understand; the baby is almost dead. One of the main valves in the heart is plugged. An emergency operation is about to be done, and I have been appointed first surgeon by Dr. Bell. I have advanced a rung on the ladder of becoming a surgeon. Emergencies do not allow for mistakes, and I am about to perform my first cardiac emergency. One stitch at a time is adding up. One brick at a time is at the top floor of the skyscraper; one stitch at a time is nearing the completion of the operation.

I discuss the procedure with Dr. Bell.

"The only chance the baby has is to take a Brock's valvulotome and push it through the valve opening and hope it works." Dr. Bell hastily makes ready for the operation by going over the valvulotome with me. "It's just like a small pencil with little side blades attached to where the lead point would be located. The trick to the operation lies in the fact that the blades protract as far out as you like. With this baby, we will barely be able to open them, but it's our only chance."

Never Give Up

I suddenly realize why Dr. Bell is letting me be the first surgeon on the case. It is not so much that I have become such a great surgeon so early in my cardiac training, but rather because it is a simple technical procedure that requires no special surgical skill other than sticking a "pencil" in the heart and blindly pushing it through the aortic valve, plus the fact the baby will in all likelihood not live, no matter who pushes it through the valve.

I expose the heart, such a miniature heart, and place a purse-string suture near the tip of the heart. Next I stab the center of the hole I have just outlined with the suture. Now the valvulotome. I gently push it through the opening I have just made. I grasp it with my right hand and push my left index finger on the base of the aorta and invaginate it momentarily. All I have to do is aim for my fingertip.

Set the dial to protract the blades.

Push. Through the valve.

Close the blades.

Pull. Back into the ventricle.

Remove the valvulotome from the heart.

Blood squirts through the hole in the heart.

Quickly tie the purse strings. Bleeding stops.

Close the chest…the baby is still alive.

There is immediate improvement, but she probably has had too much of a strain on the heart muscle to survive through the night.

She does survive, however, and two weeks later is discharged from the hospital. I feel good but not elated. I do not fully understand why I don't feel like a hero. Why am I not more proud? Probably because I acknowledge the fact that I had very little control over what happened. I didn't even have faith that the baby would make it through the first night, much less be able to leave the hospital in two weeks.

Bob is enjoying the service because I am splitting the lung cases with him. We both want to learn as much as possible about surgery on the lung, since a great deal of our surgical practice in the future will be centered on lung operations. This aspect of the cardiothoracic surgery training is not as rewarding as the heart surgery because so many of the patients with cancer of the lung are in a terminal state when we first see them. The patients are usually men who smoke one or two packs of cigarettes a day and then come to see us when it's too late to reverse the damage.

For some reason, people cannot grasp the reality that smoking causes cancer of the lung, and the more they smoke, the more they increase their chance of getting a tumor. I even try to get a patient who smokes three packs a day to make a wager with me on his chances of eventually dying of cancer of the lung. No one will take me up on the bet, but no one will quit smoking the three packs a day either. What's more, lung cancer in women is on the rise, and the most obvious reason is that more women are smoking today than 25 years ago. Try to explain the dangers to a nice-looking college coed student who has made up her mind that smoking is the thing to do, and see if it makes the slightest impression on her.

We will always have patients who continue to smoke to excess until they "grow" their lung cancer and then decide to quit smoking a week before surgery in the hopes that it will make a difference on the outcome of life-versus-death situation.

Mr. Frank Harris is being admitted to the hospital today to our service for a routine workup of lung cancer. After spending 30 minutes with him and reviewing his X rays, I get the history that he has had a bad cough for several years but thought nothing about it until one morning when he noticed there were some small flakes of blood mixed with the mucus. He dismissed it completely, but a few weeks later the same thing recurred. He mentioned it to his wife, who immediately made an appointment for him to be examined. His local physician saw him, had an X ray taken, and referred him to our service. There is a mass the size of a lemon in his right lung.

The first inquiry I make of the patient is whether there are some old X rays we can look at for comparison. If he had a film taken five years ago and the spot was present then, and it has remained unchanged since then, there would be no need to operate and take out something that isn't causing him difficulty and has almost no chance of being cancer. Mr. Harris has not had any chest films taken, however, so we are going to work him up from scratch. The workup is begun by giving him a cup to spit into in the morning; the material will be examined under the microscope in search for malignant cells that can be "shedding" from the mass in his lung and be washed out in his sputum.

The Ultimate Negative

No malignant cells are found in his sputum.

Next is bronchoscopy, the process of passing a flexible lighted tube through the nose down the inside of the trachea and into his lung to look for the tumor. The bronchoscope is introduced into the larynx and windpipe, slid down the larger air passage of each lung, and eventually into the area where the mass is located. If any portion of the mass can be seen from inside the lung, a small piece is biopsied and sent to the pathologist for diagnosis. If nothing is seen, saline is injected into the bronchoscope and then suctioned back out. The material obtained in this manner is also sent to pathology in the hope that some of the cells have been washed off the tumor, allowing a diagnosis to be made.

Bob slides the bronchoscope neatly into the area of lung in which the tumor is located. The bronchi appear clearly. He slides in a small wire with a miniature brush on the end and pushes it out the passageway beyond in hopes that the brush will either penetrate the actual tumor or brush up against it and scrape some of the tumor cells onto the brush. The brush is sent to the pathologist, who looks at it under a microscope.

Still no tumor cells; no diagnosis.

Due to the location of the mass on X ray, there is a possibility that some of the tumor has spread into the lymph nodes along the trachea. We decide to perform a mediastinoscopy, which entails making a small incision in Mr. Harris' neck and sliding a small, lighted, metal tube down alongside the trachea and bronchi. In this manner the lymph nodes can be seen and biopsies made in order to determine if the tumor has spread to this area. If it has, the chances of curing Mr. Harris by surgery are very slim.

I perform the mediastinoscopy, see several lymph nodes, and make biopsies. Mr. Harris returns to his room to await the pathologist's report.

The report comes back completely negative; no tumor is seen on the bronchoscope, no tumor cells are found in the bronchoscopy washings, no tumor cells are found in his sputum, and no tumor can be found in any of the lymph nodes biopsied on mediastinoscopy. The only way left to determine if the spot on X ray is cancer is to open Mr. Harris' chest and actually take a piece of the mass and let the pathologist examine it.

A Worthy Goal

Mr. Harris is scheduled for morning surgery. I position him on the operating table so that his right side is up. He is prepped and draped, and I make an incision through the skin beginning just under his right nipple and extend it backward, curving under his shoulder blade. The chest incisions are extensive in order to get the chest opened enough to have an unobstructed view during the operation.

The muscles of the chest wall are divided, and the chest cavity is entered between the fourth and fifth ribs. Even though the muscles between the ribs are incised, the ribs remain in the same position as always; they are pried apart with a heavy metal gadget that is slid between two ribs in order to push them apart. The ribs are separated seven or eight inches in this manner, allowing me to see inside, as well as get my hand and instruments inside the cavity to work.

"He really has the black lung," Bob says, commenting on how black Mr. Harris' lung appears. A normal lung is pink and clean-looking, but the lungs of a chronic smoker turn darker and darker until they become black with the carbon the lungs have absorbed.

I place both hands into the opening and feel the tumor mass. The right lung is separated by three lobes, or divisions, and I can feel the mass sitting in the middle lobe, close to the connection of the other two lobes.

"Bad disease," I tell Bob as I continue to explore the area with my hands. I feel for spread of the tumor in the other lobes and also in the lymph nodes around the main artery. I feel several nodes near the main branches, but none with the firm, "stuck-down" feel of cancer that has spread. "I think the only way to get it out is to do a radical pneumo on him. I'll biopsy a piece of the tumor for the frozen section."

I pull my hand out of the chest and let Bob take a feel to see if he finds anything different, or has any suggestions to make. I tell him my decision to do a radical pneumonectomy—to remove the entire lung as well as the lymph nodes situated around the trachea and the right main air passages. If the tumor were situated further out in the middle lobe, it might have been possible to remove only one lobe and leave the remaining two. However, Mr. Harris' tumor is sitting right on the main air passages, and no margin of safety is present. If we leave any tumor behind, it will prove fatal.

Truth Faced

Bob agrees with my decision. I send a small slice of lung containing the tumor to the pathologist. He sends back the report: carcinoma, squamous cell. There is cancer present.

We start the radical dissection by incising the thin pleural covering lining the cavity of the chest. As I bring the dissection down toward the lung, I include the lymph nodes that would be in the path where the tumor would spread. Next we dissect around the vessels to the lung and isolate the artery and veins. Finally the dissection is completed and the cancerous lung is removed. A tube is placed through the chest wall and the wound is closed.

The resection completed, Mr. Harris is taken to the recovery room.

"What will you tell him about what you found?" Bob asks as we leave the recovery room. This is one of the first cancers of the lung Bob has scrubbed on, and he wants to know what to tell a patient who has cancer.

"I would tell him exactly what I would want to know if I went to a surgeon with a spot on my lung and paid him to find out what it was. I think the only thing you can do is tell it to him straight and tell him what his chances are. If he doesn't want to accept that as fact, then it's up to him to deny it to himself and to anybody else he wishes."

"What if the family asks you not to tell him he has cancer or tells you to wait a few months to let him know what you found? It seems like half the families made such requests when I rotated through the cancer service on general surgery."

"I know exactly what you're talking about. In some of the cancer cases, the tumor has to be left behind and you know there is no way possible for the patient to survive the malignancy. I have had some families ask me not to tell the patient, or worse still, ask me to lie to the patient about what I have found. I assume these families try to act as if nothing is wrong and attempt to lead a normal life once the patient is sent home to await death. I know this cannot last long before the patient begins to grow suspicious of the whole setup and especially of the surgeon who explained the finding to him," I say to Bob as he writes the post-op orders on Mr. Harris' chart.

I continue: "I first explain to the family that I am going to tell the patient that he does have cancer and whether I was able to remove it. Very few families argue with that approach. Then I go ahead and tell the patient what I found during surgery. With some patients I can be straightforward, but with others, I can't. You have to make the decision based on the individual peculiarities of each patient."

With the orders written and the conversation ended, it is time to do another bronchoscopy and mediastinoscopy on a man admitted yesterday with a spot on his lung. I observe over Bob's shoulder as he glides the scope into the patient's trachea.

Habits by Repetition

I enjoy working with Bob. He is inquisitive, and this requires me to arrange my thinking well enough to be able to explain and discuss with him. I take out the *Goals Rule Book* from my pocket. I flip through the pages and realize that most of what I have written down has become habit. These habits have been formed by repetition. For example, I automatically throw out negative thoughts as they enter my mind and replace them with positive ones. The bad-apple rule has become a habit. I still make my daily lists of things to do in order of importance; it is now habit to do it that way. I look at things that need to be done, see them as immediate-action goals, and relate them to the overall structure of my intermediate and major goals.

It has also become a habit to take large problems and break them down into small, one-stitch-at-a-time items. In fact, I am already seeing myself as having finished cardiothoracic training. What was once difficult to achieve is becoming easier through habit. I also notice I am returning to my rule book less and less; I am developing good habits through repetition of the rules. My mind has taken the rules, planted them, nourished them, and is now harvesting them in the form of habits.

Suddenly a Scripture I have heard numerous times becomes real: "As [a man] thinketh in his heart, so is he" (Proverbs 23:7). I am becoming what I have kept on my mind for the past several years. Thought has become habit, which, in turn, has become character. My character as a surgeon has matured from thoughts on becoming a surgeon. The giant steps between my thoughts and the character I have developed as a surgeon were achieved only by putting my thoughts into action—the all-important immediate-action goals.

19

Seven Boys and Their Mother

I DO NOT KNOW OF ANY GREATER NATURAL LOVE than that of a mother for her child. A mother will forfeit time, pleasure, and money for the love of her child. A mother will do without so that her child can have something he would not otherwise have. A mother will give her all, even her very life, for the well-being of her child.

In surgical training, we operate on many patients without ever knowing the details of their lives. Occasionally, though, we run across someone who seems special enough to make us wonder what kind of person we are dealing with. I was about to experience such a patient.

She had the sweetest, kindest face; her conversation was equally impressive. Her children, seven boys, respected her and everything she had taught them. You could tell by the way they talked to her and treated her that they loved her dearly. The questions they asked concerning the upcoming operation left no doubt about their love for their mother or their willingness to do anything for her. I am sure that if she told them she wanted a chocolate sundae at 11:00 P.M. the night before surgery, they would have satisfied her wish. Their love for her was so great that they would have obeyed her commamds instantly.

Though I operated on these sons' mother during my residency, it wasn't until many years later I correlated the love they had for their mother with the love Christians know for Christ. I can relate to how much those sons loved their mother because I have a mother. I can comprehend the love that this mother had for her sons because I have a son. I find it more difficult, however, to fathom how much I should love God.

How does our love for God compare with our love for our mother or father? How much love does God require of us and how does it compare to the love of family? First John 5:3 makes a direct correlation between love for God and obedience to his commands: "This is love for God: to obey his commands." Just as a child's love for his earthly parents expresses itself in obedience, so should our love for our heavenly Father be expressed in obedience. What's more, our love for Him is to supersede all other loves.

Anyone who loves his father or mother more than me is not worthy of me; anyone who loves his son or daughter more than me is not worthy of me (Matthew 10:37).

At first this saying from Jesus puzzled me. Were we to love our father or mother or son or daughter any less? No; the Lord was giving us a benchmark by which to measure our love and obedience to God. He knew the intensity of our love for family. He knew that love can be overwhelming. Our love for Him is to exceed even that great love. Being His children warrants no less than that type of love.

I was soon to operate on this beloved mother whose love for her sons emanated from her every action. I was about to take her life into my hands. I only hoped she would survive so that she could continue to show her love to her sons.

As the weeks roll by, I find I am letting Bob do more and more of the lung cases and find myself actually enjoying assisting him during the surgery. In return, Dr. Bell is allowing me to perform more and more of the open-heart cases. I have been blessed with success on most of them but am quick to remind myself that Dr. Bell does the difficult ones and leaves the easy ones to me—the ones who are supposed to do well. Dr. Bell informs me of a new patient just admitted for surgery this week.

Mrs. Willis is 59 years old, an obese woman who is so sincerely friendly that I wish I could have known her when I was a child so that I might have learned some of her friendly ways. She has seven boys whose ages range from 13 (her "baby," as she calls him) to 27. They all come to the hospital to be with their mother while she undergoes open-heart surgery. They need each other at a time like this. The father was killed in an automobile accident eight years ago. They are a very close family, jabbing at each other, kidding the "baby," laughing with their mother. They talk as a unit, act as a whole. None of the boys is married; it's just them and Mom. Dr. Bell and I talk to her and the boys about the forthcoming operation. All of them accept it as a necessity and plan to take it in stride.

A Mother's Love

Mrs. Willis had rheumatic fever 20 years ago, and this left her mitral valve (the heart valve between the left atrium and the left ventricle) in a condition similar to that of a cancerous growth. The reaction to the infection has chewed at the edges of the valve. Dense scar tissue has invaded the body of the valve, making it like stiff cardboard that does not move with each beat of the heart as a soft, pliable, normal valve does. This results in a leak in the left side of her pump. Not only will the valve not close properly, but it is so scarred down that it obstructs the forward flow of blood, which normally should pass through the valve with little effort. She has been in heart failure for over a year, but "could not leave the boys long enough to have it looked after." Now she has a large, distended heart that is in chronic failure and will prove to be very difficult to get "off the pump"—the heart-lung machine.

"She'll be a difficult case, but I think she ought to do okay," Dr. Bell says after walking out of her room. "Do you want to do her? It ought to be easy to get the valve in place because she has such a large atrium."

I nod in the affirmative, hoping that nothing goes wrong with the case. I am midway through the year as chief resident and have 14 valve operations under my belt. I have had no deaths from a valve case, mainly because of the "good-risk" classification of my patients. Mrs. Willis definitely is not a good risk, but I feel confident in tackling this more difficult heart.

Counting the Risks

I speak spontaneously to Dr. Bell. "I don't think I could bear facing those boys if something went wrong. The young one asked me if it would be all right if he planned to play football with his team Friday night. I am sure they don't understand the seriousness of the operation."

"She will do all right," Dr. Bell responds assuringly. I just wish she didn't have so much calcium in her valve. We will review her heart studies on film and evaluate the valve once more.

The morning of the operation begins at 6:30. Bob and the students are already making the rounds. I go by and check the most recent post-op patients before putting on my scrub suit to get ready for the case. Mrs. Willis is supposed to be in the operating room at seven, but she isn't even in the entrance hall at five to seven.

"Who's bringing Mrs. Willis down?" I ask a nurse at the O.R. desk.

"We're shorthanded this morning, and I don't think anyone has gone after her yet."

"If you don't have someone to get the heart patients here by seven, let me know. I'll get them down myself. We can't hold up the whole team just because someone didn't show up for work." I angrily pick up the phone and call the seventh floor.

"I'm sorry, but we just don't have enough help around here," the operating room nurse repeats, shuffling the papers on her desk.

I finally get Bob on the phone: "Bring Mrs. Willis down. I'll meet you at the elevator."

I hang up and begin a brisk walk toward the elevators. *What a way to start off!* I think to myself. *I'm going to perform open-heart surgery and have to roll the patient to the operating room myself!*

Stretching for the Finish Line

Bob and I succeed in getting Mrs. Willis into the room and begin helping the anesthesiologist put in the I.V. lines. Three lines are placed: a long catheter in a vein in the left arm is threaded into one of the large veins emptying into the heart; and two other catheters threaded through needles are stuck into each jugular vein in the neck. One of these is passed into the superior vena cava (just above the heart) and connected to a monitor to measure the pressure of the blood just before it enters the heart. Mrs. Willis is awake during all this but displays no hint of discomfort. Bob and I next perform a cut-down over the radial artery in her left wrist. The artery is partially divided and another catheter is inserted about one-half inch into the vessel. This catheter is connected to yet another monitor that will record the blood pressure continuously while we are operating. Just to the right of Mrs. Willis is the large black multimonitor with numerous connects and lines, including the two pressure lines we just placed. The technicians run the monitor, which is all-important at critical times during the procedure. The top portion of the monitor consists of a screen in which the E.K.G., the venous pressure, and the arterial pressure repeatedly sweep across the face of the screen for easy interpretation by the surgeon and anesthesiologist while the patient is on the heart-lung machine.

On Mrs. Willis' left is the life-sustaining heart-lung machine, which receives blood from her and pumps blood, rich in oxygen, back into her. Mrs. Willis is put to sleep. I open the chest and incise the pericardium, the thin sac around the heart. I spread the edges of the sac apart, revealing the glistening heart muscle. There are four chambers in the heart—the right atrium, the right ventricle, the left atrium, and the left ventricle. It is easier thinking of the heart as a two-sided organ, the right side receiving blood from the body and pumping it through the lungs and into the left side, and the left side receiving blood from the lungs and pumping it into the aorta and throughout the body. The heart-lung machine works by placing a siphon hose into the heart just where the blood is entering the first chamber, and stealing the blood from the "right heart" and giving it to the heart-lung machine. The machine, in turn, will supply this blood with oxygen, doing the work of the lungs, and then pump the oxygenated blood through another tube, doing the work of the left heart. The heart is completely bypassed and can be opened, cut on, sewn, or patched while the body continues to thrive on the flow of blood coming from the miraculous heart-lung machine.

I place all the connecting tubes into Mrs. Willis' heart and pass them off the table to the technician running the heart-lung machine. He connects the tubes to his pump, and after the entire system is filled with blood he turns on the pump, which begins to push oxygen-rich blood back into her body. I open the left atrium and examine the valve. The mitral valve appears exactly as we were afraid it would—so scarred with calcium that it looks and feels like bone. The leaflets of the valve are firm, scarred, and useless. They will certainly be difficult to remove. An attempt is made to excise the valve by cutting with scissors, but this proves futile. A clamp, similar to needlenose pliers, is used to crush and chew at the calcified valve until it is broken enough to excise with a pair of heavy-duty curved scissors.

Much time elapses in removing the valve. I begin sewing an artificial valve into position with difficulty. Nothing seems to be going right. The calcium does not stop at the base of the valve but extends into the heart tissue, where the stitches have to be placed to hold the artificial valve. The needles bend as I push them through this unsewable area; the sutures pull out when tied with any tension at all; it seems impossible to get the artificial valve in place.

Finally, after much frustration and difficulty, the valve is in and ready to be tested. We have spent several hours getting the valve removed and the prosthesis sewn in. The heart muscle itself is sick as a result of battling the diseased valve, and it will be short of a miracle if it survives this added insult of surgery. The heart-lung machine is turned off gradually and the heart is given an opportunity to take over the work it has been accustomed to for such a long time.

It begins pumping some blood, but not enough, and with inadequate force to perfuse the organs of her body. We try everything in the book to aid this dying heart to beat effectively once again. Word is sent to her sons that their mother is not doing well in coming off the bypass. We decided to once again open the heart to see if, by chance, the valve has pulled loose or is allowing blood to leak around the edges, which may keep her heart from taking over again.

The valve looks just as we left it, firmly sewn in place. Her heart simply isn't strong enough to recover from the long operation, and both Dr. Bell and I know it. One more attempt is made to get Mrs. Willis off bypass, but the heart muscle has been under too much stress for too many years to be put through the strain we just placed on it. Two more hours are spent trying to get her heart to take over.

"Turn off the pump, she's gone." Dr. Bell gives the order. I look at him, knowing the most difficult task is yet to be performed. I have been first surgeon; I am the one to tell the seven boys their mother is dead. I dread talking with them. No one in the room knows how I dread it, but it must be done.

Dreading the Inevitable

"I'll go tell them." Not much else is said as I leave the room for the long walk down the corridor to the waiting room where the boys wait to hear the news about their mother. Several nurses speak to me as I meet them in the hallway, but I hardly notice them as I rehearse what to say. The nursing supervisor has placed the boys in a separate room adjacent to the waiting room. I walk in and shut the door behind me. Seven pairs of eyes stare into mine, and all remain motionless as if time has stopped, waiting for me to speak.

What do I say? Do I look at the floor? Do I look at the wall? Do I dare look at the boys? What can I say to make it seem less real? An hour of thoughts race through my mind in the brief moment before speaking.

"Boys, I'm afraid she didn't make it. We tried everything, but couldn't get her heart to work." I look at the oldest. He fights to keep back the tears, but soon his cheeks become moistened as he stands, his eyes fixed upon mine, gently nodding his head.

"We knew it. We knew the minute we were told she wasn't doing well earlier. We knew it the way the nurse asked us to step in here.

We knew it when you walked in and shut the door. Even though we knew it, we still had *hope*…until just now." His voice breaks as he turns and puts his arm around his youngest brother.

The young one whines at first, but soon begins sobbing. The other brothers grab each other for solace, and the oldest is able to thank me for trying before he sits down and buries his face in his hands.

All of the explanation in the world cannot change the fact that Mrs. Willis is dead, will never utter a sound, breathe a breath of air, or give a friendly greeting to her boys again. This is all that registers in the family's mind, all that matters to them. Yet I must try to explain to myself what happened during the surgery, what went wrong, why she died. This a surgeon has to do in order to be able to operate again. He cannot leave anything unanswered in his own mind; this is the one time he has to be honest with himself or lose his "right" to operate. Only *he* can know whether the best was done for the patient, whether death was preventable. It is a complicated problem that is never completely solved in anyone's mind. The family of the dead patient must live through this problem only once, but the surgeon must face this ever-present drama each and every time a patient dies.

I leave the room. I don't know why, but a single thought concerning the youngest son comes into my mind. Today is Thursday. Tomorrow, all the high school players have their football game. All except one.

Death is a terrible situation for any family to face, and it is also the most horrifying experience a resident will ever go through. Death is so final! There is no second chance at treatment. It is unbearably difficult to explain a death on the operating table to a family when I can't even begin to understand it myself.

Death acquires the largest portion of hatred I can muster under any circumstances. I know I must pull away from the emotional aspect of a patient dying, but I really wonder if I will ever be able to. The prevention of death, almost at any cost, becomes instilled in our minds as each day of the residency progresses. And the response to death is usually twofold: one, the empathy felt with the family; and two, even when the surgeon knows he has given the patient the best operation possible, there is always a feeling of insecurity, of doubt, of defeat when the patient does not survive. I can only hope I don't have a series of Mrs. Willises to face.

Growing with the Goal

I push on. Days turn into weeks, weeks to months. I become more proficient in running the service, and my confidence builds with each case we operate on. The hours are long but very rewarding. I become aware of a compulsive drive to work. I know that has developed over the years of surgical training, but only now am I aware of the way I do things. I have made myself strive for perfection, knowing the impossibility of the feat. I cannot explain it to myself, but I know I have realized some benefits from this attitude—intangible benefits, perhaps—but the overall gains in life cannot always be measured directly by whether we try harder on any particular feat or job. Rather, they are often measured indirectly by our overall mental attitude.

I will have to change before long. I cannot live life knowingly making myself compulsive, but must continue this frame of mind until the completion of residency. The program is far too pressing to tackle without an aggressive spirit. The *Goals Rule Book* has been a valuable asset in helping me to get as far as I have. The rules are easier and easier to apply to new situations. Life as a surgeon is becoming easier and more natural. I feel at home now.

However, there is a price paid for all this training—an amount that I do not know yet. For example, I am seldom at home, and Harriet is getting along in her pregnancy. I am not the supportive husband I should be during a time like this. We are not together enough to really call it "living together." We are pulling together, but do not seem to be making much headway. I am in a successful situation, but what a price to have to pay! Harriet and I do not discuss it because we have both convinced ourselves that this pattern is only temporary. I hold on to that belief. How can a man help direct his children if he is never around to give direction? How can a man's wife continue to support him and care for him if he is never around to be loved? How can a marriage grow and mature in a situation like this? I have many questions, but few answers. I continue on, one stitch at a time.

The week finally ends, and on this particular Saturday morning I decide not to go to the M & M conference and, instead, I spend the three-hour block of time in the anatomy room dissecting coronary arteries. I never miss the M & M conference, but Dr. Bell is away and we won't be discussing our complications or deaths. My time will be more beneficially spent in the lab studying arteries of the heart. Thousands of patients die each year from the blockage of these arteries—blockages that result in myocardial infarctions (heart attacks). Presently, surgery is being performed by taking a segment of vein from the patient's leg and using it to bypass the blocked area in the artery. One end of the vein is sewn into the aorta and the other end is sutured into the artery in the heart carrying blood around the blocked area. I decide the best way to learn the anatomical details of these arteries is to follow them out through an actual preserved heart. I am finishing dissection on the right coronary artery when an intern comes running into the anatomy room.

"Better hurry! A man just came into the E.R. who put a shotgun to his chest and blew out the whole left side." I lay the heart on the dissecting table and quickly follow him out of the room, not taking time to wash the harsh, odorous formalin from my hands. We run down the hall toward the operating room. There is a lot of excitement in the intern's voice—he is almost shouting at me, too excited to give many answers. I nod and keep running.

I enter the operating room without stopping to change into a scrub suit. A man is lying on the operating table with blood pouring out the left side of his chest, onto the table, and pooling on the floor. The anesthesiologist is in the process of putting a tube in his windpipe, and two scrub nurses are hastily opening gowns and instruments.

Immediate-Action Goals

I quickly glance around and realize I am the ranking surgeon in the room, with the responsibility to save this patient. What should I do? I am still in street clothes, standing in the midst of nurses, interns, and residents who are scurrying around trying to get sterile gowns and gloves on. All the while more and more blood pours out of the patient's chest and pools on the floor. I have never been in such a situation before. Thus far nothing in training has taught me what to do with a patient like this. No one in the room has taken any definite steps to alleviate the situation. There is no one here to look to for advice. All I have is my "computer."

"Give me a knife!" One of the scrub nurses hands me a knife, and I make an incision at opposite edges of the gaping hole in the chest in order to give me room enough to get my hand in. Groping through the blood-filled cavity I feel for the hilum of the lung, the area adjacent to the heart where the arteries come out of the heart and enter the lung. The heart is hardly beating as I slide my hand down on the hilum in an attempt to get control of the bleeding. Spreading my two fingers apart, I am able to wedge the larger arteries in between them. I squeeze my fingers together, like closing a pair of scissors; the bleeding stops as if by some magical power. I now have time to evacuate the blood and clot to see what I have. The entire left lung is in bits and pieces.

"Give me the biggest clamp you have."

The nurse hands me a large DeBakey aneurysm clamp. I place it across the area I am holding between my fingers. The bleeding stops completely. The intern and anesthesiologist busily pump un-cross-matched blood into the patient, who by some act of fate is still alive. In less than 60 seconds the situation is under control. Blood is going into his system and none is coming out.

I have a feeling of accomplishment that is indescribable. I have been placed in a live-or-die situation and right now believe the results are going to be successful. Even though I have never even thought about what to do in such a situation, I assessed it correctly and acted accordingly. This has to be one of the peaks in my training.

However, I am only one-tenth finished with the operation that faces me. The patient has not been prepped and has not been draped. I am still in my street clothes, and blood is everywhere. I accept a gown and gloves, and we clean and formally drape the patient. Assessing the situation in the chest, I observe that he has blown most of his left lung out but has caused very little damage to his heart. The remaining bits and pieces of his left lung will have to be removed and a cover has to be made for the big hole the shotgun left in his chest wall. The remainder of the operation proves to be straight-forward; by the time we finish, his blood pressure is stable and it becomes evident that we have saved his life.

After the case, I shower and change into a clean scrub suit that I will wear home, since my clothes are all covered with blood. I sit alone in the dressing room and ask myself questions I've thought about before: Why do so much to save someone who has just tried to kill himself? His last wish was to die and not have to face reality. Now I have denied him a wish so strong that he would put a shotgun to his chest and pull the trigger. The problem that made him pull the trigger will still be there in the morning, plus he will realize that he was a failure even in ending his own life. Will he ever be grateful that he was unsuccessful? These are questions I cannot answer. I suppose he will answer them for me by either trying to kill himself again or thanking me for my efforts.

Dividends

I also reflect back to my initial actions in the operating room. There were other residents and doctors in the emergency room when the patient came in. There were more physicians in the operating room. Yet no definitive action had been taken to stop the bleeding. Could the rule of immediate-action goals have applied here? Is it possible that I have trained my mind to go ahead and act now on the immediate goal of getting the bleeding stopped? Perhaps the *Goals Rule Book* is paying off in important dividends that I do not even realize.

Three weeks later I discharge the patient from the hospital. He is grateful for what I have done, but I don't really know how sincere his gratitude is. Neither do I know if the next suicide attempt will feel any appreciation for my services, but I know I will do everything in my power to give him or her that choice.

I get a few minutes to go over some thoughts on cardiac surgery with a handful of students who are sitting in our on-call room next to the I.C.U. One of them asks about the future of heart surgery. I reply, "As time passes, I become more and more intrigued with the possibilities that await the future of surgery on the heart. It is interesting to read the history of this field and realize how much progress has been made relatively recently. Surgeons and cardiologists alike have been interested for years in getting more blood flow to a heart that is ischemic—one not getting enough blood flow through blocked arteries. As far back as the mid-thirties, attempts were made to bring the 'fatty apron,' the omentum, out of the abdomen and sew it against the outside of the heart muscle in hope that some of the blood supply of the omentum would creep across and also supply the heart muscle. I learned that in the mid-forties an artery in the chest was 'tunneled' into the diseased heart muscle and actually improved the symptoms in a significant number of patients. However, the most interesting aspect of this new field began in 1958 with the introduction of actually injecting dye into the arteries of the heart and taking motion pictures with X-ray film in order to visualize blocks in the arteries to see which of the three main arteries of the heart needed to be carrying more blood. This technique opened the door to a new field of surgery on the heart.

"If you obtain a heart from the anatomy department and complete the dissection of the coronary arteries, you can correlate what you actually see in the inner walls with what you read concerning the disease process that goes on inside these arteries. They are being choked with plaques that leave the inner linings looking much like a clogged-up drainage pipe. The difference in appearance of the arteries and the pipe is mainly that the lining of the arteries is firm and covered with a smooth layer of tissue. However, the end result of both is the same—plugging the opening and preventing any flow through the pipe or artery.

"These patients with partially or completely blocked vessels usually exhibit the symptoms of angina pectoris—a squeezing, pressure-like chest pain that is commonly described as a tightness or pressing sensation felt behind the sternum. It is usually not well localized and can radiate to other portions of the body, mainly the left shoulder or down the left arm. This pain is brought on when the patient exerts himself and can usually be relieved by having the patient stop and rest.

"Some of these patients can benefit from a better supply of blood to the heart, past the area of blockage in the artery. After a patient has been studied by the dye injected in his arteries and does become a candidate for surgery, a vein can be removed from his leg and one end sewn into the aorta, and the other end sewn into the artery in the heart, at a site past the blockage."

The discussions with the students completed, I am reminded that we have a coronary bypass patient being admitted today. He has already been studied extensively by the cardiologists and has been referred to us for coronary artery bypass.

"Why don't all of you go by the lab and see what his studies show?"

Doctor Versus Mechanic

Joe Howard is the patient, and I find that he has "three-vessel disease." Each of the three main arteries in his heart is blocked to some degree, meaning that the operation will be more of a risk and more difficult to perform, and that the chances of a "cure" are less than if he had only one vessel partially blocked, with the other two branches open. Dr. Bell tells me the prognosis is even worse in Joe's case because his heart function is so borderline; it stopped beating on the cardiac catheterization table when the dye was injected into the coronary arteries during the coronary arteriograms. His heart is so starved for blood that the few moments the dye was mixed with the blood going to the heart was enough to make his heart stop beating—a very unusual event.

I walk into Joe's room and introduce myself. Joe is slightly obese, 44 years old, and covered with black hair, literally, from head to toe. He has so much hair on his chest that it looks as if he has on a black wool sweater as he removes his shirt for me to examine him. His wife is with him.

"I saw Dr. Billings and told him I am going to will my body for his students to cut on if I don't make it." He greets me with this statement straightforwardly and in all sincerity. Dr. Billings is the head of the anatomy department in the medical school and is a close friend of Joe's, and evidently Joe has discussed the possibility of donating his body to the school. Both Joe and his wife seem to sense the possibility of death more than any other patient I have ever taken care of.

"Well, we certainly won't think along those lines, Joe. Besides, you have too nice a wife to even be thinking such thoughts." Joe's wife is a very pretty woman with olive skin who wears her silky black hair tied at the back of her head. She is a "young" 38 and seems the epitome of sophistication sitting in the red vinyl stuffed chair beside Joe's bed.

Seeds of Doubt

"My chances aren't so good, are they, Doc?"

I attempt to imagine what it is like to be in Joe's place as he speaks to me. His chances aren't so good and he is intelligent enough to realize this. There is to be no small talk with him. He knows the name of the game and knows the cards he is holding. He has been dealt a bum hand. If I were in his shoes, could I talk about the possibility of death as freely as Joe? Could I really admit the fact that the odds were stacked high against me? Some people in a similar situation talk this way just to get the doctor to give them words of encouragement, but I sense that Joe is talking because this actually is on his mind—just as he is spilling it out to me.

"Joe, I am sure the operation and the risks of the surgery have been discussed with you in detail by Dr. Bell. He will be with us on evening rounds. He'll discuss that with you."

I am still uneasy discussing the risk of surgery with a patient as frank and straightforward as Joe, and I elect to take the easy way out and refer such discussions to Dr. Bell. I acknowledge to myself that before my training is complete, I will need to be able to discuss all possible complications following surgery. I must learn more than just how to perform operations.

Day One: The day for the operation arrives, and all of Joe's questions will soon be answered. I assist Dr. Bell in the operation. I make an incision in Joe's right leg and start removing the vein we will use in the bypass portion of the procedure. While doing this, Dr. Bell splits the sternum and opens the pericardial sac surrounding the heart in preparation for the bypass. Dr. Bell takes the vein I have removed, cuts it into three segments, and meticulously sews each segment into the aorta and into each of the coronary arteries. Soon there is good flow to the vessels of the heart. The operation is completed, and tubes are placed through the chest wall and into the operative area in order to drain the oozing blood that will follow surgery. Joe is taken to the recovery room for three hours and then taken to the intensive care unit. He has just survived the most critical early postoperative hours. He goes through the night with no unusual occurrences. His wife, still wearing a black dress, remains all night waiting patiently outside the unit.

Day Two: We are all pleased that Joe has come through so well. One thing bothers us, though. All of his studies are borderline normal. He is slow coming around, doesn't want to eat, doesn't want to get out of bed, doesn't want to talk to anyone, will not laugh; all in all, he has become a number-one grouch.

Day Three: Status quo.

Day Four: Joe begins developing some lung complications.

Day Five: It becomes evident by evening that Joe has pneumonia and is having difficulty keeping his oxygen saturation within a normal limit. The intern and I discuss Joe's complications as I glance rather methodically at the cardiac monitor at the foot of Joe's bed. The monitor is running 24 hours a day, and it is my habit to examine the squiggling lines as they race across the screen. Very seldom do I actually witness a significant change in the rhythm of the heart on the monitor, but I realize it is presently changing before my eyes. *Right now* something is happening to Joe's heart. Ventricular fibrillation! The ventricles are only quivering ineffectively and give a cardiac tracing on the monitor as if a nervous individual were trying to draw a straight line. We immediately begin resuscitation, including external cardiac massage. A piece of plywood is placed under Joe's back for support, and I put the heel of my hands on his sternum and begin pushing. Each time I push the sternum down, it is pushed against the heart and the grafts. I am sure each trauma can clot them off or even tear them loose.

The heart is shocked electrically and a breathing tube is placed into his windpipe. We get Joe back to a regular rhythm, but I have no idea what damage has been done to the vein grafts as a result of all the pounding during closed chest massage. At least he is still alive and now back to a regular rhythm. A successful outcome will be long in coming.

Real Life

I walk out to the waiting room to tell Joe's wife what has happened. She is sitting in the lounge with a light blanket pulled around her legs. She has been able to catch a few catnaps earlier in the night but is reading a book as I approach. I had talked her into going to a friend's house last night in order to get some sleep, but she insisted, for some reason, on staying at the hospital this particular evening. She also insists on wearing a black dress. I'm not sure what this does for Joe's morale, but I wish she would wear something red, or blue, or anything but these black dresses. She looks startled and apprehensive as I approach her. She did not hear the ever-dreadful "Code 500, intensive care unit; Code 500" which the relatives of patients in I.C.U. find out means that something drastic is happening and all available doctors in the hospital are to report to the unit. There was no such call in this instance, since we were at Joe's bed at the time of fibrillation and there was no need for further help. Joe's wife is sure she would have heard such a page if anything had happened to him. This only makes it more difficult to explain that something has happened to her husband.

"I'm sorry to have to tell you, but Joe has had a setback. His heart quit beating momentarily, and we had to give him external massage and place him on a respirator. He is holding his own now, but I am not sure where this is going to lead us. We will continue to do everything possible for him and hope for the best." She does not rise as I tell her of the situation; she only nods and stares at the floor.

"I'll be all right. I would like to be left alone right now." She continues to stare at the floor. I feel awkward as I stand over her. I want to say more, to tell her he is alive and we have that to be thankful for; that she will be able to go in and see him in a few minutes and actually talk to him; that this doesn't mean that he is going to die—that he still has a chance to make it. But there is a "sense" in the air that she will not accept any of these statements, that she knows his odds of living now have just dropped from 40 percent to 10 percent, that there is no use kidding herself about what had just happened.

"You can come in and see him," I say as I turn and walk back toward the unit. Her mood is so thick I feel almost reverent as I leave her sitting by herself. I stay by Joe's bed for the remainder of the night. She never comes to see him while I am there.

Day Six: Joe continues to slide downhill.

Day Seven: I do a tracheostomy in order to suction the secretions from Joe's lungs and try to get at his pneumonia.

Day Ten: Joe is still alive, but vascular status is unstable.

Day Fifteen: Persistent pneumonia requiring therapeutic bronchoscopy four times per day.

Day Eighteen: Pneumonia worse. Blood gases inadequate for survival. On respirator.

Day Twenty-one: Worse.

Day Twenty-three: Joe dies.

I talk with Joe's wife. We have come to know each other in a unique way during these 23 days. Yes, she will permit an autopsy to be performed—if for no other reason than to let us know what went wrong. Yes, she still wants his body to go to the anatomy department. Joe wanted it that way. No, she never thought he would live through the operation; in her mind he died 23 days ago. She will grieve her husband's death and will find it difficult to explain to her children. She thanks me for my consideration, for keeping her informed of what was going on. I finally understand why she always wore the black dresses—she was mourning her husband from the time he came into the hospital.

I never see her again but think of her from time to time over the next few days whenever I see an attractive young woman wearing a black dress. On such occasions I have to keep my mind from wandering back into the thoughts of the losing battle of those 23 days with Joe.

Three weeks later I have all but forgotten Joe Howard as I stroll through the anatomy lab. One of the students recognizes me and yells across the room, "Say, you ought to remember this one. You all did him in, didn't you?" He jokingly motions me toward his table. I glance his way and recognize the hairy body on the dissecting table. They are dissecting Joe's right leg. There is one vein missing, but I don't feel like explaining to them why it isn't there, that it was removed in a futile operation. I don't feel like explaining anything to them, not even why I am ignoring his comment and walking out of the lab.

20

The Quick and the Dead

As a young surgeon I wondered why some people lived and why some died, why some remained sick and why others were healed. I questioned why God would allow certain Christians to be healed and not others. I did not understand God's ways, nor could I begin to explain them. Many years later, these questions drove me to search the Scriptures for a possible answer regarding the way the Lord works.

Some people in the Christian faith believe in miraculous healing. Others believe that such healing took place only in the days when Jesus was on earth, and that today God uses medicine and physicians to effect healing. My questions didn't inquire about the patients who got well, but rather, those who were not healed—those who died.

One day a lady patient of mine who had cancer in her liver called the elders of her church to pray for her healing. I knew her cancer had spread throughout her abdomen and was progressively worsening even though she was on all the best chemotherapeutic agents available. I knew that her type of cancer would eventually quit responding to treatment. Her time to leave this earth was near. Her husband and children loved her very much and did not want to lose her. Fortunately, she was a committed Christian. She had faith in God and knew Jesus Christ as her Savior.

I will never forget the day she lay on my examining table, telling me about the visit by the elders of her church and the healing service they conducted. Her husband and two daughters had been present and witnessed their prayers. They believed in the Bible as God's Word and really thought she was going to be healed. When she died less than two months later, I could not help but ask myself, "What will her death do to the faith of her husband and daughters?"

I knew that God did not make mistakes, so I began to search His Word for answers. Why do not all Christians recover from their illnesses? Why do Christians need medicine? Why did this patient die? She asked in faith for God to remove her affliction. Why had He not done so?

I searched. I read of the miraculous healings Jesus performed—of blind people seeing, of lame people walking, of deaf people hearing, even of dead people being resurrected. All of that I found, but it was not what I was looking for.

Then I began to read about the apostle Paul's physical afflic-tion—a "thorn in the flesh" he called it. He asked that the Lord heal him. The Lord did not. As I read on, I saw that Paul asked a second time, but was not healed then either. This related to my question; this was my patient's situation. Like Paul, she had asked to be healed but was not. Paul even asked a third time, to no avail.

In 2 Corinthians 12:8,9 I finally found the answer I had been looking for: "Three times I pleaded with the Lord to take it away from me," Paul relates. "But he said to me, 'My grace is sufficient for you, for my power is made perfect in weakness.'"

Why don't all Christians recover from their illnesses? Why do some have to endure thorns in their sides? Why do some die? God's grace is sufficient for all our needs; we must put our complete faith in this fact.

I still do not understand why some people are healed and others are not. But I do realize that God uses a third form of healing today—the kind that He used with Paul. God's third type of healing is called, "My grace is sufficient."

I go by the office to pick up the consultation sheets from the med-icine department. I pull out the familiar blue slips marked "C-T Surgery." There are more than the usual amount for one day.

Looking at the consultation sheets I see a pediatric heart patient, a lung abscess, a carcinoma of the lung, and one sheet on a Mr. McLaughlin, who has a bad aortic valve in his heart. It says he may need an emergency valve replacement.

They've done it again. Mr. McLaughlin needed his valve replaced a year ago, and they treated him medically for so long that we are going to have to do it with him half-dead. They didn't even call me about him, but sent a blue slip to be picked up when I got around to it; I'd better go see him.

Mr. McLaughlin is dying. There is no way to save him by oper-ating on him. I'll present him to Dr. Bell. I know he will operate as a last-ditch effort, for not one patient in 20 survives under these conditions. If we spend just ten hours at the operating table on these extreme-risk patients, that would amount to 200 man-hours of surgery alone in order to possibly save one patient. Not only that, but ten times that amount of time is spent after the operation trying to keep such patients alive, but they still die. Two years earlier Mr. McLaughlin would have been a straightforward case and have been out of the hospital in ten days.

Still, we owe our best to each patient. We are not mechanics who can pick and choose the job wanted, but we are morally obliged to give this patient his one chance in 20 of surviving. This is Dr. Bell's philosophy, which results in his spending a significant amount of time on extremely poor-risk patients like Mr. McLaughlin.

One in Twenty

We cut. Six hours later we cannot get Mr. McLaughlin off the pump. His heart will not take over. He is dead. I angrily blame the medicine department for not referring him to us sooner, but Dr. Bell informs me that Mr. McLaughlin refused surgery for six months. It was his own decision.

There is little to do this afternoon since our patient died on the table. I look forward to not having the strain of keeping a close check on a post-op patient for a change. At that moment, a resident from the O.B. department pages me. Like a light switch going on, I know what is happening: Harriet must be in labor. I answer the page.

"Your wife is here and having good contractions. Dr. Ellison wants to know if you still want her to have epidural spinal anesthesia."

"That's what she said she wanted. Go ahead and start it. I'll be right over." Boy, this is exciting! I can't believe that Harriet is actually going to deliver in the daytime and at a time when I am not so busy that I cannot be with her.

The epidural is already in when I arrive in her labor room. She looks relaxed and flashes a big smile for me.

I gently rub her abdomen. "What are we going to have?"

"We'll know as soon as a few more of these contractions come, and I don't think it will be long."

Dr. Ellison comes in. He is a big man, authoritative. "Do you want to watch your little wife put this baby out?"

"No, sir. I'll just wait and let you tell me what it is and how it went."

I go out to the desk and wait while they take Harriet into the delivery room. I just hope nothing goes wrong. I pick up a pencil and make some dots on the paper on the desk. Then I try to place the point of the pencil exactly on each dot, just to prove to myself that my hands are not shaky, that I am staying calm. Some of the dots are difficult to hit.

"Girl. Both did well. Congratulations." Dr. Ellison is off to another patient.

Father of two! Harriet did well. Her name is Patricia. Harriet named her when she first became pregnant. I wonder how she knew we would have a girl.

The night brings good sleep. Patricia. It feels good going to sleep thinking about a little baby two floors up named Patricia.

Expensive Goals

I get a decent night's sleep and awaken early to begin the routine once more. We have another heart to do today. It doesn't take long to forget about patients we have lost a few hours ago and get back into the swing of operations all day long. It is more difficult to forget about Harriet and Patricia, but I force myself to think into the future—not a year from now, not a week, but only a few hours. A slight smile creeps onto my face as I think back to one of the rules I made as an intern. One stitch at a time. It works—this residency is passing one day at a time, but it will be over someday. The major goal will be reached, not in one day but in successfully completing one immediate-action goal after another. Everything is about to fall into place, and it's the greatest feeling in the world.

Today's heart case goes well, and the post-op care isn't as time-consuming as most cases. However, a late, leaking aneurysm keeps us up the best part of the night.

I check on Harriet before retiring for the night. She gets to go home in the morning. Bob and I retire to our "suite" for a coffee break. I am not sure what causes moods to change, but, for some reason, after working all day and into the night, there is something almost mystical about opening the window and letting in the cool night air. I relax on the bed and Bob stretches out on some cushions on the floor.

I manage to get four hours of uninterrupted sleep, while Bob ends up with three frequently interrupted hours. All in all, it is a fairly easy night for the two of us; we accumulate seven hours of sleep between us.

Today turns out to be fairly quiet, and we finish evening rounds at seven. I feel almost as if I were on vacation. Everything is stable at the hospital, we have an easy case scheduled tomorrow, and there is a dependable intern on call tonight. Bob and I both decide to go home for the night.

Peace in the Heart

Harriet is glad to see me. My son Ben greets me at the door and, with wild excitement, explains to me that he has a new baby sister. It feels good to be home with all the family. For the first time in a long while, we spend a leisurely and relaxed evening at home with no calls from the hospital.

As the residency progresses, time loses its meaning and value. I realize I have slowly lost the concept of morning and night. Most people think of going to work in the morning and coming home at night. Even days of the week are lost from the important pages of my mind. I am aware of this time change in my life and wonder if I will ever be able to rearrange my living pattern once residency is completed. The only day that is at all different from any of the rest is Thursday—the day we put in cardiac pacemakers. I look forward to Thursdays, mainly because it is a change. I feel I am doing a tremendous service to those patients whose hearts aren't beating at a normal rate, and the procedure is not nearly as time-consuming or mentally taxing as operating on a heart.

Pacemaker Day

Today is slack, with only one pacemaker, and I decide to give a short lecture to the students on our service. We gather in the corner of the diagnostic study room, which is used for putting in the pacemaker. I try to keep my talk informal as I begin to tell about the patients who receive pacemakers.

"Most of the patients have pure, single blockage of the small fibers that carry the impulse through the heart that causes it to beat. This blockage is a significant cause of death in the elderly, estimated to be 12,000–13,000 new cases each year in the United States. Thousands of these patients have benefited from the cardiac pacemaker. The idea is simple, and the operation to implant a pacemaker is relatively easy. Normally there is an area in the atrium of the heart that acts as a transmitter for a small electrical impulse to originate. This impulse travels through a system of fibers from the atrium to the ventricle, causing the ventricle to contract each time it is 'shocked,' or stimulated, by the impulse. The ventricle, in turn, reacts by squeezing blood out of its chamber and thus causes a 'beat' of the heart. This happens, on the average, 72 times a minute in a normal, resting individual. Now that's how it's supposed to work." The students listen intently. There is no notetaking; they will not be given a test on what I am telling them. This is for their own general knowledge of medicine.

"If you take the patient we just operated on, you will see a different picture. The aging process affected his network of conducting fibers and caused them to become scarred and impaired in the duty of carrying the impulse from the atrium to the ventricle. When this happens, theoretically the ventricle should quit beating since there is nothing there to stimulate it; but as with so many other vital systems in the body, there is a backup system that takes over when the primary one fails. The ventricle begins to beat on its own 'emergency transmitter' at the rate of about 40 beats per minute. This rate is fixed and will not increase as the patient exercises or places an increased load on the heart. Such a patient usually has blackout spells due to the fact that not enough blood is being carried to the brain. In the days before artificial pacemakers, the majority of such patients died." I conclude the short lecture on the "blocked heart" and begin to explain the role of the pacemaker.

"The cardiac pacemaker acts as an artificial transmitting station and consists of two basic parts: the transmitter and the electrodes. The transmitter is a compact unit of stored electrical energy in the form of a battery. An impulse is fired by the transmitter and carried through wires that are connected to the ventricle in some fashion. The wires are electrodes. These electrodes can be carried to the outside of the ventricle, causing a contraction and thus a beat of the heart. The rate of the pacemaker can be set to a predetermined number of impulses per minute.

"As far as actual extension of years in active life, the cardiac pacemaker has probably played a larger role than any other form of surgery related to the heart. There is not nearly the excitement of replacing a heart valve, but the pacemaker implant operation is significant." I finish the short lecture, and we start for the X-ray department to view some recent films on our patients. I realize that I am actually going to make it home again to eat with my family tonight, unless we find something unusual on rounds.

Spontaneous Initiative

Two interns rotate onto the service this month. I dislike the first of the month because the new interns know nothing about our special routine for taking care of post-op heart patients. Not all of the interns have goals set to include the rough month of our service. They just want the month to pass. However, by the end of the month, most know how to take care of the patients so well that I hate for them to leave. This month one of the interns who has just started with us has no hope whatsoever of learning how to do *anything* right. John is on every other night, and when he is on, Bob and I end up with much more work to do because he can't get the job done. John is on call with us tonight, and as soon as we finish rounds, he sits down and lights up a cigarette. Sometimes I feel like taking interns like John aside and explaining to them that, unless they change, they will always be at the bottom of the heap in everything they do. If I could force the goals book on them, I would, but they wouldn't have the initiative it takes to read it.

"John, get an X ray on Mrs. Blum in I.C.U. Bob and I have to start the case in the O.R. and will be tied up for a while. Come down and let us know what the film shows. There hasn't been much blood through the chest tubes, and I want to make sure she isn't pooling it in her chest." I explain as clearly as possible what I want John to do and why it is important for him to do it.

The usual practice on making rounds is for the intern to write down everything the chief resident wants ordered on each patient. Then, following rounds, the intern does the scut work and reports if anything is abnormal. Good interns take the responsibility of making sure everything on the list is cared for; but unfortunately there were some interns who, if they hit a snag, they simply didn't bother to finish the task. John is one of these; he does not take responsibility for getting things done. I predict to Bob that the X ray will not be done when we finish in the O.R. He doesn't understand "do it now, get it done."

Three hours into the evening, Bob and I have just finished our case and walk into I.C.U. John is standing by the patient I placed a mitral valve in earlier, the patient I asked him to get an X ray on.

"What did Mrs. Blum's X ray show?" I ask.

"I haven't gotten the X ray yet."

"For what reason?"

"They have been too busy taking emergencies."

An Excuse and a Reason

"That…is an excuse, not a reason. I bet you don't know the difference between an excuse and a reason. The excuse is that the X ray isn't done because you haven't made it your job to get it done—one way or another." I feel my face flush as my temper rises. The whole problem is a matter of immediate-action goals. John doesn't understand what "action right now" means. It is too late to teach him now. The bad part is that he doesn't realize his dilemma. He wouldn't recognize what a goal was if it hit him in the face.

If there is one thing I cannot stand, it is finding out that something didn't get done by someone who had the responsibility to take care of it. Even worse is hearing that person blame it on someone else and say, "They haven't done it," instead of, "I haven't stayed on their backs enough to get it done."

Bob, John, and I walk into the X-ray department to find several patients lying on stretchers waiting to have X rays taken. I ask about the backlog, and find there are two new technicians on call and they are running at least 30 minutes behind. It is as hopeless to ask one of them to bring a portable machine upstairs to take Mrs. Blum's X ray as it was to tell John to make sure the film was taken.

"Could I borrow you for just a minute?" I motion one of the girls toward the portable unit. "Write on this paper the settings for a portable film with a patient in a sitting position and at what distance from the patient I should put the machine." If no one else can take the film, I will do it myself—that is, if the technician will go along with my plan.

"You can't take this machine. Besides, we would have to make out the name tags and request forms for the patient, and I am really too busy to do that right now. If you will wait ten minutes, I'll come up and take the film for you."

I turn and direct my question to John. "When you made your request three hours ago, how long did she say she would be?"

"Ten minutes," he replies. At least he knows how to answer correctly.

Turning back to the technician, I see her pick up a pad and begin writing the instructions to take a portable chest film. "Here are the numbers. Be sure to center it so nothing is hanging over the edges. Destroy the film when you get through because there will not be a name on it and I will get in trouble if they find out an X ray was taken without proper identification on it." She then marches away, muttering to herself about her new job and pushy doctors.

I think I am getting the point through to John because when we roll the X-ray unit into I.C.U. he asks to see the list of instructions for taking the film. He neatly copies them on a wide piece of adhesive tape and affixes the tape inside the cabinet door in I.C.U.: "Instructions on how to take chest film when they are too busy in X ray."

Mediocrity

The X-ray shows no blood in Mrs. Blum's chest. It has taken me an extra 20 minutes to teach John the meaning of small responsibilities and how to handle immediate-action goals. Whether my efforts will ever be profitable to him in the future, I don't know. In John's case, I doubt it. Trying to teach an individual who has no goals is like trying to cut with a knife that has no blade. There will always be people like John who will never need or want a *Goals Rule Book*. These people are satisfied with what they have. They set no goals, will rarely do what they are told to do, never do more than is expected of them, and feel cheated if they don't get paid for any extra work they perform. John is one of these people. But because there are so many Johns in the world, *everyone* who takes it upon himself to work on goals will be successful. I'll bet at least 90 percent of people are just like John, with no known goals in life. If that is true, it means that only ten percent are really striving to get ahead. Simple deduction is all I need to conclude that anyone who decides to set goals and jump into this ten-percent group will become successful. Even if he falls to the bottom of the ten-percent pile, he will still be ahead of 90 percent of everyone else.

I pull out my well-worn *Goals Rule Book* from my pocket and write on the last page: "The 90-Percent Rule: No goals, no competition. Remember the Johns in life. Set goals and join the top ten percent."

21

From Rules to Habits

THE WELL-WORN PATH FROM THE RIVER to my grandfather's house followed alongside the creek. Years of use had made it a trench about a foot deeper than the ground beside the creek. With my cousins, I would walk that path at night. It was easy to keep on the path because, any time I wandered from it, I knew instantly that I was out of its groove.

My medical training was almost over; I had formulated many rules for myself as I moved toward becoming a surgeon. They were necessary rules that I had to keep in order to reach the goal of my professional career. Those rules were quite difficult to practice initially, when I began that first day of medical school. As time progressed, however, it was as if I had gotten onto a small path—the longer I adhered to the right rules, the more deeply worn that path became.

Many times I had slipped off the path, only to realize that I was out of the groove that led toward my goal. Then I would correct my steps. As the path wore deeper and deeper, my rules changed into habits. I was so firmly fixed on the grooved path that led to becoming a surgeon that all my waking time was devoted to that way of life.

Not too long after I completed surgical training, I realized something about God's will for our lives. It too is a path similar to the one by my childhood creek, similar to the one I walked during surgical training. God has a plan for my life; all I need to do is find it and stick to it.

As a medical student I had wondered what a liver, a spleen, intestines, a gallbladder, and the stomach looked like. One day we split open the abdomen of that cadaver and I saw them. Each of those organs was plainly exposed. They all were revealed in that instant. Never again did I question what those organs looked like.

God's will for my life has not unfolded to me like those organs in anatomy class. God's will has not been opened up and revealed to me in one session. Rather, He shows it to me a little at a time, day by day. It is like a path—the more I walk in His will, the more I know His will.

Many times I get out of His will, then realize that my life is not right. Once again, I return to the groove of God's plan. As I spend more time within His will, His way becomes habitual for me. Sometimes it is difficult to take a stand for God when friends see the situation from another perspective. After the initial decision to take that stand, though, it becomes easier to maintain it. The path deepens and our actions evolve into habits. God's will gradually becomes a heavenly habit.

When I was volunteering at a mission hospital in Nepal, I would rise before dawn. At first only a hint of light would emanate from behind the mountains. Then, slowly, the edges of the mountaintops could be seen. As morning progressed, the mountains came alive. First, dark purple covered the magnificent hillsides, then the snowcaps became visible; finally the brightness of the sun showed the mountains in all their splendor.

God's will for us is like that. It emerges gradually, increasingly, progressively.

> The path of the righteous is like the first gleam of dawn,
> shining ever brighter till the full light of day (Proverbs 4:18).

I want to walk that path of the righteous—in the center of God's will, habitually obeying Him—all day long. I know it's the best course to choose.

My time as chief resident is drawing to a close. In only a few more months I will no longer be a resident. Much has transpired since that first day in medical school, when I sat at my desk thinking about a structure to develop in order to get through school and become a surgeon. The framework of goals I have developed since that day has made big changes in my life. Almost every action I make now is made from habit. I have been able to change my life, to control my life by making habits. The rules have slowly changed into habits; repetition of the rules has led to automatic habits. No longer do I have to refer back to my rules. They have become so imprinted in my mind that I react automatically. That is the link that joins it all together: Set the major goal, make your rules, and persist in them until they become habit.

Life-and-Death Issues

I awaken to the fact that I need to go to the pediatric ward to see Greg Wilson, our next open-heart case. Greg is five years old and is being admitted for a workup of congenital aortic stenosis, a tightness of one of the heart valves since birth. The workup entails cardiac catheterization and injecting some dye into the heart in an attempt to determine just how tight the valve is.

Greg is too young to have the valve excised and an artificial one put in place; we will have to try to open his congenitally small valve and make it function a few more years until his heart grows large enough to accept an artificial valve.

Greg sits on the floor playing with some toys when I walk in to examine him. This is an exceptionally difficult case for me to work on because I know Greg's father and mother from our church. Greg and my son are in the same Sunday school class. This will be the first time I will have ever operated on anyone I know personally. We are not close friends, but I know the family and have empathy for what they are about to go through. I question Greg's mother about his symptoms.

"He hasn't really been sick," she tells me. "He does get short of breath if he plays hard, but the heart medicine he takes pretty well keeps him out of trouble."

Greg glances up at me and smiles. At his age he can enjoy the blessed innocence concerning worry of everyday happenings; to him, life-and-death operations are incomprehensible. Mr. Wilson and I have talked about Greg's upcoming operation on several occasions—how it will not be a very long procedure, how Greg will have to be placed on the heart-lung pump only long enough to open the aortic valve. His operation would not be much of an operation at all relative to other heart surgeries. His case sounds very simple and straightforward, but we both are aware that any time the heart is operated on, numerous events can occur that potentially could prove fatal. The chances of such events are slim, but ever-present.

"Greg, slip your shirt off and let me listen to your heart." He is a well-mannered boy who immediately pulls his shirt off over his head and comes over to where I can examine him. I place my hand on his sternum and feel a fine vibration with each beat of his heart, indicating a turbulence of blood flow as it passes through the valve. Placing my stethoscope over the region of the aortic valve, I hear the harsh sound of blood being forcefully ejected through an opening in a valve that should be large enough to accept the end of the index finger. As I listen, I picture the small, contracted hole, only a fraction as large as it should be. I hope this will be a case in which the noise the blood makes as it crosses the constricted valve is relatively louder than the severity of the tightness of the valve.

Greg undergoes cardiac catheterization and the results are disheartening. The opening in the valve is minute compared to what it should be. He goes home to await his surgery, which is planned for June.

Greg is allowed to visit his grandparents the weekend before coming back into the hospital and enjoys an early birthday party with them. Little Greg and his teddy bear are equally unaware of all that is taking place. It is senseless to try to explain the danger he is about to face: how much pain he will have after the operation; the tubes coming out of his chest; the tubes in the veins in his neck and arms; the wires and gadgets connected to his body to record his heartbeat; the tube in his bladder to measure the hourly output of urine; or the doctors and nurses constantly around him checking for any postoperative abnormalities. To tell Greg about all this would only scare him, although we do show him the intensive-care unit in which he will be placed after leaving the recovery room. Perhaps this will alleviate some of the fear he will be required to face all alone.

He is the same age as my son. I cannot get this thought out of my mind. Why should a boy this young have to suffer anything so painful and stressful as a heart operation? I have to force myself not to get involved with the unanswerable questions concerning this case. I am a surgeon, not a philosopher; the more time I spend philosophizing, the less time I have to prepare for the operation.

Unwanted Responsibility

We start the case at 7:00 A.M. and everything goes well. We place a tube into the femoral artery in Greg's leg and another into the veins going into the heart, then connect them to the heart-lung machine in order to make a closed circuit between Greg and the machine.

"Let's go on." The familiar words instruct the technician to start the pump to begin the blood flowing out of the right atrium and into the heart-lung machine in order for oxygenation to be accomplished. The pump is started and begins to "push" the blood back into the body via the femoral artery. A clamp is placed across the aorta near the malformed valve to keep blood from flooding the operative field once the aorta is opened. An incision is made in the aorta and the valve inspected.

"Look at that valve!" Dr. Bell shakes his head in disbelief. The valve area has no resemblance to an aortic valve, but looks like a clump of smooth, shining tissue resembling Silly Putty. It has no shape or form. Usually there are three cusps, or cups, making up the aortic valve, and all that needs to be done is to cut between each cup to increase the diameter of the opening. "I don't know if we are going to be able to do much to this valve. It has the look of one you would expect to see at an autopsy in an infant who died from aortic stenosis. That's no valve. It's just embryonic tissues clumped together. I don't see how he has lived this long." Dr. Bell is amazed that the heart could have used this "valve" for any purposeful effect.

We examine the valve closer and, since there are no identifiable cusps, decide to make a two-leafed valve out of it by placing two small incisions opposite each other. We are walking a tightrope with this boy's life and everything has to go 100 percent correctly or we will surely lose him.

We make the incisions in the valve.

Close the aorta.

Release the clamp on the aorta.

Begin to slow the pump in order to let the heart take over and pump more of the blood on its own.

"Let's go off." The pump is stopped and Greg's heart takes over perfectly. "Pump time" has been nine minutes—not bad, considering the fact that we had to alter the routine of incising the valve and decide exactly where and how to incise.

Dr. Bell drops out of the case since everything is stable and goes to explain to the parents what we found and what has been done. A future operation will be needed because the valve will have to be replaced as soon as the heart grows large enough to accept an artificial valve. It isn't good news, but at least we have done enough to keep Greg's heart going until that time comes for another operation.

Something Goes Wrong

We take Greg to the recovery room and begin the all-important postoperative monitoring. The first 30 minutes go well, but all of a sudden the cardiac monitor shows something irregular, more irregular—ventricular fibrillation. The heart only quivers and loses all effectiveness in beating. I immediately begin external massage as Dr. Bell gives orders to get the pump ready immediately. I crawl up on Greg's bed and continue the massage as we roll him back to the O.R. The incision is quickly reopened and we work frantically to place Greg back on the pump. We operate for two hours, knowing all the time that fate is against us. With a valve like this one in his heart, and the ventricle fibrillating, the chance of pulling him through is almost nil. A lump comes to my throat as we repeatedly fail to get him off the pump. I cannot talk. My eyes are watery as I stare at the dying heart. I feel helpless. We are doing everything we know to do, but still we cannot make Greg's heart beat again. I desperately try to think of something to do that may pull him through. I know Dr. Bell is rerunning every conceivable thought through his mind that may produce an answer as how to get the heart to work again.

God, You can't let this happen. Why don't You do something? Can't You understand we're losing him? We're losing Greg! I half-pray and half-think to myself. I become deaf to all the talking around me. Dr. Bell gives further instructions and we follow through with them, but nothing registers in my mind. We have lost him. We try to get him off the pump a few more times, but each time his heart is not strong enough to take over.

Why are we operating so long this time? Dr. Bell knows, and I know, that our chances of getting Greg back sank to less than one percent after the first 30 minutes lapsed and his heart continued deteriorating. By all logic, we both are convinced that all hope is gone; yet I can visualize Greg's heart coming back on its own and beating without the aid of the pump, can visualize Greg's parents being told that everything is all right, and that Greg is going to make it. Still, these thoughts can only be fantasy, but for us to give up is to end the life of a child. Only when that one percent of hope is exhausted will Dr. Bell give the order. Only then will we have paid our debt to death in our minds.

"Turn the pump off." It is all over. We have failed to get the heart going again. Dr. Bell says he will speak to the family. I start closing the chest. This time there is no pulsating heart pounding under the incision, no need to worry about making sure all vessels are tied off to control bleeding. Nothing matters now. Greg is no longer with us.

His body is still there, but Greg isn't. How do you explain death to a mother and father when you don't understand it yourself?

A strange quietness falls over the room, with no one saying a word. The anesthesiologist is busy gathering his equipment. He isn't needed for the closure of the wound this time. A scrub nurse stays and passes suture as I need it, but no words are exchanged. A plastic bag is brought in for the body. I finish closing the skin, remove my gloves, and head for the on-call room to be alone.

Some Answers Aren't Privileged

I sit on the left side of the bed and stare at a blank wall. The only word I can think of is: *Why?* For one hour I sit with an occasional tear running down my face. High school—yes, that was the last time I cried, and I can't even remember the reason now. It was so insignificant that I can't even remember why. But this is so different. Now I play the game of life and death with humans. I lie back on the bed and close my eyes. All I can see is that valve. *Embryonic valve,* I keep thinking. "Never saw anyone live this long with a valve like that," Dr. Bell had said. I remember his saying just that. I open my eyes. Maybe Greg should have died as an infant, or even before. Maybe Greg's parents had a few years of happiness with him when by all facts and figures he should have died sooner. I try to reason, but cannot. All I know is that Greg Wilson was playing with some early birthday toys yesterday, but now he will never play with those toys again.

I hear my name being paged for Dr. Bell's office. I elect to talk with him in person rather than over the phone.

Dr. Bell is sitting at his desk as I enter. He straightens a few misaligned papers on his desk and reclines back in his chair, as if getting ready to speak. His chin is propped between his thumb and forefinger and he focuses on the corner of his desk as I've seen him do so often when he starts to talk about a serious matter.

"There is one thing you cannot do in surgery—if you have done the best you can—and that is to blame yourself for the death of a patient. You did your best; I did my best. Greg's valve was so borderline that it couldn't take the added strain of an operation, especially one that didn't really help the dynamics of the heart all that much." Dr. Bell realizes the mental beating I have taken since the operation. He has been there before and is much the wiser for it.

I still cannot speak, only listen. He continues, "You have rounds to make, X rays to see, patients to care for, and interns to give instructions to. It is best you get back to work. We will get together in the morning and rehash the case to see if there was something we could have done differently."

Near Breakdown

I nod in the affirmative and leave his office. I am sick of going over deaths to see what could have been done differently. I am tired of M & M conferences. I don't want to discuss deaths and complications. I don't want to look at X rays. I don't want to follow any of the crazy rules I have set up for myself concerning pushing on, going the extra mile, getting it done. Right now, all is futile. The whole rotten structure of goals and residency and medicine stinks. I am mentally beaten. I am going home.

The experience of previous years tells me I cannot simply leave without making sure the service is in order, so I tell Bob to take charge of rounds, that I will return later tonight to see the patients by myself, to call me at home if any troubles come up.

I give my son an extra hug and kiss when I make it home. He doesn't understand why I hold him so long. I can't explain the action to him or the reason I do not talk with him. Harriet knows which case I had scheduled for today and senses it didn't go well.

"Did something go wrong with the operation?"

"Wrong is not the word for it. Greg didn't make it." I sit down and pretend I am looking at the newspaper. Harriet sits beside me and says nothing. Finally she says, "I'm sorry." She squeezes my hand before going into the bedroom to check on Patricia.

She is sorry, but there is no way for her to really understand how I feel. Ben is busy playing with his toy cars. There is no way he can have any understanding of what has taken place. Greg Wilson's parents have lost their son. They are grieved and hurt. But even they cannot understand my feelings now. A life is entrusted into my hands, and in a few short hours that life is no longer. How can a surgeon learn to cope with this?

"Come on and eat. You will feel better when you get some food in your stomach." Harriet knows at least one way to make me feel better. I go to the table with no appetite, but I eat.

I return to the hospital for some quick rounds and then crawl into bed for some much-needed sleep. Even Patricia's crying does not wake me.

Attitude Is the Mortar

I awake in the morning and find that I do not want to return to work. Thinking about the hospital puts a bad taste in my mouth, but I automatically pull out the bad-apple rule from the book, throw out that bad-apple thought, and replace it with the thought of reality. I am almost finished with residency, and that is a reward worth going back to the hospital for. I have to pull all my habits back together, throw out the bad thoughts of yesterday, and feed in the good thoughts of tomorrow. The bad-apple rule involves only one thing: *attitude*. How I handle this situation and all other bad-apple situations depends 100 percent on my attitude, and my attitude is the one thing over which I have 100 percent control.

I have been rewarded with a full night's sleep because there was no open-heart case to stay up with, an ironic prize for the death of a patient. The night's rest brings clearer thinking, however, about the life-and-death aspect of surgery. I determine that my immediate-action goal for today is to once again start following the rules I have set down for myself as a resident. Last night was the only time during my entire training that I have not adhered to the rules I have set up. I conceded to that one defeat, but I am back in the game this morning to win by the rules.

22

The Domino Effect

*GREG DIED. MY ATTITUDE FAILED. All my pat rules began to crumble.
I had to guard against losing sight of my goal, even if this experience
was just a small nibble on the foundation. I knew the danger of loss
of vision, even if only for a short period of time. That first small
domino so often has the power, once it falls, to knock the second one
over. Then there's no telling what can happen.*

*At first, in medical school, there is the temptation to decrease
one's study time just a little. Other students were watching television—two or three shows a week. Why shouldn't I watch just one 30-minute show?*

*As an intern, there was the temptation not to spend so much time
reading about the operation to be performed the following day. After
all, some of the other interns did not study the operative techniques
in detail because they knew they would not actually be doing the
procedure, only assisting.*

*As a resident, there was one fellow who always seemed to have
a little more time off than everybody else. He was a little slack in his
workup of patients; he had his interns doing some of the work he
should have been doing; he was frequently late for rounds. It would
have been easy to adopt some of his habits, since I needed more time
at home with Harriet. We all had to be careful not to yield to the
subtle inclination even to begin thinking along those lines.*

*Some weren't careful enough. John had the highest grades of
anyone in my senior class at college. When he entered medical
school, he began to slack in his studies. His grades dropped. He
would play Ping-Pong at the fraternity house for two hours after
supper and frequently watch television. He became decreasingly
interested in school, and eight months later, his grades hit bottom.
The falling dominoes took their toll. He quit and went home.*

*The intern who didn't prepare for operations became one of the
unfortunate ones who did not make the cut into the residency program. Again, the dominoes fell.*

*The resident frequently late for rounds was called into Dr. Eler's
office just prior to his chief residency year. Their conversation soon*

became known to the rest of us; it was one of the few times we heard of Dr. Eler apologizing to anyone for anything. He told the resident he was sorry he had not put him out of the program the year before, since it is difficult for a resident to get kicked out of one program, then obtain a position in another one at the beginning of his chief year. Dr. Eler gave him two choices: Either the resident could look for a position himself in another program, or Dr. Eler would find one that he would have to accept without even seeing it.

> The hand of the diligent will rule, but the slack hand will be put to forced labor (Proverbs 12:24 NASB).

Either way, he was out of the program. The dominoes had fallen.

To become like one of these individuals would have been easy: First, start thinking like one of the slack ones, then talk to them about how they were getting by easier than everyone else. Next, associate with them, spend more time with them, and eventually walk on their same path. Then begin to stand around with them on that path and, finally, take a seat with them in their way of doing things. Pretty soon, the last domino topples.

In studying the Scriptures, I find similar situations in which the Bible illustrates how easy it is to fall away from the narrow road. Psalm 1:1 speaks of this:

> Blessed is the man who does not *walk* in the council of the wicked or *stand* in the way of sinners or *sit* in the seat of mockers (NIV, emphasis added).

I see the same principle illustrated in the three times the apostle Paul mentions Demas. In Philemon 24, Paul speaks of him quite positively: "Demas...my fellow worker." In Colossians 4:14, Paul drops him a notch and mentions him simply as "Demas." Finally, in 2 Timothy 4:10 Paul say, "Demas, because he loved this world has deserted me and has gone." Demas slid from being a fellow worker of Paul's to being a deserter of the faith. He walked, stood, and then sat in the world's way and forsook God's way.

I had to guard against the domino effect that could erode my goal structure after Greg's death; I had to guard against it even more, though, in my walk with the Lord. We must all be on guard against Satan's attempts to tip over that first domino.

❖   ❖   ❖

I enter the last month of residency with all the feeling of competency I had following my year as an intern. It is truly remarkable that a medical student can start in a training period of surgery as soon as he completes medical school and comes out, a few years later, a surgeon. I accept the fact that it takes some intelligence to be accepted to medical school, but after that the amount of work you put into your training pretty much determines where you come out in the field of medicine. This idea is even more true in the field of surgery. So much of my training has been pure hard work and long hours. The academic portion is there to be learned, and all it takes is time to learn it. At this stage of the game I look back to decide if I have managed my time successfully. The few weeks that remain will be insignificant relative to all the hours I've already spent learning to become a surgeon. I turn all the cases over to Bob during the last two weeks with the exception of one case I have wanted to perform since the first day I decided to take the cardiothoracic residency: a triple-valve operation.

Accept Opportunities Now

Dr. Bell is going to give me the opportunity to do what I have seen and read about but never thought I would ever actually perform. I am scheduled to remove three of the four valves in Mrs. Maude Vaughn's heart and replace them with three artificial ones. Our patient has rheumatic disease in these valves and all three need replacing with prostheses. Dr. Bell has me scheduled as the first surgeon, and I know the only way I will come out with a live patient following an operation of this magnitude is to perform it without a single technical mistake.

I stand at the scrub sink this morning thinking of what has brought me to this point in my career. I am almost finished with my surgical training, have matured surgically and mentally, and have learned and formed habits both good and bad.

I think of one habit that has happened more by chance than by planning. I remember back to the day I performed my first hernia operation at the V.A. hospital as a junior medical student; I cannot recall whether I was afraid of not doing a good job or whether I wanted help. But while scrubbing my hands, I said a jumbled prayer simply asking that I do my best on that case. I have never performed an operation since when I have not repeated that prayer.

Today is no different. The only significant different now is that I started with a simple hernia operation, and today I am about to replace three valves inside a heart.

I begin the operation by removing the heavily calcified aortic valve and sewing the artificial valve in place. Next comes the mitral valve, which goes as planned. I am making good time and have a chance to get the patient off the pump without prolonged bypass time if I can get the tricuspid valve out and replaced without undue delay. The longer the patient is on the pump, the greater chance there is for difficulty in getting her heart to beat on its own. So far, so good.

All is quiet in the room. The scrub nurse hasn't said two words since we started. I haven't had to lift my eyes from the operative field; the nurse has everything ready as I need it. I feel the quietness. Everything goes better without all the gab that usually is present in the operating room. If I had my way, the mask covering our faces would mute words coming out of the mouth in addition to cutting down on the number of bacteria extruded.

I open the right atrium and find a large, dilated chamber that was made so by back leakage of blood through the incompetent valve. Such a large atrium gives me more space to work in, but it also means the atrium has been greatly overworked.

The tricuspid valve is excised and the new one put in place. Mrs. Vaughn comes off the bypass without difficulty and it looks as if she is going to do nicely on her own.

"Excellent!" Dr. Bell uses one word of praise following the case.

No Shortcut to Experience

Excellent. What I have gone through for that one word to be muttered to me one time! Initially I am flattered, but as I have time to think of the word, I begin to realize that it is not me he is talking to—not the individual self. He is talking to practice and experience—two entities that anyone can obtain with enough stamina to stick to it. With this simple understanding, my ego deflates as rapidly as it had inflated. The compliment from Dr. Bell drops from a ten rating down to a one. I have arrived as a surgeon; I no longer need compliments from my colleagues in order to do a good job. The patient is sick; I operate on him and that is that. There is no need for anyone to be in the grandstand cheering, or observing, or interested in what I am doing; it is down to a surgical relationship between me and the patient. In the past ten minutes I have come to realize that becoming a real surgeon has nothing to do with competition between interns and residents; it doesn't matter what your assistant thinks about the way you handle a knife and a pair of scissors; it is insignificant for the head of the service to pay you a compliment. The truth lies only in how well the patient does as a direct result of the way I perform an operation.

This realization is almost anticlimactic. A year earlier, if Dr. Bell or Dr. Eler had paid me such a compliment, I could have hardly waited to tell Bob First about it, or tell Harriet immediately after getting home. Now such a compliment only registers in my mind and remains untold.

Two days pass. Mrs. Vaughn is doing well, with no complications.

I sit at the side of her bed in I.C.U. to have an informal chat about how she is doing. I ask her if she can tolerate a few more days with all the wires and tubes coming out of her.

"They don't bother me," she replies. "What is getting to me is the clicking of the valves in my heart. You didn't tell me I would be able to hear them click. It's going to drive me crazy. Every time I wake up, all I can hear are those valves clicking."

"Don't worry about the clicking; you'll get used to that. The time to start worrying is when you *don't* hear the clicking," I reassure her.

I relate the incident to Dr. Bell later in the day, and he informs me there have been suicides attributed to the clicking sound of the artificial valves—sort of like a water faucet dripping as you are trying to get some sleep. The only problem is that the patient can't get up and turn it off.

The third night postoperatively, "500, I.C.U., 500, I.C.U." comes over the intercom. Mrs. Vaughn. I know it's her. There has been too much done for her to come through the operation without a single complication.

I run up the six flights of stairs to I.C.U. to see a resuscitation already in progress on Mrs. Vaughn.

"What happened?"

The intern is giving external massage and the general surgery resident who was in I.C.U. at the time is just finishing placing an endotracheal tube into her trachea.

"Her pulse rate went to zero. I heard the monitor buzz and looked over and didn't see a thing on the scope," the nurse explains as she hangs an Isuprel drip in the I.V. to stimulate the heart to beat more rapidly.

"Let's see what she has on the monitor." I motion for the intern to stop the external massage. It shows a regular rhythm and I place my hand on her groin to feel the pulse. Strong and full. Her heart is back on its own and beating normally. Mrs. Vaughn opens her eyes and looks at me without moving from her position on the cardiac arrest board under her back.

"You're okay. Your heart is beating normally. You are going to be all right. I'll take that tube out of your windpipe in a little while. Your heart stopped beating for a minute but it looks good now." I reassure Mrs. Vaughn that everything is all right, but I wonder myself exactly what happened. Why did her heart stop beating, and why is it beating normally now? Did the nurse actually check to see if the heart had quit, or did she just glance at the monitor and think the heart had stopped? I've had numerous cardiac arrests after open-heart surgery, but I have never had a situation like this before. We hadn't worked for even five minutes before her heart started beating as normally as ever. The cardiogram looks the same as it did at this time yesterday.

After an hour of observing on the monitor, I see what is happening. When Mrs. Vaughn's heart slows to a rate of 40 and I give her Isuprel, the rate picks back up to 80. Apparently the conduction fibers in the heart that carry the beating impulse from the atrium to the ventricle are not working. She is having heart block, just like the elderly patients who require pacemakers. However, the cause for this blockage is different. The blockage has to be surgically related to sewing in the last valve.

The solution to the problem is to put a cardiac pacemaker in to control her rate. I explain the situation to Mrs. Vaughn and return her to the operating room and put a pacemaker on her heart. She does well following this. Upon discharging her from the hospital I have a feeling of accomplishment that can come only after all the years of surgical training that have led me to this point in life.

I complete my last week of residency in a state of complete satisfaction with my life, with my work, and with my future. I come to the hospital the last day of work to say good-byes more than anything else. I have made friends whom I will never forget. Many incidents and many patients will remain in my memory, needing only a small reminder to bring them forth. There is no way to offer the thanks deserved by Dr. Bell and Dr. Eler, but I make an effort to tell them what their teaching and training has meant to me. There is joking and kidding with the other residents and interns, and we talk quickly of how each will remember the other. As at all times like this, we mention only the good, the fun times, the successful operations we performed together. We ask each other, "Remember the time…?" and we recall incidents we have lived through over the past several years, and we promise to get together again soon and keep in touch.

Major Goal Accomplished

Before leaving the hospital for the last time, I go by the "office" where Bob and I spent so much time to pick up my belongings. I leave my old razor, shaving cream, shampoo, and toothpaste. I am sure they will all be used by someone within a week.

I sit down on the edge of the bed and smile as I glance at the framed sheet of paper with Murphy's Laws. Talk about negative thinking! I scoot back on the bed and prop my back against the wall. I take a small worn notebook from my right-hand coat pocket and thumb through it.

The *Goals Rule Book* has proven successful. It has stood the test of time through medical school, internship, and surgical residency. There is no doubt in my mind that whatever major goal I decide to set, I can reach. Just as I understand human anatomy, I understand goal anatomy—with one exception. The reason I know I can personally achieve any major goal I set is because of some power within my mind that will never let me set an unattainable major goal. What this power is, I do not know, but I do know that if I can think of it, I can do it. Furthermore, it is a simple matter to reach a major goal by staying within the framework of the *Goals Rule Book*. The major goal depends upon the intermediate goals, the intermediate goals depend upon immediate-action goals, and the immediate-action goals mean action *right now*. The price to pay for reaching any major goal is the cost of the immediate-action goals. This can be very costly—it can cost time from family, time from leisure activity, time from sleep. But the payoff is this: If you are willing to pay that cost, any goal that your mind will let you set can be reached successfully.

I make one last entry in the goals book—something I saw on a poster one time. "Happy is the man who sets a goal and is willing to pay the price to reach it." I do feel happy. I have paid the price. The race is over. I am ready for the reward that Harriet and I have talked about so much—free time.

I leave the hospital shortly after noon. I walk out the front door alone and glance around. It seems that there should be a band playing, and that someone ought to be standing on the front lawn waving flags. There should be crowds cheering. I have just finished years of study that required unswerving dedication, and even now I don't see how I did it. I am so full of happiness I feel I could explode. I want to tell everyone. I have a smile on my face that won't change to anything else. I have just conquered the biggest goal I could possibly set in my life!

But I walk on alone, and no one seems to notice. Two young boys are playing out by the large water fountain in front of the hospital. Patients continue to come up the walk and pass me without fanfare. This is real; this is life; no one here can experience my joy. They have not experienced my life up to this moment and can have no empathy with me now.

A one-day-old intern stops me and brings my mind back to reality. "Sir, can you tell me where the interns are supposed to meet this morning?"

"You don't know?" I ask almost in disbelief. "Go to Dr. Eler's office and ask the secretary. She will get you straightened out."

I stand a moment and watch him walk away. He has a long road ahead of him. Maybe I should have given him my *Goals Rule Book.*

23

Goals for a Christian

WHEN I LOOK BACK ON THE GOAL STRUCTURE *I used to get through residency, then compare it to my walk with the Lord, I realize I have only scratched the surface in achieving spiritual goals. In fact, I believe most Christians aren't reaching their full potential for God.*

The Christian life is not a competitive situation in which one Christian vies for a spot held by another Christian. Perhaps because of this fact, many of us Christians float aimlessly in a sea of mediocrity, ambivalent to what God has for us to achieve for His glory. We have set no goals under God's direction; therefore there is no way we can either succeed or fail. We are lukewarm—not aflame for the Lord, but not really cold either.

Perhaps we hold strong convictions about some matters, but do we speak up in a crowd? Not usually. What would others think about us? We try to live the life of our worldly friends and also live the life of God. We want to make it to heaven without overdoing it here on earth. We want to live for the Lord, but we don't want everyone in town talking about it. We want to feel like a Christian without paying the price to be one. Let's be honest; what does the Bible have to say about this? What does God think of the mediocre, lukewarm Christian?

> I know your deeds, that you are neither cold nor hot. I wish you were either one or the other! So, because you are lukewarm—neither hot nor cold—I am about to spit you out of my mouth (Revelation 3:15,16).

What does God have to say about the person who wants to live the Christian life but likes the world's life also?

> No one can serve two masters. Either he will hate the one and love the other, or he will be devoted to one and despise the other (Matthew 6:24).

We need to get on our knees and ask the Lord what He would have us do to get out of this sea of mediocrity and begin realizing our full potential for Him. We need to set goals, not according to our human wisdom, but through the indwelling power of the Holy Spirit. It is possible to set a goal while relying on self and miss the fact that the Holy Spirit has greater potential for us to achieve.

We need to acknowledge the power of the Holy Spirit in our lives and then allow Him to accomplish what could not be accomplished merely by self. This is the only way we will reach our full potential as Christians.

> In all thy ways acknowledge him, and he shall direct thy paths (Proverbs 3:6 KJV)

> Commit thy works unto the LORD, and thy thoughts shall be established (Proverbs 16:3 KJV).

Let's leave mediocrity behind and daily trust the Lord to use us in achieving goals so large that only He can receive the glory for their attainment.

World Medical Mission

❖ ❖ ❖

World Medical Mission is committed to bringing glory and honor to Christ and contributes to world evangelism by providing short-term Christian medical assistance to peoples in need.

The organization is successful through the grace of God and the prayers and support of Christians who recognize the need for this ministry.

If you are interested in tithing your time in a short-term medical ministry on a foreign field—at a convenient future date as an additional way of serving your Lord, Jesus Christ—contact:

**Franklin Graham
World Medical Mission
Box 3000
801 Bamboo Road
Boone, NC 28607**

(828) 262-1980

wmminfo@samaritan.org

Other Good
Harvest House Reading

OVERCOMING HURTS AND ANGER
by *Dr. Dwight Carlson, M.D.*

Dr. Carlson shows us how to confront our feelings and negative emotions in order to experience liberation and fulfillment. He presents seven practical steps to help us identify and cope with our feelings of hurt and anger.

BRUCE & STAN'S® GUIDE TO GOD
by *Bruce Bickel & Stan Jantz*

This fresh, user-friendly guide to the Christian life is designed to help new believers get started or recharge the batteries of believers of any age. Humorous subtitles, memorable icons, and learning aids present even difficult concepts in a simple way. Perfect for personal use or group study.

WINNING OVER YOUR EMOTIONS
by *H. Norman Wright*

In today's fast-paced world everyone struggles with worry, anxiety, anger, and stress. But bestselling author Norm Wright explains that these emotions don't have to defeat us, and offers a practical, step-by-step guide to break free of worry and transform stress into positive action.

GOD WHISPERS IN THE NIGHT
by *Marie Shropshire*

Everyone experiences "winter seasons" filled with adverse circumstances, the pain of disappointment, and the discouragement of misunderstanding. Marie invites readers to rest in God's arms and let His healing touch renew their spirit and hope.

JUST ENOUGH LIGHT FOR THE STEP I'M ON
by *Stormie Omartian*

A collection of devotional readings perfect for the pressures of today's world, put together by Stormie Omartian, bestselling author of *The Power of a Praying™ Wife*. New Christians and those experiencing life changes will appreciate Stormie's honesty and candor.

A PLACE CALLED SIMPLICITY
by *Claire Cloninger*

A warm invitation to freedom from a cluttered life and a breath of fresh air for everyone who longs to slow down and find balance in all areas of life.

SURVIVAL FOR BUSY WOMEN
by *Emilie Barnes*

Step-by-step directions to help busy women organize their homes and live more stress-free lives. Revised edition with eight all-new chapters.

THE TRANSPARENT LEADER
by *Dwight Johnson*

Eighteen men at the top of their fields, including John Couch (Apple Computers) and Ken Blanchard (One-minute Manager), candidly share their triumphs and disappointments—and how faith in God is key to victorious living.